A Self-Renewing Society

THE ROLE OF TELEVISION AND COMMUNICATIONS TECHNOLOGY

N. D. Batra

UNIVERSITY
PRESS OF
AMERICA

Lanham • New York • London

Copyright © 1990 by
University Press of America®, Inc.
4720 Boston Way
Lanham, Maryland 20706

3 Henrietta Street
London WC2E 8LU England

All rights reserved
Printed in the United States of America
British Cataloging in Publication Information Available

Library of Congress Cataloging-in-Publication Data

Batra, N. D. (Narayan Dass), 1937-
A self-renewing society : the role of television and
communications technology / N.D. Batra.
 p. cm.
Includes bibliographical references (p.) and index.
1. Mass media—United States. 2. Freedom and information—
United States. 3. Communication—Technological innovations.
 4. United States—Civilization—1970- I. Title.
P92.U5B34 1990   302.23'0973—dc20   90–12796 CIP

ISBN 0–8191–7948–5 (alk. paper)
ISBN 0–8191–7949–3 (pbk. : alk. paper)

 The paper used in this publication meets the minimum requirements of American National Standard for Information Sciences—Permanence of Paper for Printed Library Materials, ANSI Z39.48–1984.

TO
My brother
Shyam Sunder Batra
who was good to the end of his life.

Also by the Author
The Hour of Television: Critical Approaches

Work in Progress
Preface to America: The Twenty-First Century

Acknowledgments

In addition to those whom I have cited in the text, I feel grateful to Dr. Bela Banathy, Director, International Systems Institute, who saw something unique in my manuscript. Dr. Michael A. Mullin of the University of Illinois at Urbana-Champaign was very encouraging in his enlightened criticism. His advice played a decisive role in shaping the manuscript. Dr. Brenda Dervin of the Ohio State University at Columbus patiently nurtured my hopes. Dr. Klaus Krippendorff of the Annenberg School of Communication made incisive observations which were very helpful. There were many other reviewers whose criticism was very beneficial in the making of the book. I am also thankful to my publisher, Mr. James E. Lyons, for his faith in me.

Norwich University does not have a "publish or perish" policy. This has given me immense freedom to set my own standards and choose my own pace of research. Since I was researching self-renewing systems, Norwich University itself became an object of my scrutiny. Coming to Norwich has been a rewarding experience.

My wife Varsha and our two children, Nikhil and Shefali, have been very supportive of my efforts. And my mother whose goodness surpasses my understanding. One could not ask for a better gift than to be blessed with such a good family.

Contents

Preface	xi
Chapter One	
Self-Renewing Systems	1
Characteristics of Equilibrium Systems	2
Cybernetics: System Controls	4
A Perpetually Self-Renewing Society	7
The Controlling Center	9
Chapter Two	
Order and Disorder Through Fluctuations.	11
The Role of Technology	11
The Bias of Technology	12
Liberation Technology	14
Technology's Reach	15
Technology and Ethics	18
Technology and Ideology	19
Chapter Three	
Freedom in the Goldfish Bowl	23
Technologies of Un-freedom	24
Terror by Data	25
Electronic Footprints	27
Sinister Shadow	30
Obtrusive Invasion of Privacy	31
The Case of Dietmann	31
No Place to Hide in the Global Village	33
Privacy and Self-Renewal	34
Controlling the Undesirable	36
Chapter Four	
Collectivization of Free Speech	37
Media Mergers and Conglomerates	40
Sovietization of American Society	42
Money and Power	45
Capturing the Narrative	46
Silence in Free Society	47

Chapter Five
The Right to Know in a Self-Renewing Society 51
New York Times v. Sullivan 53
The Red Lion Case 55
Media Access 58
The Freedom of Information Act 59
No Absolute Right 62
How Much Sunshine Can a Government Stand? 63
Imprisonment of the Unwanted 63

Chapter Six
Different Approaches to Truth 65
Free Press and Fair Trial 65
The Sam Sheppard Case 67
The Whole World is Our Jury: Cameras in Courtrooms 69
Suspicion of Television Technology 70
The Most Subversive Human Right 71

Chapter Seven
Politics in the Republic of Television 73
Communications Technology and the Electoral Process 73
Opinion Polls: The Emerging Fifth Estate 76
Good Questions and Right Questions 78
Negative Political Commercials? Why Not? 80
Direct Impact of TV Commercials 81
Political Debates in the Age of Television 82
Direct Transaction via Satellite 84
The Big Eye is Watching 85
The Weeding Process 85
Ambushing Politicians 87
Agenda-setting by the People 88

Chapter Eight
The American President in the Age of 'We The Media' 89
Televisual Presidency 91
Watergate and Television 95
Why Can't the President Hear? 98

Chapter Nine
The Electronic Age Congress 103
Televised Hearings 104
Policymaking in a Partyless Democracy 106
The Necessity of Adversarial Relations 108
Hastening the Process 109

Chapter Ten
Programming the American Mind 111
Technology and Narrative 115
Children Made for Television 116
Trashing the Child: Saturday Morning TV Programs as Commercials 119

Chapter Eleven
Communications Technology and the Human Nervous System 123
Political Consequences of the Video Cassette Recorder 126
Change through the VCR 129
What Happened in Poland? 131
The Liberation of America: Mass Communication as the Collective Nervous System 134
Domination 135

Chapter Twelve
Essentials of a Self-Renewing Society. 137
Some Theoretical Conclusions 137
What Can be Done? 140

Chapter Thirteen
Propositional Summary 145

Chapter Notes 153

Index 165

About the Author 177

Preface

A decade ago when I arrived in New York, I saw a ragged man foraging through garbage dumps in the mid-Manhattan theater district. That evening a CBS special report said that more than 30,000 homeless people in New York took shelter at night on the city pavements. I went to Kentucky after a year where I learned about a devout Christian community of snake worshipers. I was told that the people of the region were the descendants of the Scottish, the Welsh, and the English. Their superstitious and obsequious behavior puzzled me. What had happened to the people from the land of Shakespeare, Newton, and Churchill in the past two centuries? Was this Joseph Conrad's terrible idea of "the outpost of progress"?

But in my mind, the image of America "That's one small step for man, one giant leap for mankind," and " We are the world, we are the children," throbbed persistently and created a shocking dissonance with what I saw. The range of civilization from the garbage-pecking and snake-worshiping Americans to the Americans in space astounded me. I cried...for explanation.

Apparently America is not a monolithic civilization, but how do the two extremities, two subsystems of the same civilization, co-exist and communicate with each other? America seemed more like a comet with its long tail far, far away from its brightly shining head.

I was fascinated and saw a great possibility of both self-renewal and self-destruction. This prompted me to ask a revolutionary question: Is the decline and fall of a society inevitable? Will American civilization come to an end? Is perpetual self-renewal possible?

In order to seek answers to these questions, I embarked upon this study, which partly subsumes and partly steps outside the highly respected path of communication research – functions, uses and gratification, effects, agenda-setting, etc. Instead, it goes to theoretical biology for an answer. It uses the paradigm of autopoiesis (self-renewal), particularly as presented by Humberto R. Maturana and Francisco J. Varela, and to self-organizing dissipative structures as presented by Ilya Prigogine and his colleagues of the Brussels School. Conceptualizing the media and communications technology as the collective nervous system of a society can help us in understanding the continuous dying and renewing processes occurring daily in American society.

Theoretically, an autopoietic organization "constituted by a network of processes of production of components that (a) through their interactions continuously regenerate and realize the network of processes that produced them and (b) constitute the organization as a concrete unit in space and time" (Krippendorff) is capable of perpetual self-renewal. Are there some unique structural characteristics of a perpetually self-renewing society? How strong are they in American society? I was like an anthropologist who stumbled upon a bone which led him to the discovery of "Lucy" and the paradigm of self-renewal. I felt born again. My conclusions are different from those of some great historians like Edward Gibbon, Arnold Toynbee, Paul Kennedy et al. who have explained decay and death elsewhere.

Chapter One discounts the inevitability of decline and fall of American civilization, because, unlike the great civilizations of the past, it is based upon decentralized freedoms and a growing acceptance of the most subversive of human rights – the right to know. It explicates general system theory and cybernetics and their links with the paradigm of self-renewal.

Chapter Two expounds the view that technology, communications technology in particular, through audio-visual-linguistic descriptions and realization, determines and expands the cognitive domain, the knowledge base, of a society. Technology demands a re-assertion of ethical thinking, which is a necessary condition for self-renewal. It questions the patterns of beliefs and values on which a society is based.

Chapter Three discusses obtrusive and non-obtrusive types of communications technologies and their impact upon privacy, which is a necessary condition for individual and collective creativity and self-renewal. But the same technology gives opportunities to individuals and public-spirited groups to keep watch on their own as well as foreign governments and warn the people of impending man-made disasters.

Chapter Four discusses the role of the non-conforming opinion in the process of self-renewal. It asks the question, How much freedom, what kind of free speech is left when financial consortiums, conglomerates, and multinationals take control of the collective nervous system of the society? In America a new kind of central control over free speech, not by the government, but by remote national and multi-national corporations is being established; it may gradually lead to collectivization of free speech as it exists in the Soviet Union. Whether it is a corporation or a political party exercising control over ideas, the effect is the same: the self-corrective process through dissent is eliminated, and the society inevitably stagnates.

Chapter Five and Six discuss the impossibility of societal self-renewal without a collective habit of self-criticism, which cannot be exercised unless the right to know is accepted as essential as clean air and water. The chapters explore the society's struggle toward recognizing and accepting this dangerous human right through the New York Times v. Sullivan and the Red Lion cases, The Freedom of Information Act, various state and federal sunshine laws, the question of who and why a person goes to prison and his right to a fair trial in the public view, and how modern technology is helping the people to exercise their most sacred right.

Chapter Seven argues why the much decried negative political commercials are so important to the self-renewal of a society. By cutting every candidate to his proper size, the negative commercial warns us what might happen in the future. The emergence of the independent pollster is as important as was the growth of the penny press. Television debates, although imperfect at present, constitute a direct mode of communication between the candidates and the electorate. The electronic democracy would create new checks and balances in the political system.

Chapter Eight discusses how, since the time of Theodore Roosevelt, the American president has gained in power and prestige by turning himself into the most important source of news; thus, by virtually aligning himself with the press, he has weakened Congress and tamed the judiciary and has made the presidency less accountable to the people.

Chapter Nine argues that one way Congress can regain its proper constitutional role as a co-equal in power is to turn itself into a source of television news. It can counter the presidential ploy "I can't hear you" by televising events like the Iran-contra affair. Government of separate powers is very essential to the self-renewing process.

Chapter Ten examines, with the help of the symbolic convergence theory of communication, how the electronic story-teller creates the collective cognitive domain of a society which, in conjunction with the state of technology, determines how the people can solve their problems. In market-driven, advertisement-dependent programming predicated upon ratings, the repetitive narrative and rehashed stories imprison the collective mind and structurally and psychologically couple it to the same set of solutions. The chapter states that while the East is being sabotaged by the VCR, in America the child is being desensitized through purposeless violence and maimed by program-length commercials. The East is being liberated. Who will liberate the American child?

Chapter Eleven explores the cultural and political impact of the video cassette recorder in the West, in Poland, in India, and in the Arab world. The VCR is one of the greatest threats to any established political authority, particularly to those in closed societies. America has yet to realize the full significance of the VCR.

Chapter Twelve recapitulates the paradigm of self-renewal and discusses five operational steps in the creation of a perpetually self-renewing society. It concludes that it is essential to close the gap between technological and socio-cultural intelligence, that social activism and civil disobedience may become necessary to awaken society from its stupor.

Chapter Thirteen states a set of propositions which form the nucleus around which each chapter developed.

Through the methodology of historical-critical research augmented by case studies, the book explores the attenuation and enhancement of the right to know, electoral processes, the triumvirate political power structure, and the role of communications technology in programming the collective mind for self-renewal.

The book will have a wide appeal: academicians, policymakers, media professionals, students, and the general public.

– N.D. Batra
Northfield, Vermont
May 5, 1990

Modeling
A Self-Renewing Society

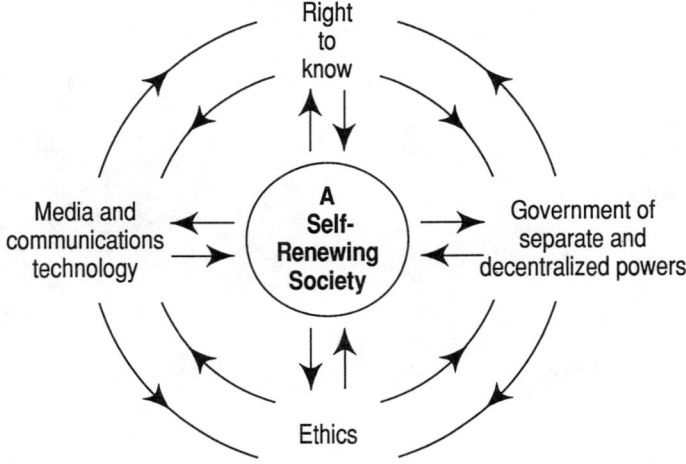

A self-renewing society is an open state of order, far from equilibrium, subject to internal re-inforcement of fluctuations which drive the society from one creative threshold to another. It is an ethical society where a critic is more honored than a hero, where the right to know is more sacred than the Word.

Chapter One

Self-Renewing Systems

> It is the business of the future to be dangerous... The major advances in civilization are processes that all but wreck the societies in which they occur...
> —Alfred North Whitehead

Is it possible for a sociocultural system to renew itself perpetually so that it can escape the fate of some of the extinct societies like that of ancient Egypt, Greece, Rome, and, not the least, many modern colonial empires like Britain, France, and others? What is the contribution of technology, particularly communications technology, the right to know, and freedom of speech in the process of self-renewal or self-destruction of a sociocultural system? These questions run against common sense and historical experience because it is believed that what began must come to an end; all systems are subject to entropy and decay. A great historian, Paul M. Kennedy, said in a 1987 symposium:

> ...the world has never stood still, and that people who think they can keep things just as they are are deluding themselves. Throughout history there have always been technological breakthroughs, which benefit some societies more than others; changing patterns of settlement, trade and demand; varying birth and death rates; changes in climate and therefore agriculture. All of these variable means that, at any point in history, some people have been more productive than others. Their greater wealth and more advanced technology usually gave them greater power as well. Their weapons were better and more numerous, and they could more easily afford to pay for security in a jealous and competitive world. At the same time, however, they also found themselves facing a dilemma. If they failed to provide for security, their wealth and well-being were in danger. But if they poured too much into armies, fortification, wars of conquest, then they would have fewer resources to renew their productive base.[1]

Professor Kennedy, in spite of his brilliant historical analysis, did not take into account some of the crucial structural and cultural factors like decentralized freedoms and free speech giving birth to the right to know, the habit of collective self-criticism, and a restless, innovative, do-it-yourself temperament – the hallmarks of American society – which, however, were, in various degrees, absent from the societies of the past. The decline and fall paradigm is inadequate in understanding America. We must look somewhere else.

Characteristics of Equilibrium Systems

The idea of perpetual self-renewal is worth exploring. The related fields of general system theory, cybernetics, information theory and autopoiesis provide some of the answers, and their explication at this juncture is essential.

General system theory was initiated by Ludwig von Bertalanfy, a biologist who postulated the concept of holistic thinking and applied it to many social and biological phenomena, hoping that one day it would develop into a logico-mathematical discipline. General system theory, according to him, is a general science of "wholeness" which up until now was considered a "vague, hazy, and semi-metaphysical concept." He attempted to integrate knowledge in various disciplinary areas and used systems theory to abstract certain general laws. He says: "An exponential law of growth applies to certain cells, to populations of bacteria, of animals or humans, and to progress of scientific research measured by the number of publications in genetics or science in general. The entities in ... question are completely different... Nevertheless, the mathematical law is the same."[2]

The integrative approach of the system theory and its capacity to explain many phenomena have given it a universal appeal, and it has been found applicable from mousetraps and missile systems to mass communications and monetary systems. One of the main objectives of the system theory is to develop those "generalized ears" that listen to cross-disciplinary communications.[3]

A simple definition of a system is that it is a set of functions, objects, units, or processes which are interrelated and constitute a whole. Systems are said to be closed or open according to the degree of their interchange with the environment.

A totally closed system will be subject to entropy, progressive internal decay, and disintegration. A burning candle encased in a glass jar will extinguish itself because its exchange with the environment will come to an end. Similarly, the sun will eventually come to an end when its core is exhausted. This is how gossips die; this is how television programs die; this is how communism is dying. On the other hand, an open system keeps up a level of exchange with its environment; it gives and receives matter, energy, information, trade, or whatever justifies its existence. It is characterized by life and growth as are, for instance, biological, sociocultural, and psychological systems. A system possesses qualities of wholeness, interdependence, hierarchy, self-regulation, environmental interchange, equilibrium, adaptability, and equifinality.[4]

According to the system theory, the whole is not the sum of its parts. The U.S.A is not the sum of fifty states or a collection of Coca-Cola, IBM, AT&T, Harvard, Praise The Lord, the Bronx, the Mafia, etc. It is the mutual dependence, constraints, and antagonism of the components in a dynamic equilibrium which make the whole so different from its parts.

Although each of its components displays some of the attributes of the whole, it is not the whole. For instance, the state of Vermont as a component is isomorphic in attributes and functions with America as a whole; but it does not, as a constituent state, presume to be the whole. In fact its interests, for instance in the prevention of acid rain, may be at odds not only with those of other states but also with other structures, such as the industry in the Midwest on which it may be dependent.

It is this dependency and antagonistic interrelationship among structures constituting the whole which give the system a form and a shape, and unique attributes. In other words, if a part or a component grows too fast, it will affect not only the other components, but also the whole – stimulating growth or causing distortion. When television began to grow too fast in the sixties and the seventies, it seemed to swallow other mass communications systems; its visual impact changed the way magazines and newspapers presented their contents. Some of the magazines like *Life* and *Look* just disappeared because they were rendered redundant. It gave rise to newspapers like *USA Today* which, in turn, spun the television show "USA Today." Similarly, the video revolution is impacting the television networks' programming practices.

When an interrelated unit changes its policy or functions or uses a new technology, it causes fluctuations in the system, leading to variations or distortions and selective adaptation and change in the whole. A new balance or equilibrium is set up among the constituents of the whole, and the system, after renewing itself, asserts its identity again. For instance, the rise of the print media made the U.S. presidency more visible, and more powerful, against Congress. It distorted the original intent of the founding fathers. That's probably one way of looking at development or societal evolution.

A system consists of subsystems which in turn may have other subsystems giving rise to hierarchy. Every revolution in the history of mankind was aimed at toppling the existing hierarchy and establishing a new one. The French Revolution, the Russian Revolution, and Mao's Chinese Revolution, although aimed at the abolition of the hierarchy and therefore hegemony, ended up in re-establishing hierarchy. Wherever there is a hierarchy, there will be power centers because hierarchy cannot exist without the establishment of rank, order, and priorities.

Therefore, all social systems are power systems, and communication in the system would reflect the power dynamics. No wonder corporate America is trying to assimilate the mass media through mergers so that they can dominate the image-making and public opinion processes in the country and assert their hegemony over the public mind, Congress and the president. This is an example of a constituent part trying to dominate the whole, and consequently, through distortion, variations, and selective adaptation, change the whole to a new whole or destroy it altogether.

It is through self-regulation and control that systems assert and maintain their integrity and reach their goals. Systems have built-in capacities for goal attainment; they are purposive, teleological, in outlook. Teleology, according to Webster's, is the use of design or purpose as an explanation of natural phenomena. A goal may be economic growth in the fifth five year plan in Russia, improvement in the overall ratings of CBS through imaginative programming, the release of hostages, or finding an AIDS vaccine.

Cybernetics: System Controls

Purposefulness and self-regulatory controls are the distinguishing attributes of a sociocultural system and require an extensive system of feedbacks, which is the subject of cybernetics. Cybernetics, states its pioneer, Norbert Wiener, "is the entire field of control and communication theory, whether in the machine or in the animal..."[5] The system concept posits purpose, evaluation, and adjustment through feedback and control.

A society fed on slogans of equality and individual freedom may abhor the idea of mechanical controls, adjustment, and course correction; but in the case of machines, the theory of cybernetics is easy to understand and its applicability easy to accept. Cybernetics, according to Stephen W. Littlejohn:

> deals with the ways systems (along with their subsystems) use their own output to gauge effect and make necessary adjustments. The simplest cybernetic device consists of a sensor, a comparator, and an activator. The sensor provides feedback to the comparator, which in turn provides guidance to the activator. The activator in turn produces an output that affects the environment in some way. This fundamental process of output-feedback-adjustment is the central theme of cybernetics.[6]

In sociocultural organizations or nation states one observes the output-feedback-adjustment process in the form of public hearings, investigative reporting, and other forms of free speech. It is only through uncontrolled and independent mass communication processes that a society corrects itself. This process might take any form: a novel like the *Jungle*, exposés like the Watergate or Iran-contra affair, sex scandals of a presidential hopeful like Gary Hart, a grand jury indictment of an auto-manufacturing corporation alleged to have sold use cars as new, a court case like New York v. Sullivan, etc.

In social terms cybernetics is a process of collective self-criticism; and mass communication, arts, and literature are some of its manifestations. Economists have developed statistical indicators to gauge the economic health of a society. When we are told that in June 1987, the U.S.A had more than $ 200 billion in foreign debt, we are heightening our self-awareness and self-preparedness for some future action. In the case of a space shuttle the cybernetic processes occur in split seconds while in the case of social systems cybernetics is a long process of collective dreams, fantasies, debates, dramas, novels, poetry, investigative reporting, negotiation and bargaining, primaries, and political conventions. Does this happen in closed societies, for instance, in Russia, China, or Khomeini's Iran?

No society can survive without some internal debate. However, debating in a closed society is limited to the people who wield power, which excludes masses, resulting in their isolation and alienation. It creates the need to keep them under control by a police state apparatus, psychiatric wards, and censorship; and hence the need and the sanctity of revolt.

In open societies, because of the diversity of sources of information and the mass media's constant practice of gauging public opinion through repetitive polls, people have a sense of control through participation. However, there may occur a progressive "sovietization" of American society, the closing of the American mind, a point which we shall pursue in a latter chapter, if the present trend of conglomeration and mega-mergers or the grabbing of mass media by corporate America persists.

Cybernetics as the essence of general system theory can be a very simple process, as in the case of a mousetrap; or it can be a very complex and long drawn-out process, as in the case of sociocultural systems. As Norbert Wiener pointed out: "This principle [feedback] in control applies not merely to the Panama locks, but to states, armies, and individual human beings... This matter of social feedback is of very great sociological and anthropological interest."[7]

A society might exercise control by providing its members a limited number of choices; a mechanical or electronic system might exercise control through a forced choice or no choice situation. When Soviet Russia's general secretary, Gorbachev, talked of "glasnost" or openness in the summer of 1987, he meant to offer more choices for the people – social control through more choices. It is not necessarily the same as decentralized freedoms or decontrolled information. A choice is a form of feedback, therefore, leading to control – as can be seen in Nielsen's ratings, which lead to program reshuffling, rescheduling, or cancellation; in short audience control. A television or theater critic might perform cybernetic functions through his positive or negative feedback in the form of criticism.

The regulatory control system in the form of the output-feedback-adjustment loop enables the system to change and adapt to environmental pressures, leading it from homeostasis to morphogenesis and to a new homeostasis. Homeostasis aims at system balance or the status quo, while morphogenesis leads to structural changes. Evolution of a society is a play between homeostasis and morphogenesis. As we shall see, technology is a major sources of morphogenesis while ideology, culture, and policy-making stabilize society, reasserting homeostasis. In a physical or biological system, excessive deviation can become intolerable and is corrected through the feedback mechanism. Body temperature in humans tends to remain within a tolerable variance range, for example. The evolutionary clock assimilates deviation, enabling man to ascend from the primate.

Sociocultural systems, on the other hand, seek morphogenesis, that is growth, through technology, free speech and policy intervention. A small invention might bring about a tremendous social change. This is called a "butterfly effect," according to chaos theory. It happened with the advent of the birth control pill, which liberated the American woman from the bondage of virginity deified for two thousand years in Virgin Mary, and set her on a road to freedom, and in some cases to singlehood, loneliness, and poverty, and to new forms of serfdom to men. This structural change due to morphogenesis in American society has affected the institution of marriage and the idea of fatherhood, giving rise to a new social concept, surrogate motherhood. Baby M was a product of technology, not Christianity or communism.

There are other ways in which morphogenesis might occur. For instance, we observe a relentless though slow increase in the interdependence between the economies of Japan-Pacific rim countries and the U.S.A on one hand, and the U.S.A and Canada on the other. The European Common Market will have transformed itself into one unified market and a new political system with unified Germany by 1992; and after a century there may be a supra-state with the center of gravity lying anywhere in the continuum. This is an example of endosymbiosis, in which several independent systems cooperate and coexist as loosely coupled subsystems to form a new whole without, however, losing their autonomy. But this kind of wholeness is not the same as is achieved through hostile takeovers, mergers, and bankruptcies and the restructuring of corporations, formation of conglomerations, or multinationals.

Since sociocultural systems are teleological, goal establishment and achievement is a constant system activity. But the same goal or the final state could be achieved by many ways. This is conceptualized as equifinality. Complex social systems subject to morphogenesis can achieve their final states or goals through many different routes and in many different environmental conditions. Japan is an example. Although its social system and culture are so different from those of the West, it has achieved the same standard of living and quality of life as prevalent in the West and the U.S.A. However, it may become essential sometime to bring about structural changes in order to achieve goals. These structural changes, as A.D. Hall and R.E. Fagen have pointed out,[8] could be brought about through a progressive centralization or decentralization – a process which is often seen during mergers and takeovers, or social revolutions; or, through subdivisions and consolidation of the subsystems, as happened during the rise and expansion of the British Empire.

In a nutshell, a sociocultural system is a set of interdependent but autonomous structures which exists in mutually supportive and antagonistic interrelations constituting the whole. Wholeness, interdependence, self-regulation, and exchange with the environment are nestled in cybernetics, which keeps the system in a spiral loop of homeostasis and morphogenesis, stability, and change. But, socio-biological systems whose sole aim is to maintain hierarchy of power and control tend to degrade humans, diminish their creativity, inhibit their innovativeness and inventiveness. The systems theory as a political philosophy can lead a society in the name of efficiency, order, stability, and equilibrium to authoritarian control and eventually, to entropy. A self-renewing system, on the other hand, creates new order through internal re-inforcement of fluctuations and moves to a new level of autopoiesis, self-creativity, and autonomy.

A Perpetually Self-Renewing Society

All open, democratic societies are destined towards totalitarianism – unless its members assert their autonomy. And the end of a totalitarian society is disintegration as happened in ancient Egypt, Rome, the medieval Catholic Church, Nazi Germany, Fascist Italy, and is happening in many of the modern ideologically-oriented totalitarian societies in the East and the West. At any given moment, an open society exhibits totalitarian tendencies which degrade its members and reduce them to units of production rather than sources of self-renewal.

Autopoietic (self-renewing) organizations are self-referring, autonomous systems which maintain their own identities and individualities and realize their autopoiesis through interactions with other autopoietic systems constituting the whole. The concept of autopoiesis originated in theoretical biology and was presented by Maturana, Varela, and Uribe.[9] It is bereft of any vitalistic perspective: human life is not driven by some ultimate vital force. In a limited sense it is "purposeless," and if it has any purpose it is in the maintenance of its autopoiesis. It has no "manifest destiny;" its members are not the "chosen ones." However, when individuals become members of a society they do circumscribe and limit themselves through interaction with others.

Since hierarchy, as discussed earlier, is the essence of all organized sociocultural systems, it gives rise to power centers; and the exercise of power becomes an end in itself, necessitating ethical choices. Maturana says:

> the stabilization of human conduct always entails a restriction of creativity through a restriction of the possible interactions of the individual human beings outside those prescribed by the society that they integrate. The extreme case of this, of course, takes place in a totalitarian society of any kind. Or, in other words, the spontaneous course of the historical transformation of a human society as a unity in a given medium is towards totalitarianism; this is so because the relations that undergo historical stabilization are those that have to do with the stability of society as a unity in a given medium, and not with the well-being of its component human beings that may operate as observers. Any other course requires ethical choice; it would not be spontaneous, it would be a work of art, a product of human aesthetic design.[10]

The properties of components of a physical system are easy to stabilize and control because they do not interact through linguistic/audio-visual description but through electronic-mechanical feedback, as explained earlier. But in the case of human beings, the nervous system developed over millions of years of evolution makes them observers of themselves and their environments; and as observers they live in a domain of description, and through description they can indefinitely increase the complexity of their cognitive domain.

Communications technology latches itself to the human nervous system, extends its power to observe, and enhances its power of linguistic/audio-visual description. Natural and social phenomena as observed and communicated by humans are technology dependent. Reality is what the state of our communications technology, which is our collective nervous system, permits us to describe. To describe is to realize, potentially.

In a self-renewing society humans as observers question the forces which tend to destroy their autopoietic nature. Organizationally and biologically all kinds of societies, from South Africa to Switzerland, are possible; but all are not equally desirable to live in.

An authoritarian society isolates dissidents so that they may not persuade others into accepting their critical positions and question the regime's orthodoxy and power structure. It specifies and legitimates certain experiences and by exclusion creates a powerful but decadent elite, as happened in ancient Rome, ancient Egypt, imperial Britain, and has happened recently in Romania, China, and Russia. A society which demands little surrender of human dignity and individuality, in which an individual is not dispensable, where one can be an observer and a full-fledged member, is a self-renewing society.[11]

An observer is a critic of the system which supports him and which is created by him. Tolerance of dissidents and their activities is a measure of the openness and a condition for self-renewal because it is through dissidence that the mainstream is purified. But for Luther, Christianity might have perished because of corruption. The automotive industry in America has survived thanks to Ralph Nader, the consumer movement, and competition from Japan.

Dissidence opens up new possibilities and alternate descriptions of reality and becomes a contender for the truth. This is the source of tragic conflict: society, as it becomes more complex due to technological advancements, tends to be more hierarchical and totalitarian; individuals, in order to be creative and thus a source of self-renewal for the society, need to assert their autonomy, their differences from the society which they constitute. That's their essential autopoietic nature.

The study of political and economic power, how it is attained and used by individuals and groups, how that power could be decentralized and dispersed in order to prevent its misuse, and how to recall those in power is crucial in a self-renewing society. Constant vigilance of those in power – whether in Wall Street or Washington, D.C. – is the price of self-renewal.

The Controlling Center

Although general systems and autopoiesis theories differ in some fundamental respects and are similar in many other ways, they do not answer a critical question: What makes one society so different from another? We might divide the world into ideological camps, but that does not answer the question either. Why is China so different from Soviet Russia since both are communist societies waiting for the state to wither away, as Karl Marx predicted? Or, why is Britain so different from the United States even though both are secular democracies?

A society is held together by a centralizing symbol, a core, which is the sum total of all its values, a set of constants, a radiating center that suffuses the entire society with its energy. Take away that organizing symbol or the centralizing core, and the system collapses. This controlling center of the system is not transplanted but develops historically as the system moves spirally through a continuous process of homeostasis and morphogenesis, novelty and confirmation.

American society is held together and is organizationally controlled by the free marketplace of goods and ideas – a symbiosis of the First Amendment and free enterprise.[12] Class in Britain, apartheid in South Africa, the Communist Party in Russia, Khomeini's Islamic orthodoxy in Iran, for instance, are the controlling centers and organizing symbols of those societies. That's why sociocultural systems do not reproduce themselves through their offsprings as humans do. But they have the potential to renew themselves through a process of recursive self-description, internal debates, free speech, the right to know, protests, and demonstrations – in short through the assertion of human dignity, autonomy, their autopoiesis.

American civilization is unique, as was Roman civilization; but it need not meet the same fate if the process of self-renewal is pursued through ethical and policy choices. As America moves towards the twenty-first century information society, as technology spins society inside outside and humans cry for stability amidst a whirling flux, ethics and policy will become very critical to decision making. Left to historical forces or unimpeded technological processes, there is no reason why America should not degenerate into a totalitarian society, or become a grotesque giant by overextending itself overseas. The sovietization of American society could be achieved very painlessly if those who wield economic and political power were left alone.

A self-renewing society maintains its open state of order through plurality and the right to know, which create internal re-inforcement of fluctuations and keep it in a state of dynamic internal non-equilibrium. Such a system, says Erich Jantsch, "continuously renews itself and maintains a particular dynamic regime, a globally stable space-time structure. It seems to be interested solely in its own integrity and self-renewal."[13]

Equilibrium systems are structure-preserving systems while non-equilibrium open systems are evolving, self-renewing systems which move from one threshold of creativity to another. While the general system theory over the past decades has searched for conditions basically with respect to stabilization and preservation of structures by means of negative feedback and control, the paradigm of autopoiesis (Maturana et al) and order through fluctuation[14] (Ilya Prigogine) and self-renewal explains the "self-organization of systems, the inner dynamics which drive them to reconstitute themselves in new structures."[15]

Chapter Two

Order and Disorder Through Fluctuations

The next hundred years will be a period of transition between the metal-and-silicon technology of today and the enzyme-and-nerve technology of tomorrow....
—Freeman J. Dyson in *Infinite in All Directions*

Is the idea of what is to be human disappearing, along with so many other ideas, through modern skylight? In its fearless exploration of inner and outer worlds, modern culture has evidently reached a turning point – a kind of phase transition from one set of values to another. Crossing the barrier that separates the phases is another kind of disappearance....

The transition that is occurring in modern culture is ... frightening and often confusing, but ... at no other time in history have conditions been more exciting or more filled with promise – for beings on a small planet hurtling through the vast darkness of space toward an unknown and unimaginable future which they, themselves, are creating.
—O.B. Hardison, Jr. in *Disappearing Through the Skylight*

The Role of Technology

A society is constantly dying and constantly being reborn, and through the process of death and rebirth the socio-cultural system enacts self-renewal and moves from one state of dynamic non-equilibrium to another. Or, if the self-destructive acts of a society, for instance drug consumption, crime, and violence overwhelm creative springs and self-renewing processes, collapse of the system through tyranny is inevitable. The self-renewing and self-destructive forces are ushered in and nurtured by science and technology, religious and social movements, new ideologies, and migration. The protest movement of the 1960s, apart from the anti-Vietnam War social and political actions, also gave birth to a free love-making generation which through its over-indulgence nurtured AIDS in the 1980s.

Social scientists have explained changes through various evolutionary and developmental models. Developmental models are incremental, involving step-by-step transformation of a simple system from stages of lesser complexity to functionally greater sophistication. Evolutionary models, on the other hand, are multi-dimensional, involving both the transformation of a system and its diversification.

Evolution may involve directional increments as well as discontinuities and quantum leaps. One might say that development could take place without evolution, but evolution, without development is inconceivable. Evolution and development have caused confusion amongst social scientists. Marion Blute pointing to "an incredible array" of "stage theories" says that "organic history is a process of descent with modification."[1]

Organic history can also be seen as a process of dissipation and self-organization of a society which takes place through variations and selective retention triggered by technology and shaped by policies and exercise of power. While power prescribes and proscribes social and political actions, technology tends to have its own momentum, its own autonomy. Technology necessitates new descriptions of reality; it cries aloud to be used; it creates tantalizing thirst for more and better of its kind; and in the process changes man and his institutions, for better or for worse.

The Bias of Technology

The essential logic and thrust, the bias of technology, is to solve problems by providing its users with choices and alternative modes of actions – a way out of a maze. But each technological solution creates newer problems and a need for better technology.

Technology is Janus-faced: it creates self-confidence and anxiety, a sense of power and powerlessness, a promise of stability and a threat of destabilization. It benefits some sections and hurts others, extends man's senses and imprisons his mind, enlarges his freedom and puts shackles on him. Not the least, each new technology creates a cultural lag and ethical issues.

Since technology makes the once seemingly difficult task easy and tempts its own use, it enhances our feelings of self-worth. And since self-worth in America is measured in the marketplace, the uses of new technologies are determined not by its inventors but by marketers. Only when technology challenges the fundamental values of a society – as is happening in the case of birth-control technology – does the judiciary step in to resolve ethical, moral, and legal issues. Left alone, it creates opportunities for some while it plunges others into anxieties. For instance, color film and television technology revolutionized the electronic media and made home viewing of sports and entertainment programs a delectable experience. But the technological search never stopped there, and as soon as the computer and media technologies began to converge, the quest for coloring old films took possession of the researcher and the marketer, leaving the artist in a whirlpool of anxiety. As Woody Allen says:

> Since they have computers that can change such masterpieces as *Citizen Kane* and *City Light* and *It's A Wonderful Life* into color, it has become a serious problem for anyone who cares about these movies and has feelings about our image of ourselves as a culture... What's at stake is a moral issue and how our culture chooses to define itself. No one should be able to alter an artist's work in any way whatsoever, for any reason, without the artist's consent...I believe the people who are coloring movies have contempt for the audience by claiming, in effect, that viewers are too stupid and too insensitive to appreciate black and white photography – that they must be given, like infants or monkeys, bright colors to keep them amused...Most civilized governments abroad, realizing that their society is at least as much shaped and identified by its artists as by its businessmen, have laws to protect such things from happening. In our society, merchants are willing to degrade anything or anyone so long as it brings in a financial profit.[2]

Technology combines and recombines to form newer technology, thus creating ever increasing opportunities for its use or misuse. The technology-created high anxiety can be seen in various sectors of American life today. A report[3] in *The New York Times* said that due to rapid development of technology, productivity in the service sector of the industry was declining. As technology takes quantum leaps, it creates exponential needs for services in the maintenance and training areas, and to solve this cultural lag more and better technology is offered as the solution, thus creating heightened anxiety in the people who cannot cope with the rapid technological changes. As the report said, "Nearly a generation after American technology companies unleashed new computers, telecommunications gear and electronic equipment, executives and employees are discovering that instead of saving labor, the sophisticated machines in many cases have been hampering their work..."[4]

Rapid technological innovations and the psychological drag they create in the wake of their adoption have also intensified anxiety in the minds of federal officials and economists who have warned that the "anemic in the efficiency of service companies could have serious consequences." The nation cannot be competitive if service industries which account for 68 percent of GNP and 71 percent of all jobs in the U.S.A shows stagnation in productivity. Moreover, economists worry that "meager growth rates in service-sector productivity could eventually raise business costs, slow the explosive growth of service jobs and erode the United States' standard of living."[5] None – businessmen, bureaucrats, artists, or authors – are immune from the technology-produced high anxiety.

Those who control the use and deployment of technology have a great sense of power and persist in their advantage until they encounter situations in which the very technology which made them feel so invincible makes them powerless and impotent; and then they cry for more sophisticated technology. Mephistophelian and Frankensteinian legends have a universal appeal and are frequently nurtured and re-inforced by such events as Chernobyl in Soviet Russia and Three Mile Island in the United States. A hole in the ozone layer will make all mankind naked before ultra violet radiation.

The case of Lieutenant Colonel Oliver North, President Reagan's "national hero" and an instigator of the Iran-contra scam, is stranger than fiction. Never was a mighty man made so helpless by the technology which he thought would rescue him from infamy. During his heroic efforts to save America, he used computers to write his self-incriminating messages about the Iran-contra deals to his superiors in the National Security Council, which became not only a part of the Tower Commission Report but are now in the public domain. The computer, which is a modern man's source of strength and an amplification of his brain, betrayed Lieutenant Colonel North because, like Frankenstein, it is its own master and exists according to its own laws and jurisdiction. Lieutenant Colonel North was deluded by computer technology[6] much as President Nixon was trapped by tape technology.

An earlier generation of Americans had discovered the powerlessness of military technology in Vietnam, as the new generation is rediscovering its helplessness in Lebanon and the Persian Gulf. Russians' humiliations in Afghanistan call for no less eulogy. Power to destroy the world through "star war" technology goes hand in glove with the inability to save a tiny oil tanker in the Persian Gulf or a president in Washington, D.C. Technology not only induces delusions of omnipotence but also creates tremendous moral and ethical dilemmas in the process of solving our problems.

Liberation Technology

The birth control technology which has enabled animal farms to produce better pigs and chickens has also given rise to the concept of surrogate motherhood. About 500 children[7] born during the past decade will learn that their mothers had acted like commercial trucks and carried them for nine months for a contractual fee of about $10,000. The birth control technology which is such a solace to infertile couples has destroyed the sanctity of motherhood a central concept to many major religions. The case of Baby M has become a landmark case.

There are some who would like to push the technology to its limit without realizing that the expanding empire of technology leaves a trail of blood and tears whatever region of human affairs it claws through.

Reproductive technology has made it impossible to enact new laws without a full understanding of the long-term consequences of surrogacy on the children involved.

"Researchers have suggested that children might be traumatized by the knowledge that their natural mother was paid to bear them... The ethical issues raised by surrogate motherhood are perhaps the most difficult of all to resolve."[8] The consequences of social experiment in parental relationship and reproductive technology will be evaluated in the next century. Someone has to pay the price now.

The birth control technology that has made test-tube babies and surrogate motherhood possible came, initially, as a liberation for womankind. Liberation led to living together, pre-marital, extra-marital, and indiscriminate sex, teen-age pregnancy, and now fear of AIDS. Instead of self-renewal, technology is leading society to self-destruction. Women's exodus to the promised land has become a march to loneliness and death. More than ten million teen-age girls became pregnant out of wedlock during the 1980s. Half of them aborted or had miscarriages – in a society where infertile couples are willing to do anything to adopt babies and surrogate motherhood is becoming an immoral trade. One-third of all the abortions done in America were done on teen-agers. A society which has a 10.8 per 1000 infant mortality rate,[9] which cannot cope with its technology but is still lusting for more of it, needs to check whether it is growing or dying. The self-renewal rate compares poorly with the self-destructive acts generated by adverse effects of technology, absence of policies, and the cultural drag.

It is very important to have a model which simultaneously measures the technology-induced self-renewing as well as self-destructive acts which are occurring daily in the United States – in every society, in fact. There is nothing like linear progress – from dawn to dawn. It could be from dawn to darkness, to long darkness, as happened after the decline of Graeco-Roman civilization and the dominance of Europe by the Catholic Church until it was liberated by the Gutenberg technology and the Lutheran Protestant reformation movement.

Technology's Reach

Technology undoubtedly extends the cognitive domain of humans who are otherwise limited by their senses. Echoing what Marshall McLuhan had said earlier, Everett M. Rogers points out:

All communication technology extends the human senses of touching, smelling, tasting, and (especially) hearing and seeing. Such extensions allow an individual to reach out in space and time, and thus obtain information that would not otherwise be available...Media technologies provide us with 'a window to the world,' and as a result we know more about distant events than we could ever experience directly.[10]

Take, for instance, a less noticed innovation, toll-free calls, which brought about a veritable revolution in social, political, and marketing communications in the United States. According to Andrew L. Yarrow of *The New York Times*, "The 800 number – that 10-digit tie line to a mind-boggling array of products and information – has mushroomed into a multibillion-dollar business and is entrenched in American popular culture."[11] In 1986, toll-free operators, scattered and invisible, answered four billion calls facilitating the hotel and travel industry, catalogue sales, product information services, and inquiries about IRS, AIDS, cancer, second-opinion referrals about surgical operations, drugs, missing children, suicide, runaways, army recruitment, etc. Think of any significant social, commercial, or political problem, and most probably there will be an 800 number to call for help. In the United States people in distress do not pray to God for succor, they call an 800 number. Even senators have 800 numbers. Toll-free Live-Aid for Africa on July 13, 1985 brought in half a million pledges.[12] But that wasn't before television had brought to our dining table ghostly pictures of famished Africa.

While the 800 number gives a person free access to the global village, a variation on the theme, 900, gives access for 50 cents to instant polls, sports, and stock market information, and maybe some hot adult conversation. More than any other institution, television is using 900 numbers for audience reactions and opinion polls, asking their opinions on everything from the New York vigilante Bernhard Goetz (whether he was guilty) to whether the New York Giants would win that season. In 1989 there were 128,000 lines[13] which were used for information about sports highlights, financial news, weather reports, etc. Mostly television stations use 900 numbers to assess audience instant reaction to news events, current affairs and, entertainment programs or pilots. Surprisingly, straw polls are becoming a unique form of access to the mass media.

Technology and the marketplace have converged once again to determine, without human intervention, what is right and what is wrong. And like many American innovations such as fast foods, slot machines, and other forms of instant gratification, the 800-900 culture is spreading into other countries. The potential uses and misuses of 800-900 numbers for democratic and undemocratic societies are mind-boggling.

Consider how music technology – instrument pickups and cordless microphone – is changing rock concerts and other stage performances. It has freed singers and guitarists from their umbilical cords to amplifiers, and they are free to weave creative patterns and stage aesthetic choreography.

Performers not only have freedom on the stage, but they can also go into the audience and draw them into participation. Maybe some venturesome artist will annihilate the distinction between proscenium and auditorium and create a new kind of performance – more participative and ritualistic, a new kind of musical-theatrical experience, enveloping, and involving. John Rockwell, the noted music critic, said, "Technology always makes its first appearance in imitation of something older and more familiar – early movies as silent filmed plays for instance, or early photography as super-realist portrait painting, or sound recording as preserved concerts. But the technology comes into its own only when it fires a visionary artist to re-invent art on the brand-new terms suggested by that technology."[14] Technology enables man to create new art forms and demands new aesthetic standards and new approaches to criticism as one can see in television programming.

Strangely enough, because of satellite communications technology, Americans today know more about the dying people of Lebanon and Ethiopia than the dying farmers of Iowa or the teen-agers of the Bronx. The question is if technology – communications technology in particular – can be a "window unto ourselves". We want some technology to help us in strengthening family ties, or bringing up children in a drug-abused and crime-ridden society as we ring in the 21st century.

Each new technology manifests both creative and destructive aspects, and demands serious analysis in order to understand its long-term and short-term impact on society. In technology's cash register, every credit must equal and explain every debit.

The boom in the information technology in the 1980s, for instance, led to a boom in inside trading in Wall Street. Computer technology has made exchange of intangible assets and financial operations quick and easy, but it has also put incredible strain on a system built for a slower pace. There is a mismatch between computer-controlled operations and the economic processes they are supposed to symbolize, encouraging predators to cheat the system and amass unprecedented fortunes.

The information revolution demands new social justice and newer public controls, the absence of which might create great social upheavals. Every time an Ivan Boesky is apprehended for an inside trading deal shaking the public's faith in a mighty institutional structure like Wall Street, or a televangelist is defrocked, robbing devotees of their faith in the house of God, the mass media respond by resurrecting their old files on ethics rather than suggesting new social policies to regulate social behavior. Here is one typical media response:

> Ethical introspection, after all, is at odds with the pragmatism of national culture. It is not accidental that the country's favored metaphor is sports:

a factual world of detailed rules and final scores, where armchair disputes can be resolved by instant replays. Questions of what constitutes right and wrong are far more troubling, but there comes a time in the life of a nation when they must be addressed, not avoided... Against the societal backdrop of value-free self-indulgence, it is not surprising that some in the Administration have been motivated by a desire to advance themselves rather than the public interest.[15]

Technology and Ethics

Today lawyers, politicians, doctors, preachers, journalists, teachers, and businessmen are roaming through lush ethical jungles raised by technology which is growing faster than their minds and morals can comprehend. "Be all you can be" and "You have only one life to live" are the slogans which constitute woofs and warps of the public discourse in the United States today. Imagine the dilemma of the gynecologist at Dartmouth's Mary Hitchcock Memorial Hospital when he was requested by an infertile couple to artificially inseminate the wife with her husband's brother's sperm.[16] Would it be all right if any woman in a family volunteers to become a surrogate mother – mother for her daughter, for instance? What is incest then? Technology forces humans to abandon old attitudes and redefine old values and concepts. It makes the sacred profane, and the profane sacred. "The real challenge would then become a redefinition of wants so that they serve society as well as self, defining a single ethic that guides means while it also achieves rightful ends," says Ezra Brown of *Time*.[17]

As technology dislocates the ethical base of society, the cry for legislative controls will pierce the skies; more technology may mean more controls, less freedom. Jacques Ellul says in *Presence of the Kingdom* that technology tends to annihilate existing moral values without providing guidance for an alternative. When technology arouses hopes of the kingdom to come here and now, why not go for it?

Ellul reminds us that for the sake of efficiency, people in power will do anything, "as in ancient days men put out the eyes of nightingales in order to make them sing better."[18] In medieval kingdoms in the Middle East slaves were castrated so that they could serve the Sultan's seraglio and harem more efficiently. So it is efficiency, cost effectiveness, profitability – values measurable in the marketplace – which count and determine values and social conduct. When God spoke to the televangelist Oral Roberts, didn't He ask him to raise $8 million or He would "call Oral Roberts Home"?

New technology, initially, appears as an innovation, improvement, or extension of the existing technology and generates new optimism; but eventually, through convergence with other technologies or as a spin-off, it establishes its new identity and asserts its demanding character by questioning traditional ethics, laws, orthodoxies, vested interests, and ideologies or anything else which stands in its way. It demands to be used on the promise of plenty, or by offering solutions to intractable problems.

No one knew a few years ago how microchips would affect our daily lives, as few know today how superconductivity will affect life on the earth in the next decade. All that scientists are doing now is to indulge in hi-sci fantasies – the cradle of all scientific inventions – that the whole transportation system might be very different; that there may be new highly efficient long-distance transmission lines; that there may be miniature supercomputers with functions unimaginable at present. Eventually, superconductivity technology might run into headlong confrontation with the automobile industry and in the course of time destroy it, as the automobile itself destroyed a lifestyle associated with the railroads. When the marketplace and superconductivity converge, there will be massive social upheaval in the United States. It will question our ethics, our laws, our ideology.

Technology and Ideology

Ideology pretends to explain all facts and natural phenomena and has normative functions; it aims at "total explanation ... by the application of a single idea to the various realms of reality."[19] This view of ideology makes it a closed paradigm. Its practical application in politics, as historical experience shows, has led to totalitarian terror. Ideology, sometimes, dwarfs the human mind. Ideology, according to J. Gould, "is a pattern of beliefs and concepts (both factual and normative) which purport to explain complex social phenomena with a view to directing and simplifying socio-political choices facing individuals and groups."[20] Since it lays down norms of behavior, it has ethical content embedded in it for the survival and expansion of the group which practices it. So ideology is not only an intellectual system but a daily practice, and thus rivals religion in its hold on the people. Both prescribe formulated and well-defined ends to be pursued, and proscribe ideas and practices to be shunned.

In his intellectual pursuit, an ideologue will uncover lies and deceptions in other systems, and in his practice he will proselyte and persecute the non-believers. It would appear that the Soviet Union, China, Khomeini's Iran, etc., have been treading ideological paths while societies like the United States are ideology-free, which is of course not true because no society can be built or last long without a broad, acceptable pattern of beliefs, concepts, and values. It is a question of the enforcement of those set of values necessary to the survival and prosperity of the society.

The United States is not ideologically free but ideologically open: all systems of beliefs and values are tolerated so long as they do not question the controlling center or the core of American society. That's the free marketplace of goods and ideas, the First Amendment and free enterprise. That explains the lure of America as a place where one can tell one's rosary or chant one's mantra and also pursue one's material dreams. In ideologically closed societies, humans feel suffocated until someone like Luther ushers in a liberation theology or some alternative ideology.

Every new technology questions the existing ideology because it offers different ways of doing work, leading to alternative explanations of phenomena and the questioning of ethics based upon previous explanations. Technology is also an enemy of utopia because like ideology, utopia, too, aims at establishing forever an earthly heaven, excluding other possibilities.

Technology creates other possibilities only by destabilizing the present actualities. In other words, technology tends to open up a closed ideology, as one can see happening in Russia under Gorbachev and China under Deng Xiao Ping (before the massacre in Beijing in the summer of 1989) . The two communist giants, in order to catch up with the West, will adopt newer technologies, necessitating giving up their rigid ideologies. Diffusion and adoption of technological innovations require free debate at some level, and if free debate is an anathema to a society, adoption of newer technologies will be hindered or slowed down. In other words, Russia and China will always be trying to catch up with the West.

Technology, like art and literature, is criticism of a society because it, too, questions the assumptions on which the society is based by suggesting alternatives. It tends to break down orthodoxy and ideological rigidities by making the impossible plausible and by freeing man's imagination. It is not surprising, therefore, that scientific and technological imagination has supplanted the artistic imagination as we enter the last decade of the twentieth century. It is in this sense that technology is not merely technique or applied science but a critique of culture. Culture, in the words of A. L. Kroeber and C. Kluckhohn, consists of:

> patterns, explicit and implicit, of and for behavior acquired and transmitted by symbols, constituting the distinctive achievements of human groups, including their embodiments in artifacts; the essential core of culture consists of traditional (i.e. historically derived and selected) ideas and especially their attached values; culture systems may, on the one hand, be considered as product of action, on the other hand as conditioning elements of further action.[21]

Since the essence of a self-renewing society lies in the worth of the individual – an autonomous, self-determining individual who resists domination and power – privacy, decentralized freedoms, the right to know, dissent, and a self-critical attitude become necessary, although not sufficient, conditions for self-renewal.

Whenever a new communications technology appears in the marketplace, the question the policy makers and the public have to ask is if the new gadget and the culture it creates will eventually dwarf the individual or enhance his capacity to assert his autonomy and self-worth. For instance, what is the effect of satellite-delivered global television programming on the child, on the woman, on the innocent who are unaware of its consequences? Will it return political control to the people if another Nixon rises? Will it destroy individual privacy – the right to be left alone to make one's imaginative world from which spring all the inventions? Will it create a gilded cage for us? These are some of the questions which shall engage us in the following chapters.

Chapter Three
Freedom in the Goldfish Bowl

... that man must shape his tools lest they shape him.[1]

Technology extends man and his senses. But it can also shrink him and reduce him to a moral Lilliputian. More than any other people in the world, Americans are being watched, scrutinized, profiled, quantified, segmented, and targeted for political, commercial, and other propaganda. Wouldn't it be easy to manage people if some technology could give the authorities access to the thought processes and inner recesses of individuals? What is good for the efficient running of a stable system may in certain circumstances be detrimental to its self-renewal, its autopoiesis. Self-renewal to a degree depends on a state of internal non-equilibrium, pushing the system across one or more instability thresholds to a new stage of evolution, as discussed in the previous chapters.

Individual creativity can only incubate in privacy. It is individual creativity that generates the necessary internal ferment and fluctuations in a society which, in the course of time, lead it to the beginning of a new order. Crazy and creative people continuously test the stability of a society.

Invasion of privacy[2] was a humiliation in the past, but today it can be a nightmare. Not long ago, a TV reporter, Lucille Rich, and a camera crew from WCBS-TV, in order to look for a scoop, barged unannounced into a posh restaurant, LeMistral,[3] in New York City and started shooting in order to record their story for a series on health code violations in the catering industry. The sudden splash of dazzling lights and the whirring of cameras sent the patrons helter-skelter for some hiding place. The shock was not because the diners' infidelities were exposed. Exposure to the public through the camera's eye was a most flagrant act of indecency and violation of their right to eat alone. It is this kind of invasion of privacy which normally attracts attention in America. The more sinister forms of invasion of privacy which occur in the act of data-gathering, recombination, and manipulation of data from diverse sources about individuals and groups go unchallenged because they are unobtrusive and seem harmless.

The concern about the obtrusive kind of invasion of privacy goes back to the last century, when two young lawyers from Boston, Samuel D. Warren and Louis D. Brandeis, wrote an article in 1880 in *Harvard Law Review* entitled "The Right Of Privacy." The authors thought of privacy in terms of defamation and trespass on property. As they said:

> The press is overstepping in every direction the obvious bounds of propriety and decency. Gossip is no longer the resource of the idle and of the vicious, but has become a trade which is pursued with industry as well as effrontery. To satisfy a prurient taste the details of sexual relations are spread broadcast in the columns of the daily papers. To occupy the indolent, column upon column is filled with idle gossip, which can be procured by intrusion upon the domestic circle. The intensity and complexity of life, attendant upon advancing civilization, have rendered necessary some retreat from the world, and man, under the refining influence of culture, has become more sensitive to publicity, so that solitude and privacy have become more essential to the individual; but modern enterprise and invention have, through invasion upon his privacy, subjected him to mental pain and distress, far greater than could be inflicted by mere bodily injury.[4]

Privacy is the cradle of creativity. It is the encroaching technological civilization with its capacity to monitor and record man's every whisper and heartbeat and explore even his genetic code which has made privacy more than a necessity for individual self-renewal. To be left alone, to be autonomous, to engage in intrapersonal communication, to re-examine one's life without being primed and probed has been always difficult, as Justice Peters of the California Supreme Court opined, because "extended family networks, primary group relationships, and rigid communal mores served to expose an individual's every deviation from the norm and to straitjacket him in a vise of backyard gossip, which threatened to deprive men of the right of 'scratching where it itches.'"[5] It is more than the scratching of body and soul which will be haunting Americans in the future.

Technologies of Un-freedom

Invasion of privacy can be obtrusively sinister, as when Ron Galela pursued Jacqueline Kennedy Onassis with his camera. But more destructive, although less noticed, is the loss of personal freedom due to a combination of computer and satellite technologies, especially when they are wedded to sophisticated research methodologies developed by marketing and advertising companies to isolate groups and target them for narrowcasting their messages. The deadly technological combination has made the advent of soft and prolonged tyrannies possible. A distinguished Harvard law professor, Arthur Miller, said: "The same technology that sends information to our astronauts on the moon moves information about us from its point of generation to distant files in institutions which probably have no sense of the conditions under which the original data were generated, the purpose for which they were generated, and the standards – especially the evaluation standards – of the initiating organization."[6] A combination of computer technology, sophisticated data gathering techniques, methods of programming, and message targeting can destabilize individuals and deprive them of decision-making powers. American society might regress and relapse into the sheep-and-shepherd concept in the new century. It is not the horrors of the Orwellian world or Huxley's brave new world order but the softer tyrannies of technology which tend to close the mind. Individualized direct-mail, personalized propaganda, the evanescent, subliminal commercial: they cast invisible chains on the American people.

It will be much easier for the Koreans, Chileans, Chinese and Russians to revolt against their harsh and cruel governments than for the Americans because the latter do not feel the sweet tyrannies of corporate America. A combination of segmented and target-seeking mass communication messages – computer individualized and personalized – may skew democracy away from the people. They may not feel it because every time they lose a bit of freedom they will be overly compensated by dazzling varieties of consumer goods available at affordable prices in acres of air-conditioned malls. Jacques Ellul says that in the technological society the town hall concept of democracy is being replaced by the idea of a shepherded democracy: "If propaganda involved calm exposition of political theories among which the citizen might choose intelligently, contradictions would be beneficial and would leave the citizen a free man. But this is an impossibility, from the moment the propagandist possesses material means for exerting action on the mob and knowledge of the secret recesses of the human psyche."[7]

High speed computers with their immense capacity for data storage and retrieval have made it possible to collate and correlate data from different individuals and collapse them into new information neighborhoods.[8] Once these information neighborhoods are recognizable, it becomes easy for a Madison Avenue rhetorician to create messages which give the sender direct control over his millions of dispersed receivers. As reception and assimilation of the message become more efficient, communal dialogue and democratic participation recedes. People don't talk back; they listen. A nation whose people don't talk back is a slave nation.

Terror by Data

At any given time in America, thousands of data collectors, some door-to-door, others via telephones, are unself-consciously accessing innocent citizens and asking them questions about their interests, opinions, recreational preferences, and culinary likes and dislikes along with age, ethnic background, and other demographic details. The non-threatening low-level data collectors yield place to sophisticated data analysts, most of them having research degrees in statistical methodologies. They in turn manipulate the data for multi-dimensional scaling and clustering to identify groups which respond to the underlying assumptions, and hence messages. Computerized statistical methods have become so refined that the realm of probability has become a realm of near certainty. The next step of matching a segmented audience with message, channel or media selection and daypart or timing is easily done by computers. It is a kind of sophisticated dating service which, strangely enough is also being performed increasingly by computers.

In 1988, Equifax and TRW, Inc., two of the biggest list marketers in America, initiated services that enable direct marketers to target consumers selectively based on the prospects' level of available credit or the non-zero balance of their credit cards. TWR now gives information on revolving credit lines rather than mere credit-worthiness. All video rental companies keep a list of their clients, and it is not difficult to profile a customer from his reading and video habits and then target him politically and commercially. The greed of corporate America might cause consumer paranoia. A regulatory measure like The Video & Library Privacy Protection Act might be a corrective measure against corporate abuse.

Through cable narrowcasting and digital addressability (which allows the cable operator to record what is being watched and sell that information to others), direct mail, and specialized magazines, a multimedia approach to audiences may chain American people into electronic slavery. There will be qualitative difference between the electronic slavery of the future and the feudal slavery of the past. Modern man will not feel that he is a slave because he will be drowned with the excesses of technological plenty. His greatest freedom will lie, as it does today, in listening to the commercial speech, which is increasingly replacing the free political speech as enshrined in the First Amendment. It is not big brother but the corporate brother who threatens the privacy, autonomy, and potential for autopoietic self-renewal of the individual in America.

There are no protests and violent demonstrations about this erosion of privacy because the process is slow, invisible, and non-obtrusive. We don't see our enemy, but like a lump in the throat or dull pain in the breast, it is there; and we have fearful apprehensions which we ignore. Imagine you go to a fashionable store and buy a costly fur for your girlfriend and pay with your American Express Card. Before you get out of the cashier's line the Universal Product Code (UPC) is computer scanned. Your credit card and the various items of purchases can be used by a research company, say Information Resources Inc., and through a research methodology called Behaviorscan[9], the company can analyze your lifestyle and cluster you with others and sell the information to companies whose purpose may be far from commercial – it could be sinister. You wonder why Sears & Roebuck or J.C. Penny sent you a birthday greeting card and how they came to know about your birthday when your husband forgets about it.

It is difficult to deny information to data collectors. The most avid collector of data about the American people is the Census Bureau, which develops the data for altogether different purposes. Although it does not release the data about individuals, corporations and businesses could use the micro and macro data fraudulently. Something which makes the bureau's activities popular is the publication of the Statistical Abstracts of the United States. But the marketing research companies use the data in other ways. After supplementing the census data with their own surveys, they use them for market segmentation and target clustering. The census blocks are turned into community types. For instance, a cluster identified in rural Vermont may have a commonalty with a similar cluster in Texas and both the clusters may receive similar messages, political or commercial, from a political candidate or an advertising-marketing company. It is this isolation of clusters of interests, or taste collectivities as mentioned elsewhere,[10] which has become so important to sellers and buyers of information.

The whole idea of neighborhood and local community has been changed by the information gatherers of today. We are all for sale, like the slaves of the olden times – though we don't feel it; we are busy with our push-button fantasies.[11]

Electronic Footprints

One of the richest sources of information about the American people is the Social Security Administration; another is the Department of Health and Human Services. Both of them combine and correlate data to discover fraud and abuse and in the process open newer possibilities of data combination and patterning through computer interconnections. Whatever modern man does or does not do, he leaves his electronic footprints, which become the database for statistical analysis in a society like the U.S.A, obsessed with quantification and measurements. No bit or byte is useless.

A byte that cannot be used today may be used tomorrow. Researchers and information scientists of today are waiting for tomorrow's technologies so that they can develop newer methodologies of data manipulation and patterning. It is the pattern-making capabilities of modern computers which have given so much power to corporations and wealthy groups and have left the common man in America so helpless.

The selling of a message has become much more important in America than the product itself, as was seen during the 1988 presidential election. The choice-making capabilities of individuals who based their decisions earlier on deliberations, discussions, and debates are being pre-empted by remote political and commercial interests. What matters now is not a public debate about national issues but the mobilization of public sentiments or emotions in a particular direction. If the Iran-contra affair had not demobilized President Reagan, he would have gone down in history as the "great communicator," so successful was his image-building and direct access to the people via television.

One might argue that all is not lost since society does take care of Watergates and Irangates, that the players of the Watergate and Iran-contra affairs were different from those who should be making decisions about their local communities, schools, and environmental pollution. But the consensus among the wielders of power in the U.S.A is that what matters is not political debate but the management of public sentiments and prejudice through population segmentation, clustering, and manipulation. As Burnham pointed out in *The Rise of the Computer State*, that in an age when "computerized direct mail machines are spitting out scores of different but not necessarily inconsistent messages directly aimed at the mailboxes of millions of prescreened voters, the truth about a candidate and his promises may be obscured for both the individual voters and even the most aggressive reporters."[12] Or, maybe the aggressive reporters are persuaded to take more interest in the extra-marital behavior of a political candidate, as happened in the case of Gary Hart, than question the candidate's stance on national and international issues. Trivia pursuit might engage all the nation's energy.

People are genuinely concerned about their privacy, as various opinion polls and surveys show. A survey carried out in 1983 showed that 84 percent of the respondents felt that it would be possible for someone to construct a master profile about them which would invade their privacy, and urged criminal sanctions against the commercial interests whose data-collecting activities violated an individual's right to privacy.[13]

It is not only surveys and instant opinion polls but also home banking, home-shopping services, information services, home and personal security services, home study courses, special entertainment options, and organizational fund-raising which strip our souls and bodies naked. Through insinuating questionnaires, a very delicate and critically significant pool of personal data is collected from respondents which then is sold as a high-priced commodity for commercial purposes, for confidentiality breaches to criminal elements, and even for legitimate purposes to various government agencies.

Those who use electronic banking have reason to live in fear. Banking data centers have already collected massive amounts of data about millions of individuals. Marshall McLuhan and Bruce Powers said that "private identity which was tied to a specific time and place is already gone" and the Electronic Fund Transfer users are painlessly sliding into an electronic slave society: "Armed with your account number, outside investigators can now find out your bank balance as easily as a criminal can...The future holds for us a corporate individual who will accept the goldfish bowl as a natural habitat, having recognized that electronic espionage has already become an art form."[14]

Americans would rather give up their privacy than avoid contact with the EFT system at all. The electronic funds transfer system, apart from handling accounts efficiently and providing resources to a conglomeratized and multinational-controlled economy, is the most unobtrusive system of surveillance in a "free society." As technology enhances system efficiency, privacy tends to shrink, and self-renewal of the individual and society is threatened. It is not over-commitment abroad, but invasion within the country which threatens American civilization as it faces the 21st century.

The National Commission on Electronic Fund Transfers identified different ways in which the system could hurt privacy: by creating financial transaction records when none existed before, by recording not only the details of a checking system but also the exact place and time of the transactions, by the ease of the retrievability of electronic data and by the on-line and real-time operational capacity of the system which could locate instantly the person who entered the transaction. One might cite the advantages of EFT by the number of small-time crooks and murderers who have been arrested and convicted because each transaction takes place on a video-tape camera. It happened in the 1986 conviction of a man who killed a well-known Seattle attorney and left his electronic footprints while using the attorney's bank card. But the big time crooks who mine the foundations of Wall Street have no way of being detected.

By linking the various EFT systems in the country and using Social Security numbers as codes, governments, private businesses, and criminal organizations have already got an immense data base from which to operate. The government has taken perfunctory note of the problem by enacting the Electronic Fund Transfer Act of 1978, which deals mostly with regulatory issues like EFT card issuance, civil and criminal liabilities, and the disclosure policy of banks. The Electronic Communications Privacy Act of 1986 extends eavesdropping restrictions to the new communications technologies like mobile telephones and computer mail.

One could be satisfied with the facts that the law enforcement officers cannot intercept such communications unless they have court orders and the unauthorized interception or destruction of such data can lead to prison terms. But neither of these two facts can stop various systems from being linked together and the data to be reorganized, manipulated and put to use in a way for which they were not intended. It is not the interception of data which is such a serious problem but the misuse of the legally obtained data by collating it with other data and using the emerging patterns and profiles for group control and political and commercial purposes.

Sinister Shadow

The deregulation of the cable industry has already made a mockery of the Cable Communications Act of 1984. The act's provisions that the cable operator notify the subscriber in writing about any personally identifiable information, obtain the subscriber's permission before data collection, not to release any information to a third party without written consent, and to allow civil action in case of grievance have been nullified by a recent court judgment declaring that the cable industry is beyond the pale of the Fairness Doctrine. Wayne Walley reported in the *Advertising Age* that "Direct marketers may become unexpected benefactors of cable deregulation when they are allowed to buy cable subscription lists. The relaxation of government controls, in addition to allowing cable operators to set their own fees, gives most systems the option of selling their customers' names."[15]

Cable systems could collect a lot more information than they are now doing, and under pressure from cable-mail operators and the lure of huge unearned incomes, data collection for the cable companies could become a more important business than the operation of the cable itself. As Burnham suggested: "Even if laws and procedures are devoted to provide each subscriber with an ironclad guarantee that individually identifiable information will never be improperly shared, neighborhood patterns of book reading, television watching, banking and electronic shopping will give commercial and political marketing experts a powerful new tool to burrow into the psyches of unsuspecting customers."[16]

Most of the states allow individual and class lawsuits when there is an invasion of privacy. While individual harm can be shown, it is difficult to prove harm leading to a class action. Class action takes place when members of a group who have a common grievance against a party file a collective suit on behalf of the entire group. Such collective harm is difficult to prove because it is not easy to transform dispersed aggregate cable users into a socially self-conscious active group. An individual may not know where the logic of data manipulation placed him according to a particular underlying need of the system manager. It is not an individual's file which is in danger of being probed for a particular bit of information, but how that file fits into a wider network of relationship and how it assumes a new meaning because of new configuration, has become a crucial question today. As stated by Boorman and Levitt in a *New York Times* article: "This is because block modeling classifies people on the basis of where they fit in a larger web of relationships. Therefore one has to be concerned with many more "files" than just one's own – some belonging to people no one has connections with....the new technologies frequently pick out less than obvious groups where members may easily fail to recognize that they are being targeted in common."[17]

Sex-crazed evangelists in America have probably succeeded in building their ungodly empires of the gullible by cluster-targeting.

Obtrusive Invasion of Privacy

Defamation or obtrusive invasion of privacy is a public event, more like an act of aggression which does not go unnoticed. Although intrusive technologies invade privacy, the thirst to know more about the government, corporations, and celebrities too has been increasing. Consequently, the Privacy Act of 1974 and the Freedom of Information Act of 1966 limit each other. They also epitomize the society's dilemma. Under the Freedom of Information Act, the public and the press have the right to know and have access to all information except that which "would constitute a clearly unwarranted invasion of privacy." As several court cases have shown, the courts normally weigh public interest as the deciding factor when there is a conflict between the right to privacy and the right to know.

Although the tort of intrusion of privacy ranges from illegal entry into a house and window-peeping to surreptitious tape recording, it is the camera which has been a nuisance to some people. But as we pursue this inquiry, we find that the same person who complains of invasion of privacy does not mind appearing before television and even stripping before it provided there is money for him or her.

The Case of Dietmann.

A. A. Dietmann was suspected of practicing medicine without a proper license. The State Board of Health of California and a Los Angeles district attorney entered into a cohort arrangement with *Life* magazine to trap the con man. On the face of it, it was professionally wrong to cooperate with state authorities because pressmen are supposed to be independent of governmental authorities. Jackie Metcalf, a *Life's* reporter, and William Ray, a *Life* photographer, gained admittance to the house of A.A. Dietmann by giving a false reference and pretending that Jackie Metcalf had a medical problem. While Dietmann examined Jackie Metcalf, the photographer secretly took pictures. A hidden transmitter relayed the "patient-doctor" conversation to a nearby van where it was tape-recorded and listened to by California state officials. A. A. Dietmann was convicted of practicing medicine without a license, and he in turn sued for damages for invasion of privacy. The court awarded Dietmann damages amounting to $1,000. Judge Shirley Hufstedler, disregarding the argument that electronic instruments were important tools of investigative reporting, made interesting observations about sleuthing and investigative reporting: "The First Amendment is not a license to trespass, to steal, or to intrude by electronic means into the precincts of another's home or office. It does not become such a license simply because the person subjected to the intrusion is reasonably suspected of a crime."[18] Dietmann's case is a warning to journalists who use cameras, electronic transmission devices and video tapes in order to exercise their right to know as the public's surrogate.

More than the law, it is a question of ethics. For instance, most of the sates permit recording of conversations provided there is one-party consent. It is called consensual monitoring, which means that only the third party is forbidden to tape conversations. However, one of the two parties in conversation can tape without the knowledge of the other party, and most journalists carry a miniature tape recorder. Every time technology throws up a new product in the market, new ethical questions arise which cannot be brushed under the carpet. Ethics reflect and protect the set of constants or invariants which constitute the inner core, the controlling center of a society. They come under attack whenever a communications tool is given to humans.

As the mass media scavenge for scoops to increase circulation or boost ratings, they become insensitive to ethics and bulldoze into private lives, where the truth begins to hurt. It is the pressure to feed the hungry media machine which makes journalists blind to what is the public interest and what is the domain of privacy. A case in point is Virgil v. Time, Inc. in which *Sports Illustrated* published an article about a surfer, Mike Virgil. Mike Virgil, after giving consent for an interview, withdrew his consent for the article. Nonetheless, the magazine went ahead with publication and was sued for invasion of privacy damages. Circuit Judge Merrill said that publicizing private facts was not protected by the First Amendment unless the subject was newsworthy, and that the newsworthy aspect of an event should be decided by community standards and mores: "The line is to be drawn when the publicity ceases to be the giving of information to which the public is entitled, and becomes a morbid and sensational prying into public lives for its own sake, with which a reasonable member of the public, with decent standards, would say that he had no concern."[19] The judge warned journalists not to misuse the media technologies and seek application regardless of the consequences.

The mass media thrust many unknown people into the limelight, and the public longs to know more about such instant celebrities. Media and publishing companies hasten to turn the public inquisitiveness into cash by rushing into movies and docudramas which occasionally land them into privacy suits. Potentially every one's life is waiting for some hack writer to turn it into a mini-series or a movie. In such cases the right to privacy becomes a publicity right – in essence a property right. Actors like Bela Lugosi, who acted as Count Dracula, and legendary personages like Elvis Presley hold their name and fame beyond the grave, and have a tremendous cash value – thanks to media technologies serving the free marketplace of goods and ideas.

But the assault on privacy does not matter so long as one gets paid for it, nor does anyone mind being naked in a naked society so long as one's topless act is paid. When the cash register rings in America, most people forget their privacy.

No Place to Hide in the Global Village

Remote-sensing satellites which have been circling the globe for about two decades are used to locate mineral deposits, assess farm crop conditions, and uncover patterns of deforestation. The same technology was used for detecting the Chernobyl nuclear accident, discovering the Soviet Union's space center in Asia, and natural disasters like floods and droughts.[20] At present commercial satellites can't read a license plate or photograph a nude on the beach, but the technology is moving fast in that direction. The U.S. LANDSAT satellite system has a resolution of 30 meters; the French SPOT gives a resolution of 10 meters. The military satellite system can spot a tennis ball in your backyard. What belongs to the military today could be in the commercial domain tomorrow, raising serious privacy issues.

The Land Remote-Sensing Commercialization Act of 1984, which regulates the operation of private land remote-sensing satellites aims to "preserve and promote the national security of the United States..." [21] Except from requiring that the data be supplied on non-discriminatory basis, it does not refer to privacy issues. But as high-resolution satellite technology becomes commercially feasible, it may raise the constitutional issue of unreasonable searches by government, the tort of intrusion into privacy by the news organizations, and the area of trade secrets.

The Fourth Amendment states, "The right of the people to be secure in their persons, houses, papers, and effects, against unreasonable searches and seizures, shall not be violated, and no warrants shall issue, but upon probable cause, supported by oath of affirmation, and particularly describing the place to be searched, and the persons or things to be seized." Remote-sensing satellites so far have not run afoul of the Constitution. The closest cases wherein the parties raised objection to the aerial surveillance of their properties by law enforcement officials without search warrants were by a California marijuana grower[22] and Dow Chemical Co.[23] Although in these two aerial surveillance cases, which come close to remote-sensing operations, both the plaintiffs lost, the majority opinion does seem to limit the use of remote-sensing satellites.

Justice Warren Burger said in the Dow case that "the surveillance of private property by using highly sophisticated surveillance equipment not generally available to the public, such as satellite technology, might be constitutionally proscribed absent a warrant."[24]

But as the resolution capabilities of remote-sensing satellites increase and computers begin to enhance and interpret images with greater sophistication, law enforcement authorities will be increasingly tempted to use them in observing criminal activities such as drug operations, marijuana growing, and illegal immigration. And for internal security reasons, the courts might change their opinion and allow an uninhibited use of remote-sensing satellites without much regard for individual privacy.

Would the courts stop a newspaper or a network doing investigative reporting if they were to use satellite technology in gathering data? What if they were to use the rental facilities of foreign satellites in gathering information, thus bypassing the domestic constitutional hurdles? While it sounds legitimate to use remote-sensing communications technology in apprehending auto-theft gangs, marijuana growers, drug traffickers, and the violators of pollution and environmental laws, the question is how to prevent its misuse.

Communications technology, which gives government and corporate America control over the people, can create opportunities for determined individuals and public-spirited groups to keep a watch over big brother. In 1985 some Swedish journalists started an independent, commercial information service called Space Media Network which monitors important military programs of the Superpowers and other international thugs. It was this group, now owned by a Swedish philanthropist, which first reported the Chernobyl disaster of 1986; some of us thought, erroneously, that it was Gorbachev's glasnost policy which had brought about honest reporting. Media Space Network discovered "secret preparations for a Soviet space shuttle, powerful laser installation, which could be made to serve a Soviet 'Star Wars,' advance evidence of resumed Soviet nuclear tests, the site for Chinese missiles in Saudi Arabia, a huge new cocaine-growing region in South America, giant forests fires in China.... Technology is allowing ordinary people to break down the information monopolies that can decide their fate. This time little brother is winning a round."[25] The fate of the earth may depend on how ordinary people organize themselves and exercise their right to know.

Privacy and Self-Renewal

Privacy puts one in charge of one's destiny – good or evil. Justice Louis Brandeis considered privacy "the most comprehensive of rights and the right most valued by civilized men." As intrusive communications technologies invade privacy, a condition of being civilized – to be left alone – is being taken away gradually. It is during moments of fearless solitude and retreat that humans do personal verification, self-testing, and self-affirmation. This leads to self-renewal and re-birthing of individuals who give new meanings and interpretation to the world around them.

From an innovative society, America might slide into an imitative society – waiting for someone else to develop technology and then rush to copy it as is done in Russia and China. The very technology which needs innovation and creativity to sustain it may be destroying its own source of fecundity if the policy-makers kowtow to the profitmakers. To be a scientific explorer and a moral agent, an individual has to be anchored in his own "respect-worthiness," as Manfred Stanley calls it. According to him individual dignity shares in "world building or world destroying actions," and thus "does not rest on intention, moral merit, or subjective definitions of self interests. It rests on the fact that we are, in this fundamental way that is beyond our intention, human. We are moral agents."[26]

To be a moral agent is to make choices, which is the essence of creativity and self- and societal renewal, autopoiesis. In privacy, in dignity, an individual can make and unmake worlds without public ridicule. A person can afford the luxury of self-criticism, self-reflection, or course correction and bring about other adjustments required to face the world without any loss of face. The public person and the private person thus enter into a process of mutual renewal. Alvin Gouldner pointed out:

> To make matters 'public' means to open them even to those who are not known personally, to those who do not ordinarily come into one's sight and hearing. On the paradigmatic level, to make things public is to take them (or allow them to go) beyond the family, for communication that may, in consequence, be cryptic, allusive, seemingly vague... One could be a public being, with all the exhaustion and tension that it generates, only because there was a place – the private sphere – to which one could retreat for repairs; a place in which one could find support for efforts that had failed to find public support. The private was a place here one could speak the silences of the public to a sympathetic and validating hearer.[27]

Effective control of many aspects of our lives has now shifted to outside forces, and in fact "individuals may be denied rights, privileges, and benefits based, not on past performance, but on a prediction of future tendencies."[28]

Imagine, in the future, an adventurous reporter, instead of invading a political candidate's privacy, uses a computer database to profile a political candidate and make predictions about his or her future political tendencies. The methodology for consolidating datafiles from diverse sources and predicting patterns of behavior based on the convergent datafiles is being perfected.

Controlling the Undesirable

Are there some undesirable people who should be subjected to electronic surveillance? The answer to this question depends upon our individual position in society. A housewife, a mother of teen-age children, a senior citizen, might want drug dealers, rapists, drunken drivers, and the like to be put under surveillance; law enforcement officers may want to put anyone under surveillance whom they suspect of criminal intentions; political incumbents would like all their rivals to be put under surveillance; corporations probably would wish to put governments under surveillance so they could manipulate decisions affecting them.

For every individual there is someone who is undesirable and unfit to live and roam freely and should be subjected to surveillance. It is this kind of dangerous thinking which encourages some of us to believe that the tentacles of the information society should be used to control undesirable elements. One might argue that in an age of increasing violence and the spread of epidemics like AIDS, society would benefit if datafiles of some social elements were kept under close scrutiny; but in that case, we all shall be under scrutiny.

Technology creates abundance of material goods, and sometimes imbues us with false confidence. An illusion of omnipotence leads to disastrous consequences, as happened during the Watergate crisis and the Iran-contra affair. Yet the temptations of technology are so great and sometimes so evil that the very freedom and privacy which led to the resurgence of technological innovations is threatened by the technology itself.

Communications and computer technologies have a built-in bias and thrust towards the control of uncertainty to ensure predictability, and consequently they re-inforce the existing power structure and make change difficult. Instead of increased freedom, which is the promise of technology, we may have a regimen of tyranny. As Paulo Feriere pointed out in *Pedagogy of the Oppressed*: "Any situation in which some men prevent others from engaging in the process of inquiry is one of violence. The means used are not important; to alienate men from their own decision-making is to change them into objects."[29] While living organisms grow and die, social systems have the potential of perpetual growth and self-renewal if individual dignity, worthiness, and privacy are held inviolable. There were societies in the past which could have lived forever, but they perished because their built-in tyrannies destroyed them.

American society, which rests on the twin foundation of free speech and a free market economy and has the potential of eternal self-renewal, may become a victim of not only the uncontrolled excesses of communications and computer technologies but also the unholy alliance between the mass media and corporate America.

Chapter Four
Collectivization of Free Speech

That's the slave's lot, not to speak one's thought.
 —Euripides, *Phonecian Women*

That something one might call the poetry of transgression is also knowledge.
 —Susan Sontag, *Style of Radical Will*

A free society shaped and structured by the First Amendment and open market would be adversely affected if the mass media were controlled by a dozen or so conglomerates.

John Milton's rhetorical question "... who ever knew Truth put to the worse, in a free and open encounter?" needs to be tested again in a society where the marketplace of ideas is being regulated by some remote economic interests. His exalted ideas, however, have inspired generations of social and political thinkers from John Stuart Mill and Thomas Jefferson to Thomas I. Emerson and Alexander Meiklejohn. In his essay "On Liberty," Mill, for instance, argued that a suppressed idea may be true and the accepted opinion may be false; that the accepted truth needs to be tested again and again; and most important of all, "... when the conflicting doctrines, instead of being one true and other false, share truth between them; and the non-conforming opinion is needed to supply the remainder of the truth, of which the received doctrine embodies only a part."[1] Mill's relativist approach places the value of all ideas into the realm of probability, and therefore their control by any central authority or a conglomerate is something to be questioned.

Description of reality is dependent upon the state of technology and to some extent upon those who have economic and political power. As technology changes, the perception of truth will change unless it is suppressed by the people in power. A simple example is that of the application of genetic DNA coding in solving crime. According to the criminal justice system in the U.S.A., certain evidence, even if it is relevant and crucial to a case becomes unacceptable if it violates any constitutional provision. This has allowed many criminals to go free because their crimes could not be proved beyond a reasonable doubt.

Now DNA "fingerprints" give away a criminal beyond any reasonable doubt, thus satisfying a legal dictum that it is better to let ten criminals free than punish an innocent one. Thus the discovery of truth or description of reality is aided by DNA technology. But the courts play a significant part in determining what is or should be truth.

The courts in America and legal scholars, particularly after WWII, have kept social good and the public interest in view while interpreting the First Amendment. Zachariah Chafee, Jr. in *Free Speech in the United States*, for instance, emphasized social interest as the chief goal of free speech: "The true boundary line of the First Amendment can be fixed only when Congress and the courts realize that the principle on which speech is classified as lawful or unlawful involves the balancing against each other of two very important social interests, in public safety and in the search for truth."[2]

Chafee was re-iterating Justice Oliver Wendell Holmes' clear-and-present danger test developed in the landmark case Schenck v. United States: "... the words used are used in such circumstance and are of such a a nature as to create a clear and present danger that they will bring about the substantive evils that Congress has a right to prevent."[3] Although Chafee did recognize the value of free speech as a contribution to individual good, he was wary of extending the First Amendment protection to profane and indecent speech which must yield place to the larger societal interests of "order, morality, the training of the young, and the peace of mind of those who hear and see."[4] Chafee's categorization of free expression as socially useful and therefore deserving protection, and socially unredeeming, therefore necessitating testing and regulation, had a profound effect upon judicial thought.

Another legal luminary of the twentieth century, Alexander Meiklejohn, also divided free speech into two categories, one absolute and the other requiring social control and regulation. Free speech in relation to self-government needs absolute protection so that all political and social issues are decided in a free and robust discussion as happened in the town meetings of olden times. As he said, "What is essential is not that every one shall speak, but that everything worth saying shall be said," in the manner of an orderly debate which may require procedural regulation but must not arouse the fear of reprisal.

He argued that Article 1, Section 6 of the U.S. Constitution grants members of Congress an absolute protection for their speeches in either House so that no member of Congress shall be questioned in any place. He wanted to extend the same absolute privilege to political debate outside Congress, also without the test of clear and present danger. Rejecting the views of Justice Holmes and Chafee, he said: " ...individuals have, then, a private right of speech which may on occasion be denied or limited, though such limitations may not be imposed unnecessarily or unequally. So says the Fifth Amendment. But this limited guarantee of the freedom of a man's wish to speak is radically different in intent from the unlimited guarantee of the freedom of public discussion, which is given by the First Amendment."[5]

Meiklejohn wanted absolutely no control over political expression in order to ensure that listeners can make wise decisions regarding their communities' affairs. It is the listeners' right which is of paramount importance. As a corollary to the town hall debate model which he propounded, the listeners' right to know emerged as an important post-war political and legal concept and has guided broadcasting in America. He placed free speech and expression on a continuum from zero protection to absolute protection. Commercial speech, which makes exaggerated claims, and socio-political speech, which serves as a corrective to those claims, cannot be equated and cannot be given an equal right of protection under the First Amendment.[6] What is protected, he said, was the discussion of public issues and political ideas which contribute to decision-making. In this process of decision-making novels, dramas, paintings, or poems may be relevant and would need absolute protection.

Another important First Amendment scholar, Thomas I. Emerson, in his famous book *The System of Freedom of Expression* propounded the expression-action theory of free speech. Emerson's ideas about freedom of speech bring him to center stage as American society moves toward the twenty-first century. He not only reaffirmed the traditional view that freedom of speech includes the right to disseminate one's views and beliefs to others through any medium including art, literature, or music, but also believed that it encompasses the right of access to the opinion of others and various sources of information, as well as the right of assembly and association.

The fourfold functions and values of a system of freedom of expression in an open society are: (a) self-fulfillment of the individual; (b) discovery of truth and knowledge; (c) participative and democratic decision-making and (d) a process of "maintaining the precarious balance between healthy cleavage and necessary consensus."[7] The U.S. Supreme Court judges, too, had expressed a similar opinion. In Whitney v. California, Justice Brandeis, for instance, commented that those who won our independence believed that "public discussion is a political duty; and that this should be a fundamental principle of the American government... Believing in the power of reason as applied through public discussion, they eschewed silence coerced by law – the argument of force in its worst form. Recognizing the occasional tyrannies of governing majorities, they amended the Constitution so that free speech and assembly should be guaranteed."[8]

Justice Brandeis' ideas about clear and present danger as a test expressed in 1927 found a systematic expression in Emerson's expression-action theory which he applied to four troublesome areas viz., sedition, defamation, obscenity, and provocation to anger. The touch-stone of his theory is that "a fundamental distinction must be drawn between conduct which consists of "expression" and conduct which consists of "action." "Expression" must be freely allowed and encouraged. "Action" can be controlled, subject to other constitutional requirements, but not by controlling expression..."[9]

Emerson's expression-action theory gives absolute protection to expression but permits constraints on action. However, when we critically examine the four functions and values of his theory, it becomes difficult to assign priorities if ever there is ever a conflict among them.[10]

Emerson asks a troublesome question: "Can the system of freedom of expression survive the shift from the liberal laissez-faire to the mass technological society?"[11] Or, when the mass media have been grabbed by financial consortiums, conglomerates, and multinationals, how much freedom is left? How can people think and discuss political and social problems freely and discuss economic priorities rationally when the town hall meeting, in a manner of speaking, is overrun by profiteers, auctioneers, and salesmen?

Media Mergers and Conglomerates

In the spring of 1987 Rep. Edward Markey (D-Mass), chairman of the House Energy and Commerce Committee's Telecommunications Subcommittee, held three days of hearings to determine if legislation was needed to re-stabilize the television industry, which had been shocked by the takeover of two networks. Fred Friendly, a veteran journalist, a former president of CBS, and now a professor at Columbia School of Journalism, lamented that the public trust has been turned into "a midway of junk entertainment." It was painful to hear him urge the legislators to force broadcasters to be more responsible. He said, "Sadly, I must tell you that the television networks of which I was a part are mercantile shadows of what they once were. Those in Congress, those in the FCC, and people like myself who stand idly by, are as guilty as the Wall Street traders who have changed something once licensed 'in the public interest, convenience and necessity' into a midway of junk entertainment and headline service news."[12]

When the public mind is fed with trivia, it becomes easy to take control of it. Serious economic and political issues are sidetracked because they don't sell and bring revenues. Ben Bagdikian, a celebrated media critic and a professor at the journalism school at University of California at Berkeley, addressing the subcommittee, repeated his warning which he gave in his 1983 book *The Media Monopoly*: "Those who have great media power usually insist that they will never abuse that power... and many of them are sincere. But history is not reassuring on that point. When the stakes are high enough, everybody will use whatever power is needed."[13] During the eight years as chairman of the Federal Communications Commission, Mark Fowler deregulated standards for television stations and, according to Bagdikian, "sanctified greed." Professor John Kenneth Galbraith was equally harsh about television's obsession with profits: "The test of achievement is what produces profits... and, alas, in the very short run. In broadcasting, the audience rating and the advertising reaction are the test... These are not theoretical dangers. The future is already here... Edward R. Murrow wouldn't now be hired by CBS, and if hired, considering his capacity to offend, his job might not be secure. Can anyone think that this is good?"[14] The socially useful speech in the form of discussions, documentaries, investigative reporting is being driven out by advertising and public relations communication.

The relentless concentration of media power has continued, despite antitrust laws. Over the last decade and a half many voices of protests, mostly in the wilderness, have been uttered: "Why the Government can't Stop Press Mergers," "America's Press: Too Much Power for Too Few?" "Busting the Media Trust," "Can the networks Survive?"[15]. Ben Bagdikian lamented the rise of "...a new kind of central authority over information – the national and multinational corporation."[16] The loyalty of these multinational corporations lies in earning profits, not helping society to discover the truth through unhindered debate.

The total number of media outlets in the U.S.A. (daily papers, magazines, radio and television stations and networks, book publishing companies, and movie studios) is 25,000, and they are controlled by 43 national and multinational corporations.[17] All the media outlets, however, are not equally important. Most of the outlets are merely distributaries and conduits, having dependency relations with larger information-originating centers which in turn are controlled by an ever decreasing number of owners. For instance, by the end of the century, according to *The Washington Post Study*, most of the newspapers in America will be owned or controlled by fewer than two dozen major communications conglomerates.[18]

Since this alarmist study, the trend toward ever-growing chains, conglomeration, and gigantism has been relentless. In 1985, in a manner of speaking, a gnat swallowed a camel. Capital Cities Communications bought ABC for $3.5 billion, a first time cohabitation between a large publishing company and a major network. The resulting giant has 90 radio, television, and cable stations, 36 weekly newspapers and shoppers, 10 daily newspapers, and many magazines with a total revenue of $4.5 billion. During the same period *The Washington Post* bought 17 percent of Cowles Media; Advance Publications bought New Yorker Magazine, Inc.; Rupert Murdoch's News Corp. bought 50 percent of the 20th Century-Fox Film Corp.; Gannet company bought *The Des Moines Register*; Time, Inc. purchased *Southern Living* and other media properties; CBS, Inc., which itself was a target of a hostile takeover engineered by Ivan Boesky et al., acquired a dozen consumer magazines from the Ziff-Davis Publishing company.[19] Is some oligopoly trying to control access to the American mind or establish hegemony over "the eyeballs of America?" Or is it a desire for profits only? According to media analysts, media companies, have become desirable acquisitions.

Advertising and circulation create massive cash flows, and the profitability of the communications industry is very high, tempting corporate raiders with inside information like Ivan Boesky and many others to go on a rampage. The merger mania wouldn't have assumed such a rage if the 7-7-7 rule had not been changed to the 12-12-12 rule in 1985 by the FCC under Mark Fowler's chairmanship. The new rule meant that a company could own 12 AM stations, 12 FM stations and 12 TV stations provided its TV stations did not reach more than 25 percent of households having television. The deregulation policy of the Reagan era has let loose bloodhounds on the free marketplace of ideas.

The soft and quiet voice of intelligence is being drowned by the loudmouth ruckus of game shows and trivia. In the print media, the Newspaper Preservation Act of 1970, originally created to keep alive competing editorial voices in major cities at a time when newspapers were closing because of cutthroat competition, was sabotaged by President Reagan's Attorney General, Edwin Meese, 3rd. He allowed two of the biggest newspaper chains, Gannet and Knight-Ridder, to combine their business operations in Detroit when their newspapers were not failing. Under the act the failing newspapers must compete for news but they can combine their business operations. In the case of Gannet and Knight-Ridder, the deal meant $3 billion in the pot and creates "the biggest link up of metropolitan dailies in American history.... circulating more than 1.2 million copies a day, making it the second-largest metropolitan daily newspaper in the country, behind the Daily News in New York."[20] The newspaper industry, instead of being one of the most competitive ones in the country, would become, like utilities, one of the most monopolized, with a devastating effect upon free expression. Tons of titillating printed trivia masquerading as free speech in a free country would drown debate and discussion of critical issues.

Sovietization of American Society

Control of mass media outlets by 50 or fewer corporations has certainly not brought American society close to a totalitarian state, but a glacially slow pace toward the sovietization of American society can be discerned. Those who exercise market power in the communications media will also exercise mind power over American society.

The potential good of the free mass media can be discerned, for example, in the Jerry Lewis Labor Day 1983 Telethon which raised the highest highest amount ever – $32,074,566 in pledges – for the Muscular Dystrophy Association. It is this goodness in America which is being threatened.

Parade (January 1985), which is distributed with 135 newspapers every Sunday in the U.S.A., has a circulation of more than 25 million compared to *TV Guide's* circulation of 17 million and *Reader's Digest's* average of 17.8 million.[21] The control of such massive media outlets by a group mind is comparable to the Soviet communist party's hegemony over the Russian mind. The process of mind control in Russia or China is crude, but its refined version could be made acceptable to the American people.

Concentration of media power in the hands of those whose chief aim is not an open, participative government but an unquestioned right to earn profits will shift to corporate centers, which in turn may be controlled by a board of guardians constituting a supra-party. The decentralized freedoms or the dispersed decision-making processes which have been the foundation of American society will shrink into a few autonomous corporate centers rather than in many geo-political centers, as ideally it should be in the interest of self-renewal. Imagine, the United States of America, consisting of fifty states, controlled by fifty pan-American or multinational conglomerates whose interests are in worldwide profits. Their chief concern will shift from accountability to the people and Congress to manipulation of their minds through a judicious product-geographic media mix. As Bagdikian has pointed out: "In countries like the Soviet Union a state publishing house imposes a political test on what will be printed. If the same kind of control over public ideas is exercised by a private entrepreneur, the effect of a corporate line is not so different from that of a party line."[22] The real political power will pass from Congress, the judiciary, and the executive to a caucus of media conglomerate.

The difference between Soviet society and American society is basically who controls the access to information. What the Chinese and Russian communist parties achieved – central authority over information – through violent revolution, corporate America is achieving through modern technology, mega-mergers, and conglomerates. The sovietization of American society will be non-violent and therefore more lasting.

The interlocking media and financial interests control the consciousness of America. Why is this so harmful to society? A condition for spiritual and material self-renewal of a self-regulated system is that its various structures are simultaneously interdependent and autonomous, that each structure sustains itself by sustaining others. If one structure takes over the functions of another, the whole system receives a blow.

One of the most important functions of an autonomous structure like the press is to perform surveillance inside and outside the system. Surveillance within the system – Watergate, the Iran-contra affair, acid rain, toxic waste dumps, political protection for drug-traffickers, financial racketeering in Wall Street, etc. – saves the system from self-poisoning and allows it to breathe freely. This function can be performed by the media only when it is uncontrolled, unbridled, and unchained. A chained media may listen only to its master's voice, instead of being a community watchdog for the internal environment.

The self-monitoring functions which American society has evolved through 200 years of history, are being eroded through a re-definition of the mass media as business and industry with the charge to make profits. Let's listen to the soft voice of an intellectual who says that the "First Amendment should be restored to its true proprietors – the reader, the viewer, the listener. Freedom of the press must be something more than a guarantee of the property rights of media owners."[23]

The American Constitution, as Jerome A. Barron states, protects expression once it has been created but does nothing to encourage it, or is totally "indifferent to creating opportunities for expression."[24] The mass media get away with verbal and visual garbage without creating critical self-awareness, internal monitoring or environmental surveillance necessary for perpetual self-renewal. While Barron proposes re-interpretation of the First Amendment in a manner which constrains both the government and the owners of communications of media, this study argues that access to media is a condition for self-renewal.

Media access threatens people in power and makes them accountable. Thomas I. Emerson suggested that newspapers may be placed under the purview of the Fairness Doctrine that would require them to provide their readers not only a balanced perspective but also go out of their ways to search for and publish unpopular and minority ideas.[25] The U.S. Supreme Court in Miami Herald v. Tornillo (1974) rejected the argument of the access to media theory but failed to provide conditions for the efficient functioning of the press as a critical internal environment.[26]

It is ironic that technology and the free enterprise system, instead of giving expression to unheard voices, have led to the collectivization of free speech. In America it is not the individual but the corporation which is free, in a manner of speaking. And corporations speak not only through their owned and controlled media outlets but also through their public relations, advertising, and marketing departments.

As commercial speech advances in America, political and social speech retreats. Political debate is increasingly being replaced by political commercials whose repetitiveness dulls critical faculties and leads to acceptance and quiescence. Hidden persuaders are taking over the arena of the free marketplace of ideas.

Money and Power

Senator Paul Laxalt of Nevada was asked at a private dinner party in New York as to who had the greatest chance of winning the Republican Party nomination for the 1988 election. He replied that the person who would emerge as the Republican nominee would be the one who raised the greatest amount of money. The power of the political dollar was of far greater significance than political issues, or personal character. As Harold Evans, a contributing editor for *U.S. News and World Report,* pointed out, "The voters may have distinct preferences between the rivals – but only if they are aware of them as individuals and know what they truly stand for. And that takes money. It is hard for a challenger to make himself known through the news. He has to spend money on promotion. Just to get early name recognition among more than 1 or 2 percent of the national electorate can take millions."[27]

A politician has to compete with those time-and-space buyers who need media outlets for commercial speech. A thirty-second spot during prime time may cost more than $250,000. How can political speech be free and the First Amendment be served in a society which has allowed media outlets to be choked by advertising?[28] Debate is being replaced by propaganda in America, and this will eventually lead to self-poisoning of the system. Harold Evans' suggestion may provide a self-corrective measure: "Ban paid political TV spots. Give the candidates rational free time. There is equity in this. The airwaves are a franchise. They belong to the public, and the public interest requires fair use of them at elections."[29] This would save political offices from being sold to the highest bidder. The shameless spectacle of a political candidate hosting a dinner party and charging his guests $5000 a plate would come to an end.

There are other remedies which could cure the system of aphasia caused by excessive internal propaganda, advertising, and marketing: the de-chaining and de-conglomerating of the media industry. In Associated Press v. United States (1948), Justice Hugo Black while applying the Sherman Anti-trust Act said: "Freedom to publish means freedom for all and not for some... Freedom of the press from governmental interference under the First Amendment does not sanction repression of that freedom by private interests." In a lower court opinion, in the same case, Justice Learned Hand had earlier expressed the same ideas with greater rhetorical force and a clearer vision that "right conclusions are more likely to be gathered out of a multitude of tongues than through any kind of authoritarian selection. To many this is, and always will be, folly; but we have staked upon it our all."[30]

The foundation of American democracy has firmly rested on the ambiguity of the First Amendment prohibiting Congress or any government agency from constraining free speech or expression. The biblical style "thou shall not" has occasioned many interpretations of the clause and has allowed American society to adapt to many technological and political changes. The press and broadcasting have performed functions independent of other institutions such as the church, universities, the judiciary, executives, legislatures, the military, and corporations. They have extended their surveillance to all the institutions and performed self-regulatory functions. Ideally they should act as the conscience of America.

But today news and information are being turned into commodities and packaged like goods. When the press and broadcasting are independent, other institutional structures, government, the judiciary, Congress, corporations, universities, local governments, etc. become accountable to the press. But when corporations and banks take over the fourth estate, other institutional structures – instead of fearing the press and being responsive to it – will look to corporate America for survival. Political control will shift permanently to a few corporate hands. Instead of free speech and expression, America will be surfeited with advertising, public relations, and marketing communications which will not be much different from party propaganda in a communist society. As the rape of the mass media by corporate America continues, the sovietization of American society, less rigorous but more effective than in Russia and China, will become irreversible.

Capturing the Narrative

Not only is the corporate America taking control of the collective nervous system, the mass media, and consequently the cognitive domain of the American people, but it is subtly infiltrating the story line also. For instance, only a few years ago household products seen on television entertainment programs had generic names like soda pop, candy, or soap; but now many network prime-time series are showing products with recognizable names, which is a sneaky way of breaking down consumer resistance built up by regular television commercials. This is a variation on the theme of hidden persuaders which the Communications Act of 1934 cannot stop from being put into practice. The act forbids the mention of any product as an unpaid advertisement "unless it is so furnished in consideration for an identification in a broadcast of any person, product, service, trademark, or brand name beyond an identification which is reasonably related to the use of such service or property on the broadcast."[31]

What a smart company has to do nowadays is to select a program which is reasonably close to its product and provide the product gratis to the producer. For instance, a sitcom like "Cheers" could show any brand name bear or soda without violating the law. While all this is being touted in the name of realism, the commercial implications have been clearly grasped by companies. Product manufacturers rush to supply household goods on sitcoms and prime-time entertainment programs, giving rise to a new kind of service industry called product placement companies.

Apart from grabbing commercial air time and thus making political speech difficult and expensive to reach the audience, corporations have begun to crowd cultural programs. Breaking the psychological barriers created by fatigue due to the profusion of commercials has become a new market game. This could take the form of dummy packaging in which the product looks like the original but isn't the same; it could be unabashedly the original product like Busch or Stroh beer in "Cheers", Rolling Rock in "Thirtysomething," Nintendo in "Growing Pains". The placement could be subtler in the sense that the product's brand name or label is not recognizable, the viewer still feels familiar with the product like Hershey bar, Cuisinart, Heins, Lysol, Sven Jansen crystal, Oneida silverware placed on "ALF," " The Equilizer," " Dallas" and "Dynasty". Products in general like milk or diamonds may be promoted by the Dairy Board or the Diamond Information Center.

The managing director of Krown Entertainment, Russ Krasnoff, said, "Audiences today are advertising resistant.... But if you're in the body of the show, viewers think the character uses the product because he likes it."[32] Since humans live in descriptions and narrations, access to the story time has become crucial to all segments of American society; but only corporations have the money to control that access, and consequently the collective mind of American society. It is another victory for Madison Avenue. It is a kind of subliminal seduction to which there is no answer – a topic which was first discussed in Wilson Bryan Key's book *Subliminal Seduction: Ad Media's Manipulation of a Not So Innocent America*. Key's major emphasis was how sex was being exploited by advertisers.[33]

Although Key might have exaggerated his claim of discovering sex in every advertised product, there is no gainsaying the fact that Madison Avenue is wedded to the ideology of the domination of the American mind by corporate America.

Silence in Free Society

Between libel suits and commercial speech, America is being choked to death. Suing the press has become an act of heroism nowadays. Juries have become notorious in returning mega-verdicts. Carol Burnett's suit against the *National Inquirer* brought her not only extraordinary national attention but a jury award of $1,600,000 in damages which was, however, subsequently reduced substantially. Testifying in court she said: "It hurts, because words, once they are printed, they've got a life of their own. Words, once spoken, have a life of their own."[34] Another notorious case of libel which drew international attention was General William Westmoreland's suit against CBS, in which he sued the network for $120 million. In controlled bitterness, the general asked the court whether "CBS had an obligation to be accurate in its facts before it attempted to destroy a man's character, the work of his lifetime."[35]

Other famous people, wielding tremendous power and enjoying immense wealth in society, who have sued the mass media for staggering amounts are Johnny Carson, Lillian Hellman, Shirley Jones, Jerry Falwell, Elizabeth Taylor, Norman Mailer, Ralph Nader, Paul Laxalt, Mohammed Ali, Wayne Newton, Clint Eastwood, Woody Allen; and the list is growing. This may be a sign of decay in a society in which the powerful prevent the truth from being disclosed by threats of ruinous libel suits. It casts a chill on smaller newspapers. The corruption at local levels goes unnoticed because small county newspapers have turned themselves into rags of advertisements and public relations propaganda.

The discovery of truth involving public figures entails occasional mistakes, which a society must tolerate in order to keep the debate going and remain healthy. Those in power must be exposed even if it hurts. Justice Louis Powell, delivering the opinion of the Court in Gertz v. Robert Welch, Inc., said that in order to keep the debate going and make powerful and influential people responsive to society, even falsehood might have to be tolerated: "Under the First Amendment there is no such thing as a false idea. However pernicious an opinion may seem, we depend for its correction not on the conscience of judges and juries but on the competition of ideas. The First Amendment requires that we protect some falsehood in order to protect speech that matters.[36]

It is true that in almost every libel case the amount of damages has been reduced but that does not reduce the cost of litigation, which sometime takes from several months to more than a year. In a major case the defendant might spend several million dollars, which sometimes leads to an out-of-court settlement. Out-of-court settlements tempt nuisance suits and make the media easy targets for exploitation. Only the big media establishment companies can afford to defend themselves in the courts; only they dare speak the truth. But whose truth? The truth which serves their owners' interests. It is only the outrageous speech which sets a society free and helps it to renew itself continuously.

It may be difficult for the nation to compete with the resurgent Europe of 1992 or Japan of 2001 because the American mass media, which is the collective nervous system of the society, seem to have been drugged and lies in stupor. Free mass media create a state of internal non-equilibrium and re-inforce fluctuations. It is through fluctuations at multiple levels that a new order is established and societal self-renewal takes place. If the mass media are controlled by a dozen or so conglomerates, American society at best will transform itself into a conservative equilibrium society – a society without change or growth. Or, it will solidify like a crystal into a closed system. All closed systems slide into progressive internal disorder, disintegration, and death. Other societies will rush pass it.

One way of countering the evils of media conglomeration and mergers is to legalize and sanctify the people's right to know.

Chapter Five

The Right to Know in a Self-Renewing Society

> Only the emergency that makes it immediately dangerous to leave the correction of evil counsels to time warrants making any exception to the sweeping command, "Congress shall make no law... abridging the freedom of speech."
> –Justice Holmes

A self-renewing or autopoietic society needs information about its own activities so that a collective habit of self-criticism is routinized; it is necessary to gather information about other societies in order to establish a climate of competitive co-existence; and it must have a system of seeing itself as others see it lest its own perceptions of reality degenerate to collective hallucination. In such a society the right to know is the ultimate human right because it leads to decentralized freedoms which constitute a necessary condition for perpetual self-renewal.

The right to know, in the final analysis, means sharing information and control, resulting in participatory and trusteeship management of public affairs. Justice Brandeis observed that the founding fathers of the nation knew that "order cannot be secured merely through fear of punishment for its infraction; that it is hazardous to discourage thought, hope and imagination; that fear breeds repression; that repression breeds hate; that hate menaces stable government; that path of safety lies in the opportunity to discuss freely supposed grievances and proposed remedies; and that the fitting remedy for evil counsels is good ones."[1] Throughout history, Americans have valued free speech as fundamental to carrying out their civic duties. They have also feared that the weakening of freely elected authorities will "set up a prima facie case for a reversion to authoritative control, to the loss of that mental power on which social progress depends."[2] The laws must be obeyed, but the lawmakers and enforcers must be kept under continuous watch.

Although there can be no social organization where some form of free speech and free exchange of ideas does not exist, truly democratic societies have a very broad base of free expression so that even ordinary citizens can have a voice in the affairs of the state. But even in this kind of society where freedom of speech and expression is comparatively broad-based, social controls can be in the hands of a narrow elitist minority. True democracy, where individuals surrender their autonomous existence only to the extent it is absolutely essential, recognizes the right to know not as a mere concession but as a necessity. Great civilizations in the past have flourished without freedom of speech and expression, but they have perished because they denied their people the right to know without which the self-corrective process can not come into operation. The right to know, in the general system and cybernetics terms, gives the control to the people rather than to those in power.

In a totalitarian society, communist or capitalist, one speaks and the rest listen. In the times of Mao Tse-tung, Mao's thoughts were used to brainwash the Chinese into total submission. That led to the disaster of the cultural revolution. When Hitler spoke and Nazi Germany listened, there was the Holocaust. Capitalist democracies have a much wider base of free speech, but essentially it is a debate model in which a few debate and the rest listen and make up their minds about social and political affairs. At best, capitalist democracies are based upon periodic consultations, but decisions are left to an elitist minority. Alexander Meiklejohn said during the unsettling times after WWII, "Shall we give a hearing to those who hate and despise freedom, to those who, if they had the power, would destroy our institutions? Certainly, yes! Our action must be guided not by their principles, but by ours. We listen, not because they desire to speak, but because we need to hear."[3] Meiklejohn was not protecting the right of speakers so much as emphasizing the need of voters to hear all arguments so that they can make proper decisions. "What is essential is not that everyone shall speak, but that everything worth saying must be said."[4] He was keeping in mind the town hall meeting in which the final aim is not the words of speakers but the minds of listeners and the voting of good decisions.

It is worthwhile remembering that Hitler, too, captured power in Germany through town hall rhetoric abetted by his storm troopers. Nixon came to power through the open democratic process. Debates can be dominated and societies can be held hostage to deadly rhetoric, as happened in America during the McCarthy era. No doubt much more is necessary for self-renewal than free speech. In America, the debate model of free speech was not only erected by the philosophical tracts of Alexander Meiklejohn but also by what had happened in Europe during WW II. There was some erosion of faith in the rationality of the common man in America, which found expression in the warnings issued by the Commission on Freedom of the Press in 1947. The commission feared that the press, which is the equivalent of a nationwide town hall meeting, could be captured by some fascists. Its recommendation that the government should not keep aloof from what was happening in the town hall meeting and should intervene actively was worse than the malaise it was supposed to remedy: "Nor is there anything in the First Amendment or in our political tradition to prevent the government from participating in mass communication: to state its own case, to supplement private sources of information and to propose standards for private emulation. Such participation by government is not dangerous to the freedom of the press."[5]

Ironically, government does participate in mass communication through manipulated press conferences, deliberately planted leaks, and by creating barriers to a free flow of information about its activities. In a 1944 case, Thomas v. Collins, which involved union organizers' right to speak and the workers' right to be informed about their choices, Justice Jackson had opined: "The very purpose of the First Amendment is to foreclose public authority from assuming a guardianship of the public mind through regulating the press, speech and religion. In this field every person must be his own watchman for truth, because the forefathers did not trust any government to separate the true from the false."[6] The debate does continue without the overseeing authority of the government. The emerging debate model that had begun to appeal to the courts in post-war America found its supreme expression in a landmark case, New York Times v. Sullivan.

New York Times V. Sullivan

When on March 19, 1960, an editorial in *The New York Times* uttered the sublime apocalyptic warning "Let Congress heed their rising voices, for they will be heard," it ushered in a silent revolution which in a generation transformed America into a genuinely free society. One might say the actions of *The New York Times* in the early sixties brought Abraham Lincoln's Civil War to its final end; because, even though the Civil War had materially come to an end in 1865, the South had never accepted its spiritual consequences.

The last few battles of the Civil War were fought in the courts of Alabama in the 1960s, and finally in the Supreme Court of the United States in New York Times v. Sullivan (1964) – a legal battle whose deep import historians have not understood. It was not merely a libel case whose significance could be measured in terms of punitive or general damages. It was more than an example of the Supreme Court "deeply affecting the fabric of everyday American life." It was more than an exemplar of "the intersection of three dominant themes in modern American experience: the power of the federal judiciary, the role of the press as an agent for social change, and the slow and painful struggle of black Americans for legal and social equality."[7] It was an act of autopoiesis, self-renewal, and re-birth whose energy will radiate through the nation's life for several generations to come and eventually metamorphose its collective nervous system and extend its cognitive and spiritual domain.

It is unfortunate that Americans pay more attention to a painful war like the Vietnam War, which will be soon forgotten but do not comprehend how New York Times v. Sullivan changed their lives forever. As Rodney A. Smolla points out: "And therein, as forcefully as any legal case in American history, was presented both the glory and the unique fragility of the First Amendment.... that suppression of free speech always carries the potential of double evil for the speaker, for it both inhibits the accomplishment of the speaker's underlying goals (such as the elimination of Jim Crow laws), and it diminishes the speaker's dignity, individuality and autonomy."[8]

The New York Times v. Sullivan case originated from a 1960 advertisement in *The New York Times* which, on behalf of several prominent individuals, protested several acts of police cruelties during the civil rights movement done to blacks under the leadership of Dr. Martin Luther King, Jr. in the state of Alabama. The police commissioner of Montgomery, L. B. Sullivan, an elected official, demanded a retraction from *The Times*. Although the advertisement had not mentioned the plaintiff by name, he alleged that he was clearly libeled because he was in charge of the police and therefore all references pointed to him.

There were several inaccuracies in the advertisement and *The New York Times* could have easily checked them from information in its own files. It was an apparent case of negligence, and the trial judge charged that the statements were libel per se, and if the jury decided that the charges concerned the plaintiff, then he would be entitled to general damages. The jury returned a verdict of $500,000, which was upheld by the Alabama Supreme Court.

But the Supreme Court of the United States, echoing the philosophy of Alexander Meiklejohn, overturned the judgment, saying that what was happening in Alabama was not merely a matter of some individuals' being libeled but events of great public importance which required free, untrammeled discussion. Delivering the opinion of the court, Justice William Brennan said that libel must be measured by the standards which meet the rigor of the First Amendment: "Thus we consider this case against the background of a profound national commitment to the principle that debate on public issues should be uninhibited, robust, and wide open, and it may well include vehement, caustic, and sometimes unpleasantly sharp attacks on government and public officials."[9] Quoting Madison, Justice Brennan continued: "Some degree of abuse is inseparable from the proper use of every thing; and in no instance is this more true than in that of the Press." False statements are inevitable in an open society where public actions depend upon free discussion. And then quoting Judge Edgerton in an earlier libel case, he said: "Whatever is added to the field of libel is taken from the field of free debate."[10] Neither factual error nor injury to official reputation warrants suppression of free speech because public affairs need not only free discussion but also information. Libel laws should not be allowed to become a substitute for the Sedition Act of 1798, the controversy over which "first crystallized a national awareness of the central meaning of the First Amendment."[11]

Newspapers cannot serve the cause of the First Amendment if they are subjected to a succession of punitive verdicts because "The constitutional guarantees require, we think, a federal rule that prohibits a public figure from recovering damages for a defamatory falsehood relating to his official conduct unless he proves that the statement was made with 'actual malice' – that is, with knowledge that it was false or with reckless disregard of whether it was false or not."[12] And in this case, Justice Brennan concluded that facts did not support actual malice.

The expression 'actual malice' means reckless disregard of the truth or telling falsehood knowingly. The Supreme Court, thus, raised a high barrier of 'actual malice' for a public official to cross if he wanted to recover damages to his reputation. Some inaccuracies may be acceptable in public debate but deliberate falsehood has no place because the listener and the voter must be informed properly, and irresponsible speakers must be stopped from capturing the public mind through their manipulations. The listener in the public debate was very important.

The new fault requirement of 'actual malice,' as subsequent cases like Curtis Publishing Co. v. Butts, Associated Press v. Walker, and Herbert v. Lando showed, has led the Supreme Court to inquire into the newsgathering processes of reporters and the state of mind of editors, indirectly establishing the right of the people to know as to how the mass media, which process reality for us, actually act. Thus has emerged the noblest of all human rights, the right to know, which no other civilization in the past ever thought of conferring upon its people – a right which is the key to the perpetual self-renewal, autopoiesis, of a society.

The Red Lion Case

The decision in the Red Lion case, which confirmed the Fairness Doctrine, was one of the most enlightened deeds which the Supreme Court of the United States had done in its 200-year history. The repeal of the Fairness Doctrine in 1987 by the FCC was a retrogressive step because it short-changed the people of their right to be informed.

Red Lion Broadcasting v. FCC questioned the legality of the personal attack rule of the Fairness Doctrine. Section 315 of the Communications Act of 1934 enjoins a broadcaster who sells or offers free time to a political candidate for an office during election time to give equal chance to rival candidates for the same office. This is called the equal opportunity clause and is legally enforceable. This was done by an act of Congress. However, the Federal Communications Commission developed in the 1940s a two-part Fairness Doctrine which established the primacy of the listeners' and viewers' right to be informed so that they can exercise not only their right to vote but also to retain political and social control in their hands.

The first part of the doctrine enjoins upon broadcasters to air issues that "are so critical or of such great public importance that it would be unreasonable for a licensee to ignore them completely." Secondly, if a broadcaster covered a controversial issue of public importance it must make arrangements for opposite views to be presented to listeners. If a station gave editorial support to a political candidate or opposed him editorially, an equal opportunity for reply to opposite views must be given. In the course of time a third rule emerged which became operational when during the expression of views on a controversial issue of public importance, an attack is made upon the honesty, character, or integrity of an identified person or group. The rule demanded that a notice and an offer of equal opportunity to respond to personal attack be made within reasonable time. The rule was tested in the Red Lion case.

On November 27, 1964 Rev. Billy James Hargis, in one of his regular programs of the "Christian Crusade" series aired on a Pennsylvania radio station owned by the Red Lion Broadcasting Company, indulged in character assassination of an author, Fred J. Cooke. While reviewing Cooke's book *Goldwater – Extremist on the Right,* Rev. Hargis said that the author was a fellow traveler, had defended Alger Hiss, attacked J. Edgar Hoover and the Central Intelligence Agency; and that his latest book was meant to smear and destroy Barry Goldwater. Cooke, under the provisions of the Fairness Doctrine, demanded free reply time because the broadcast constituted a personal attack. But the station declined to give Cooke free time. The FCC, however, agreed with Cooke that Rev. Hargis' broadcast constituted a personal attack, and the station must meet its obligation under the Fairness Doctrine to send him a tape, transcript, or summary of the broadcast and offer him reply time whether he paid for it or not. The Court of Appeals upheld the FCC's position as constitutional.

The Supreme Court of the United States, while it affirmed the judgment of the Court of Appeals of the District of Columbia, presented arguments which strengthened the emergence of the people's right to know as a fundamental right. Justice Byron White, while delivering the opinion of the Court, traced the history of broadcast to show how Congress, due to electro-magnetic spectrum scarcity and the necessity of traffic control in radio frequencies, had given the FCC a mandate to regulate broadcasting in the public interest. This mandate included its authority to make new rules to re-inforce the provisions of the 1934 Act provided they fall short of the abridgment of freedom of speech and the press, and of censorship as proscribed by section 326 of the act.

Although print and broadcasting receive the same protection under the First Amendment, technology demands that broadcasting be treated differently from the print media. "Just as the Government may limit the use of sound-amplifying equipment potentially so noisy that it drowns out civilized private speech, so may the Government limit the use of broadcast equipment. The right of free speech of a broadcaster, the use of a sound truck or any other individual does not embrace a right to snuff out the free speech of others."[13]

Due to the scarcity of radio frequency, "it is idle to posit an unbridgeable First Amendment right to broadcast comparable to the right of every individual to speak, write or publish... Because of the scarcity of radio frequency, the Government is permitted to put restraints on licensees in favor of others whose views should be expressed on this unique medium. But the people as a whole retain their interest in free speech by radio and their collective right to have the medium function consistently with the ends and purposes of the First Amendment. It is the right of the viewers and listeners, not the right of broadcasters, which is paramount. It is the purpose of the First Amendment to preserve an uninhibited marketplace of ideas in which truth will ultimately prevail, rather than to countenance monopolization... It is the right of the public to receive suitable access to social, political, esthetic, moral, and other ideas and experiences which is crucial here."[14] Regulation of broadcasting, including the Fairness Doctrine, creates the necessity of time sharing, otherwise "station owners and a few networks would have unfettered power to make time available only to the highest bidders, to communicate only their own views on public issues, people and candidates, and to permit on the air only those with whom they agreed. There is no sanctuary in the First Amendment for unlimited private censorship operating in a medium not open to all."[15]

The court also rejected the view that spectrum scarcity was entirely a thing of the past. "Advances in technology, such as microwave transmission, have led to more efficient utilization of the frequency spectrum, but uses for that spectrum have also grown apace... The rapidity with which technological advances succeed one another to create more efficient use of spectrum space on the one hand, and to create new uses for that space by ever growing numbers of people on the other, makes it unwise to speculate on the future allocation of that space."[16]

While it is important that the marketplace of ideas should be free and open to all, it is equally imperative that no one should corner the marketplace and deny access to others whose voices should be heard. Scarce resources should be shared equitably, particularly when they impact openness and accountability of those in power. Good government depends upon the listener's knowledge of public events. The right to know is a key to self-renewal – and it seems a dangerous right to all those in power.

Media Access

In 1974, in Miami Herald Publishing Co. v. Tornillo, an attempt was made to open access to the print media. Its success would have strengthened American political culture and hastened the process of self-renewal. Pat Tornillo, the executive director of the Classroom Teachers Association, sought election to the Florida House of Representatives in 1972. *The Miami Herald* published editorials critical of Tornillo's candidacy and his role as the leader of the teachers' collective bargaining agency. Tornillo sought remedy under section 104.38 (1973) of the Florida statute – a right of reply statute which provided that if a candidate for election was attacked by a newspaper regarding his personal character or official record, the newspaper was under an obligation to print free of cost any reply the candidate might like to publish. Failure to give the candidate the right to reply constituted a first-degree misdemeanor. The circuit judge viewed the statute's vagueness as restricting and stifling free expression and dismissed plaintiff's petition. However, on direct appeal the Florida Supreme Court reversed the lower court decision. It held that free speech was broadened and not abridged by the Florida right-of-reply statute, that in fact it enhanced the free flow of information to the public.

The state of Florida, in this matter, was much ahead of the rest of the country in recognizing the public's right of access to the print media and their right to know. The Supreme Court of the United States reversed the judgment of the state supreme court since "the Florida statute fails to clear the barrier of the First Amendment because of its intrusion into the function of editors."[17] Although the court unanimously declared the statute to be unconstitutional, it did recognize merit in the right-to-reply argument. The court said, "The First Amendment interest of the public in being informed is said to be in peril because the 'marketplace of ideas' is today a monopoly controlled by the owners of the market."[18] In a footnote it said: "Freedom of the press is a right belonging, like all rights in a democracy, to all the people. As a practical matter, however, it can be exercised only by those who have effective access to the press. Where financial, economic, and technological conditions limit such access to a small minority, the exercise of that right by that minority takes on fiduciary or quasi-fiduciary characteristics."[19]

During the 1960s the Supreme Court of the United States established two models of public speech: the debate model for the print media, where the speaker is supreme even though the listeners is recognized; and the right-to-know model for the broadcast media, where the listener is more important than the speaker. This contradiction has enriched American political life. And if the Fairness Doctrine is enacted into a law, safe from the meddling whims of politicians, America will have created a very important condition for self-renewal.

The Freedom of Information Act

Governments routinely gather and create massive amounts of information, ranging from product safety and license plate numbers to individual income tax returns and data-gathering by remote-sensing satellites. Some information is released to the public without any hesitation while other information is withheld as secret and classified because its disclosure might prove dangerous to the nation's security. And when government withholds information on security grounds, it becomes hard to prove that access to the information was denied in order to hide some wrongdoing, like the Iran-Contra affair, or some other stupidity of the government. In 1967 Congress adopted the first version of the Freedom of Information Act; it was given final shape in 1975.

Between 1967 and 1975, the country went through traumatic experiences: Watergate disclosures; CIA intelligence gathering within the United States, in violation of the law; Vice President Spiro Agnew's no-contest plea to income tax evasion and his subsequent resignation; and President Nixon's lying about his secret tapes and his resignation. All these events had pressured Congress to seek more openness in the government, and the act was amended in 1975 in spite of President Gerald Ford's veto.[20]

Under the act federal agencies have to make available, within thirty days, for inspection and copying the decisions of administrative tribunals, policy statements, and staff manuals of instructions which have direct bearing on the public. Agencies must explain in writing if they delete information affecting an individual's privacy. For obvious reasons, major users of the Freedom of Information Act have been business firms eager to exercise their right to know about their competitors, and society has been none the worse for it.

The term "agency" includes "any executive department, military department, Government corporation, Government controlled corporation, or other establishments in the executive branch of the Government (including the Executive Office of the President), or any independent regulatory agency." The Freedom of Information Act cannot be used to get information from the president and his immediate advisors; Congress, its committees, and the few agencies under its direct control, principally the Library of Congress and the General Accounting Office; and the federal judicial system. The revised act gives comparatively more access to classified documents and investigatory records. Requests for information have outstripped the agencies' capacity to comply within stipulated time; also, lawsuits too have increased because the agencies have become increasingly protective of information.

The Defense and State Departments, the FBI, the CIA, and business firms seeking to protect trade secrets complained that too much information was being released to the public. This prompted President Reagan in 1982 to issue an executive order making it easier for agencies to classify documents to protect national security. For example, the operational files of the CIA are exempt from disclosure. While the act does apply to local branches of federal agencies, it does not cover state and local governments, which have their own laws, varying from state to state and city to city.

Apart from the nine exemptions, the Freedom of Information Act is limited by the Privacy Act of 1974, which excludes access to personal files of an individual "regarding his education, financial transactions, medical history, and criminal or employment history..."[21] collected by government. The Privacy Act safeguards the individual from the abuses of the Freedom of Information Act, particularly now when all data collection and storage is computerized.

Journalists under the Freedom of Information Act demanded access to the notes of telephone conversations made by Henry Kissinger while he served President Nixon, first as foreign policy advisor and later as secretary of state. Normally, the notes of conversations of the secretary of state would be subject to disclosure because the Department of State is an "agency" as defined by the act; but Kissinger had already transferred the notes to the Library of Congress under terms which gave him substantial control over their release. Since the Library of Congress is exempt from the FOI Act, the Reporters Committee [22] petitioned the court to compel the State Department to regain control over the Kissinger notes. The Supreme Court, reversing the judgment of the lower courts, ruled that a third party cannot compel an agency to take control of documents no longer under its control.

Although, as it turned out, Henry Kissinger had acted illegally, the Library of Congress could not be compelled to surrender documents in its possession; only the attorney general could take such an initiative. Kissinger had very cunningly prevented authors from any access to information; he used those notes himself in writing his own book of memoirs.[23]

Once a party releases information to a government agency, it cannot prevent the agency from the information being disclosed to a third party, as Chrysler Corp. learned in 1979.[24] The Supreme Court said that the FOI was designed to encourage the release of information, and exemptions were not mandatory. It was an important message from the Supreme Court that if an agency wanted to release some information in the public interest and under the FOI, it could do so. But those in power will always be afraid of sharing information with others. The Supreme Court's message went unheeded.

The nine exemptions crafted into the FOI Act limit the full idealistic force of the act. They have been justified on the grounds that the government must protect its secrets from its own people as well as from its enemies if it has to run efficiently: for instance, secrets concerning national security, current investigations by law enforcement officers, memoranda in regard to government policies, and the briefs of government lawyers need protection. Moreover, personal records, medical records, trade secrets, financial data used in compiling statistical records, tax returns, and other information of a personal nature receive confidentiality.

But government agencies have misused the nine exemptions and crippled the people's right to know, thus putting a drag on the nation's capacity to renew itself through self-examination. For instance, in the 1970s, the government declared that it planned to conduct a nuclear explosion under one of the Aleutian Islands, near the coast of Alaska. There was genuine concern among the members of congress that the waters of the Pacific Ocean might be polluted by the escaping radiation.

The Defense Department, when asked to release an environmental impact report, responded that the report was top secret. When the case reached the Supreme Court, the court said that it had no power to review the agency's refusal and that the act must be interpreted as Congress had passed it.[25] Until the act was amended in 1975, agencies safeguarded information with the same awesome taboo as the ancient Egyptian and Hindu priests protected their esoteric knowledge. Now the courts can examine whether the information has been classified properly and whether its release will offset the intended benefits. But the courts, too, have not understood the full significance of how the right to know can save American society from its predicted decline and fall.

The FOI Act does not mean that all information must be disclosed indiscriminately. For instance, in Miller v. Casey, the U.S. Court of Appeals, District of Columbia circuit, affirmed the CIA's refusal to disclose information about its alleged efforts to infiltrate Albanian guerrillas between 1945 and 1953.[26] The release of information, although of historical significance, would have revealed the wisdom of the CIA's covert actions.

Courts have mostly upheld officials' claims for a need for secrecy, even though the release of information might have led to greater public safety. In the late 1970s, Consumers Union, publisher of *Consumer Reports*, learned that some people had been hurt when the picture tubes of their television sets exploded while they watched television, and that the Consumer Product Safety Commission had been investigating public complaints. Television manufacturers, led by GTE Sylavania,[27] sought an injunction from a Delaware court to prevent the commission from releasing data to *Consumer Reports*. The Supreme Court of the Unites States upheld the lower court's decision that the Consumer Product Safety Commission may not release information to *Con-

sumer Report, noting that the law forbids the commission to release any information reflecting adversely on a product.

Thousands of deaths due to car accidents, drugs, and other manufactured products could be prevented if people were allowed to exercise their right to be informed properly rather than allowing business firms to hide their misdemeanors under the pretense of trade secrets.

No Absolute Right

This is not to argue for an absolute right to know because no civilized society, least of all a complex information society like American society, can sanction any absolute right to anyone; but it must examine circumstances under which a piece of information must be withheld and for how long. United States Department of State v. Washington Post Co.[28] is a case in point which illustrates how the release of information might have mortally endangered the lives of people. *The Post* learned from a tip that two Iranian officials in Khomeini's revolutionary government held American passports; in other words, they were American spies. *The Post a*sked the State Department to confirm the information but the agency's decision not to divulge information was sound, as the subsequent developments leading to rabid anti-Americanism and hostage crisis showed.

Some of the important court battles involving the FOI Act have been in the area of investigatory records compiled by the FBI and CIA. A journalist, Howard Abramson, was investigating some well-founded fears that President Nixon had used the FBI for political purposes – particularly against those individuals whom he considered his political enemies. When Abramson asked the FBI to give him access to the data in its files, his request was rejected on grounds that it was an invasion of privacy covered by the exemptions to the Freedom of Information Act.

This was a clear case of misuse of exemptions because the privacy of any individual was not in question. The chief executive was allegedly using a federal agency for his own political ends. When Abramson sought the court's help, the FBI released eighty-four pages of information from which some vital information regarding eleven political figures was deleted. Apparently, the information gathered by the FBI was not for law enforcement purposes and was not subject to exemptions, noted the court of appeals. But the Supreme Court reversed the judgment[29] of the appeals court, saying that information contained in the remaining pages not released to Abramson was part of a memorandum personally sent by J. Edgar Hoover to John D. Ehrlichman, presumably for investigatory if not law enforcement purposes, and therefore was protected from disclosure. Abramson's purpose, however, was not to reveal to the public some unsavory and embarrassing facts in the private lives of political figures, but to focus the nation's attention to the inroads made by the executive into individual autonomy and civil liberties – activities which may gradually reduce the American way of life to the Soviet way of life. America needs more sunshine.

How Much Sunshine Can a Government Stand?

In many ways the state of Florida has been more advanced in political culture than the rest of the country. For instance, its right-to-reply statute in regard to the print media which was unfortunately declared unconstitutional by the Supreme Court in 1974 was indeed a sign of the future. Similarly, Florida has another sign of superior political thinking, as evidenced by its sunshine law, which opens the door of many of its governmental activities to public scrutiny. And Congress, learning from the experience with the Florida sunshine laws passed in 1976 a federal "Government in the Sunshine Act" which declared that "the public is entitled to the fullest practicable information regarding the decision-making processes of the Federal Government," and the government must "provide the public with such information protecting the rights of individuals and the ability of the Government to carry out its responsibilities."[30] The act enjoins upon all federal agencies headed by boards of two or more persons appointed by the president to hold "every portion of every meeting" open to the public. Adequate notice about such meetings must be given, and if a meeting falls within one of the exemptions, the agency is required to make available to the public a transcript of the non-exempt portion of the meeting.

Law enforcement authorities should give free access to journalists as the people's surrogate to visit any public place, including prison, to perform their newsgathering duties.

Imprisonment of the Unwanted

One of the most important concerns of a civilized society is who and why anyone goes to prison, and how a person is treated once in prison. As Henry David Thoreau said, "Under a government which imprisons any unjustly, the true place for a just man is also prison."[31] But how can one know whether a person is unjustly held unless journalists and others have a right of access to a prison? In the Soviet Union, prisons are sometimes called psychiatric wards, and most of the dissidents find a place there. There is no evidence that anyone has come out reformed from the Soviet psychiatric ward or prison system. The American prison system, too, does not have the capacity to turn inmates into law-abiding citizens.

A prisoner does not give up all his rights once he is incarcerated. He should have the right to tell his tale to a journalist. In 1974, two parallel cases, one, Pell v. Procunier,[32] involving a ban on press interviews with certain inmates in the

– 63 –

California prison system, and the other, Saxby v. Washington Post Co.,[33] concerning a similar ban in the federal prison system, the Supreme Court upheld the ban noting that the Constitution does not impose upon the government "the affirmative duty to make available to journalists sources of information not available to members of the public generally." Justice Potter Stewart observed that "newsmen have no constitutional right of access to prisons or their inmates beyond that afforded the general public." Justice Powell, writing in dissent, said, "The administration of these institutions, the effectiveness of their rehabilitative programs, the conditions of confinements they maintain, and the experiences of the individuals incarcerated therein are all matters of legitimate societal interest and concern... In seeking out the news the press therefore acts as an agent of the public at large. It is the means by which the people receive that free flow of information and ideas essential to intelligent self-government."[34]

In another case, Justice Paul Stevens, Justice Brennan, and Justice Powell made acute observations about the role of the free flow of information in a self-renewing society: "... the First Amendment protects not only the dissemination but also the receipt of information and ideas.... Our system of self-government assumes the existence of an informed citizenry... It is not sufficient, therefore, that the channel of communication be free of governmental restraint. Without some protection for the acquisition of information about the operation of public institutions such as prisons by the public at large, the process of self-governance contemplated by the Framers would be stripped of its substance.[35]

Every organized society based upon privilege, power, or private property necessarily embodies brute force, which inadvertently creates criminals to be put aside. The question is how much the society is doing to rehabilitate the victim as well as the criminal and whether their human rights are being respected. Worse than capital punishment is the brutalization of a criminal in prison. Journalists, on behalf of the public, should be able to assess the truth.

Chapter Six

Different Approaches to Truth

... that knowledge is hard to get, that man must break through again and again the thin crust on which he walks, that the certainties of today may become the superstitions of tomorrow; that we have no warrant of assurance save by everlasting readiness to test and test again.
    –Justice Learned Hand

Free Press and Fair Trial

Although both journalists and legal professionals seek the truth based upon evidence, their approaches and methodologies are quite different. Tips, rumors, and illegally obtained information have no place in a courtroom trial, but the same evidence may be the beginning of an investigative report for a journalist. Journalists' method of inquiry is through trial and error, and they go on correcting their errors as they receive more or better evidence; sometimes they pay through their bleeding noses when they are hit with a libel suit.

The jury-dependent system of justice in America is very fragile because it is well-nigh impossible to keep the jury impartial when the mass media bombard them with a continuous flow of news. When journalists report a crime they consciously or unconsciously introduce biases which the potential jurists cannot escape. No jury can ever be impartial. And if judges try to guide or gag the press, they overstep the judicial authority and violate the press's First Amendment rights.

Since the courts interpret the Constitution as well as administer justice, their unfettered right to know has never been questioned. For instance, they reserve the right, especially during libel trials, to delve deeply into the newsgathering process and into how editorial decisions are made. They can ask for any document in the possession of journalists and use their contempt powers to induce compliance. The mass media, on the other hand, have no power to probe the judicial system and how the minds of judges work. It is therefore an unequal battle: the courts have the coercive power to extract truth and exercise their right to know; the media use their field observations, clandestine investigations, and logical deductions to arrive at some modicum of truth. What if the journalists, too, were given the same power and the right to know? The society will be better and healthier because of the free flow of information.

The Sixth Amendment to the United States Constitution provides that "In all criminal prosecutions, the accused shall enjoy the right to a speedy and public trial, by an impartial jury of the State and district wherein the crime shall have been committed..." and the accused will "be informed of the nature and cause of accusation; to be confronted with the witnesses against him; to have compulsory process for obtaining witnesses in his favor..." Journalists have been forced to testify about their secret sources and surrender their notes and documents in order to satisfy the accused's constitutional rights. The important question is whether the accused's right to a fair trial can be reconciled with the people's right to know. There are instances when the media, in their function as a watchdog of the public interest, have followed a blood trail and investigated the crime to its source, thus helping rather than hindering the administration of justice.

A pending trial may become prejudiced if articles and editorials influence jurors one way or the other. The accused, instead of being granted a speedy jury trial, gets trial by the press. The press thus usurps the functions of the judiciary. The watchdog becomes a trial judge. However, no one can be sure about the jury's impartiality because prejudice can arise from any source: color of the skin, religion, political affiliation, etc. Traditionally, jury impartiality has been achieved through initial screening called "voir dire" which enables the judge and the lawyers to check bias and screen out those suspected of prejudice. If after the jury selection it is found that jurors are dishonest or biased, the defendant can seek a new trial.

It is the rule of exclusion – that certain type of evidence is not permissible – which explains why the legal profession sometime thinks the press is unhelpful. The first rule of exclusion is that an accused's previous criminal record is not to be taken into account unless the defendant himself wants it admitted as evidence. The mass media, on the other hand, are prone to dig into an accused's past and try to prove a psychological continuity in his behavior in order to make the story credible and probable. Secondly, unless confessions have been voluntarily made and only after the accused has been given the "Miranda Warning" and informed of his rights, such confessions cannot be used in a trial. But the press would certainly highlight such confessions which might affect the jurors' minds. The third kind of evidence which has to be excluded from trial is what is obtained by illegal searches. But journalists, used to investigative reporting and cultivating their clandestine sources, might thrive on such revelations.

The courts would like to keep jurors away from being exposed to such inadmissible evidence so that the accused's constitutional rights are not violated. While that helps many defendants go free because there is a limit to the kind of evidence acceptable in the courts, the press, following its own methods of knowing the truth, portrays a different picture of crime and the criminal. The legal community wants jurors to reach a verdict based on the testimony offered in the courtroom, not what is heard or read outside of it. Consequently, a drug-pusher or a rapist might not have committed a crime if admissible evidence were not available even though the whole world had watched the crime committed. In order to create a mythical body called an impartial jury, the courts have resorted either to gag orders or withholding of information altogether.

Occasionally, the media's lack of restraint and unethical conduct does mess up a trial, as happened in the case of Dr. Sam Sheppard.

The Sam Sheppard Case

In the quiet early morning hours of the Fourth of July, 1954, Dr. Sam Sheppard, a Bay Village, Ohio, osteopath, found his pregnant wife, Marilyn, beaten to death in their upstairs bedroom. Dr. Sheppard, too, had received neck injuries, a swollen eye, and seemed to have been in shock. If he was his wife's murderer, then he was a bad liar, too, because he gave the police a very incredible account of what had happened: After their son had gone to sleep in his bedroom, Dr. Sheppard's wife also went upstairs, leaving her husband to doze off on a downstairs sofa. It was then that Dr. Sheppard heard his wife cry and that he ran upstairs to find a bushy-haired man standing next to his wife's bed.

In grappling with this ghostly form, Dr. Sheppard was knocked unconscious by a blow to the back of his neck. He went to his son's bedroom and found him unharmed. Hearing a noise downstairs, Dr. Sheppard ran down only to see the ghostly form leaving the house. Dr. Sheppard pursued the apparition to the shore of the lake where, once again, he was knocked down unconscious. When he dragged himself to his home, he called his neighbor, the Bay Village mayor Spence Houk, to report the incident. The case, known as Sheppard v. Maxwell,[1] became a cause celebre of American jurisprudence and was the subject of a docudrama. The trials and tribulations of Dr. Sheppard were probably the most sensational and notorious media reportage of the century, and the case is cited as an exemplar of the free press-fair trial controversy.

It would have been unusual for the people and the press to let the case be decided in silence by the court because Dr. Sheppard's cock-and-bull story had made him a prime suspect in the case. People's rage found expression in the Bay Village policeman who told Dr. Sheppard that the lie detector test was infallible and added, "I think you killed your wife." The coroner was reported to have said, "Well, it is evident the doctor did this, so let's go get the confession out of him."² Many newspaper reporters and photographers were invited to the coroner's inquest and the inquest was broadcast with live.

There was a flood of editorials, some of them on the front page of newspapers with screaming headlines, 'Why No Inquest?' ' Why Don't Police Quiz Top Suspect?' 'Why Isn't Sam Sheppard in Jail?' 'Quit Stalling – Bring Him In.' When the case finally reached the United States Supreme Court, Justice Tom C. Clark reviewed news coverage and publicity about the arrest of Sam Sheppard as follows: "The publicity then grew in intensity until his indictment on August 17. Typical of the coverage during this period is a front-page interview entitled: 'Dr. Sam: "I Wish There Was Something I Could Get Off My Chest – but There Isn't."' Unfavorable publicity included items such as a cartoon of the body of a sphinx with Sheppard's head and the legend below: "'I will Do Everything In My Power to Help Solve This Terrible Murder." – Dr. Sam Sheppard.' Headlines announced, inter alia [among other things], that: 'Doctor Evidence is Ready for Jury,' 'Corrigan Tactics Stall Quizzing,' 'Sheppard "Gay Set" Is Revealed by [Bay Village Mayor Spence] Houk,' 'Blood is Found in Garage,' 'New Murder Evidence is Found, Police Claim,' 'Dr. Sam Faces Quiz At Jail on Marilyn's Fear Of Him.'³

Justice Clark also noted that the trial judge, Herbert Blythin, was a candidate to succeed himself and that the chief prosecutor was a candidate for common pleas judge. More than the news media were to blame for the denial of a fair trial to Dr. Sam Sheppard and caused him "to be deprived of that 'judicial serenity and calm to which [he] was entitled,'" noted Justice Clark. He added further "that bedlam reigned at the court house during the trial and newsmen took over practically the entire courtroom hounding most of the participants in the trial, especially Sheppard."⁴

Apparently, it was a failure of judicial leadership in controlling the carnival atmosphere because courtrooms are under the control of the court. Several other measures were available to the trial judge to nullify the effect of pre-trial publicity and playing to the press by police officers, witnesses, and the counsel for both sides. Dr. Sam Sheppard's case took twelve years to resolve, ending with the reversal of his murder conviction on the grounds that pre-trial and during-trial publicity had denied him a fair trial. But Justice Clark's ringing criticism of the press, the police, the coroner, and the trial judge included observations which recognized the people's right to know in order to keep watch over those who wield judicial powers:

> The principle that justice cannot survive behind walls of silence has long been reflected in the Anglo-American distrust of secret trials. A responsible press has always been regarded as the handmaiden of effective judicial administration, especially in the criminal field. Its function in

this regard is documented by an impressive record of service over several centuries. The press does not simply publish information about trials but guards against miscarriage of justice by subjecting the police, prosecutors, and judicial processes to extensive public scrutiny and criticism.[5]

Restrictive orders like "gag orders" on the press, gagging everybody but the press, closing pre-trial hearings and opening trials have been resented by the press, and the court orders have been challenged many times.[6] In Richmond Newspapers v. Virginia (1980), Justice Brennan made a unique observation about the constructive value of the right to know: "Open trials assure the public that procedural rights are respected, and that justice is afforded equally. Closed trials breed suspicion of prejudice and arbitrariness, which in turn spawns disrespect for the law. Public access is essential, therefore, if trial adjudication is to achieve the objective of maintaining public confidence in the administration of justice."[7]

The judiciary as the third pillar of the power structure, as a coequal in constitutional power, must be open and accountable to the people. Its thinking and judicial decision-making processes must be exposed just as the press's news-gathering and editorial decision-making processes are liable to judicial scrutiny. In a self-renewing society, no institution is hermetically sealed.

Every institution must be demystified. And the television camera is a great demystifier.

The Whole World is Our Jury
Cameras in Courtrooms

There is a mystique about the judicial system in every culture. The pompous dignity of the judge and the finality with which judicial decisions are uttered arise out of cultivated secretiveness. Laborious slowness is presented as judicial serenity. The courts have always resented anyone probing deeply into their methodology of discovery of the truth and reaching judicial decisions. Having established direct inspirational links with some ultimate source of wisdom, judges have always feared communications technology prying into their faces and making them look ordinary and fallible. There is nothing more ludicrous than undressing a judge because most of the fabled wisdom of the judge is in his attire. But in this age of the ordinary, the courts have not been able to resist the invasion of television cameras.

"The Lindbergh Case," involving the trial of a poor German immigrant Bruno Hauptmann, was the beginning of the courts' hostility against communications technology trying to open the doors of the judiciary to the public. In 1932, the 19-month-old son of the famed aviator Charles Lindbergh was kidnapped and later found murdered and buried in a shallow grave in the woods outside the Lindbergh family home in New Jersey. But it took the police two years to arrest Hauptman and charge him with the kidnap and murder of the Lindbergh child.

The trial of Bruno Hauptmann (who was described by the press as a "thing lacking in human characteristics") was attended at times by 150 to 700 reporters at times.[8] His execution led to a collective guilt, and all the blame was passed on to the media. To expiate the guilt, instead of examining the jury system, an 18-man special committee consisting of lawyers, editors, and publishers condemned the Hauptmann trial as "the most spectacular and depressing example of improper publicity and professional misconduct ever presented to the people of the United States in a criminal trial."[9]

The American Bar Association, in response to its committee's report and to salvage the judicial system, adopted in 1937 Canon 35 of its Canons of Professional Ethics. Subsequently this was replaced by ABA Canon of Judicial Conduct 3(7): "A judge should prohibit broadcasting, televising, recording, or taking photographs in the courtroom and areas immediately thereto during sessions of court or recesses between sessions..."

Suspicion of Television Technology

The courts became increasingly suspicious of television technology because of its presumed capacity for interfering with the administration of justice.[10] The case known as Estes v. Texas (1965) about a flamboyant Texan swindler, Billie Sol Estes, did not much help the cause of television cameras and the people's right to view live telecasts of the courtroom proceedings. Justice Clark denied[11] that refusing television cameras in the courtroom was tantamount to discrimination against the electronic media. Televising and photographing criminals in no way helped the process of justice; on the contrary, the presence of television and photographic equipment was nothing short of mental harassment, making the task of the judge the more difficult. However, it was Justice Harlan's suggestion that "...the day may come when television will have become so commonplace an affair in the daily life of the average person as to dissipate all reasonable likelihood that its use in courtrooms may disparage the judicial process."[12] For the next ten years all electronic equipment, photographic and televisual, was barred from courtrooms.

It was the development of the lighter and less obtrusive electronic equipment, accompanied by some subtle negotiations carried on by member of the press with the bar, which resulted in an easing of the suspicion about television cameras in the courtroom. Today all but Indiana, Michigan, Mississippi, Missouri, South Carolina, Texas, Utah, and Virginia allow some camera access to their courtrooms.

The landmark case which tested the public's right to know via the television camera what happens in the courtroom was tested in Chandler v. Florida.[13] It showed that the Supreme Court of the United States had undergone a sea change in its attitude about the presence of electronic equipment in the courtroom. The case raised the issue whether the presence of cameras made a fair trial impossible, and whether they could be used in spite of the objections of some party. In a parallel case, In re Petition of Post-Newsweek Stations, Florida, Inc., the supreme court of Florida ruled that electronic coverage of the courtroom trial did not necessarily amount to denial of a fair trial; nor did the electronic media have any constitutional right to be present in the courtroom. It left the decision of the television and photographic coverage of the courtroom to the presiding judge. Following that decision, TV coverage of the state courtroom trials has enabled the public to see for themselves some of the most dramatic trials without any loss of dignity to the majesty of the court.

Improved communications technology has enabled the promise of open public trials to be fulfilled, without denying a fair trial to the accused. This new openness enabled the people to watch live on CNN in 1984 what was known as the "Big Dan's" rape trial of six men from New Bedford, Massachusetts accused of gang-raping a woman in a pool hall.[14] The case had already become a cause celebre, and public interest had been very much aroused. It became a test case whether the press could act responsibly and let the viewers see a real rape trial without being outraged and sensationalized. As it turned out, the trial of this complex and controversial case was conducted with great dignity. The judiciary lost its fear of communications technology, and the technology in the process became domesticated and has ceased to be threatening.

Even though state courtrooms, subject to varying restrictions, have become open to television cameras, the Supreme Court of the United States has stubbornly refused to open its proceedings to the public eye.

The Most Subversive Human Right

Essentially, the right to know is nothing if not a person's right to ask questions of those in power and authority. Unquestioned authority and unaccountable power have led to internal corruption, decline and fall of civilizations in the past. Historians like Paul M. Kennedy see a parallel between Edwardian Britain of 1903 and the U.S.A. of 1988.[15] There are some superficial resemblances between the empires of the past and the U. S. A. of today. America's commitments include its extension into space. Annexation of space is not immoral, but the annexation of territories (as with past empires) was immoral, and their decline and fall was a part of the script which the empires acted out.

Few civilizations in the past granted to its people the most subversive of human rights – the right to know, to ask questions, to challenge those in authority and power and, thus, prevent their decline and fall. Empires of the past were built on the suppression of human rights at home and of tyrannies abroad. American society is the first in the history of mankind to make a beginning toward perpetual self-renewal by granting its people the right to know about who lives in prison and why and how; about the internal working of courts, political and executive decision-making processes, access to media, etc. Each time a scandal like Watergate and the Iran-contra affair is publicly discussed via television, America renews itself. And the process of autopoiesis, perpetual self-renewal, will continue so long as the most subversive of human rights – the right to know – is not denied to the American people.

Chapter Seven
Politics in the Republic of Television

All kinds of societies are biologically legitimate. Yet not all are equally desirable as systems in which an observer human being may wish to live...A human society in which to see all human beings as equivalent to oneself, and to love them, is operationally legitimate without demanding from them a larger surrender of individuality and autonomy than the measure that one is willing to accept for oneself while integrating it as an observer, is a product of human art, that is, an artificial society that admits change and accepts every human being as not dispensable.
  –Humberto R. Maturana

Communications Technology and the Electoral Process

If the democratic model is epitomized in the oft quoted words "of the people, by the people and for the people," the critical question is whether communications technology is leading to a self-renewing society where the power is exercised by the people, or toward a slow centralization of power, which is the essence of the Soviet system.

Each new communications technology is an incitement to sabotage the existing patterns of political behavior because it makes information available to the dispossessed. In the later part of the 19th century, when the upper classes in India learned English and their contacts with the British through books and travel increased, they began to question the rationale of the British Empire. Either every subject of the British Empire should have the same rights, or the Empire had no ideological rationale, Gandhi argued. The network of roads which the Roman soldiers used to establish and consolidate a far-flung empire was also used by the early Christian missionaries to convert Europe to Christianity. In both cases, the dispossessed broke the empire.

Technology subverts ideology by widening the base of knowledge, enlarging debate and creating dissent. Today's new technologies like satellites, computers, cable, videotex, cellular radio, video-conferencing, computer-networking, and many others have led to their ingenious uses in political processes as seen in the political campaigns of the 1988 presidential election and the 1989 political turmoil in Eastern Europe and China. Some scholars and politicians foresee the possibility of representative institutions – a legacy of two hundred years – withering away; others see newer communications technologies ending the era of political action committees and lobbyists. At present special interests virtually drown the voice of the people.

Communications technology holds the promise to help the people re-assert their collective voice. Would this voice be pluralistic or plebiscitory in nature? The emerging thesis is that the existing representative democratic institutions under the pressure of communications technologies will develop a new check and balance in the form of plebiscitory democracy. Scientific opinion polls, and the 900 number overnight quick polls, will become important because the "present forms of government have weakened under the stress of size, increasing demands upon them, citizen dissatisfaction, and growing awareness that the people on the street are often as capable of making decisions as their representatives."[1] This subversive thought, that an average American is as capable as his representative, might be an antidote to the rise of political carpet-baggers.

Most scholars are prescriptive in their attitudes and suggestive of reforms in the American political system to make it more responsive to a complex world. They propose experimental strategies leading toward a kind of political utopia as if American society could be formed anew. They would like to put society into a crucible and recast it. But technology brings about continuous changes, and American society cannot return to the revolutionary conditions of 1776. It is a matter of formulating policies which enable the politically dispossessed to use communications technology to exercise control so that Watergate and the Iran-contra affair do not become cyclical events.

It is worth bearing in mind that technology is not the sole determinant of social change because "changes for our political institutions will result not just from technology, but from complex interactions among several streams of American life: developments in telecommunications hardware, patterns of corporate investment and marketing, changes in consumer acceptance and preferences, independent changes in our political institutions, and the public policy climate."[2] The marketplace will push new communications technologies to impact the working of political institutions. There may be an alternative to representative institutions, which themselves were a product of communications technologies of earlier times.

Most of the observers of the political scene today fear that representative democracy – debates, face-to-face group political communication, voting, and all that goes with traditional democracy in America – is being eroded because television cannot effect a deliberative process and a shared sense of responsibility which constitute democratic political culture.[3] Political conflicts which invariably involve bargaining and compromise cannot be solved without a representative mechanism, it is argued. But representative democracy, they forget, has become a prisoner of the lobbyists, the political action committees, and the special interest groups.

Congressmen and state legislators do not heed their constituents as much as a paid lobbyist knocking at their door. The cost of being a people's representative is so heavy that lawmakers don't get time to listen to their constituents... unless they happen to be rich. Electronic democracy would bypass the intermediaries and the power brokers and bring the people and their representatives in direct, close contacts. Electronic democracy is not meant to supplant representative democracy but to supplement it and to provide a new form of checks and balances.

In a continental size nation with a diverse population and pluralistic culture, it is difficult to make the executive and legislature accountable to the people, except periodically at election time. Instead, the executive and the legislature listen to special interest groups and lobbyists in a spirit of mutual give-and-take, occasionally leading to scandals. The rise of the modern press seemed to make a difference because the press occasionally did act as a surrogate of the people.

Since the time of Theodore Roosevelt, who as president initiated the practice of the press conference at the White House, the press has turned itself into an instrument of a personality cult, which consequently led to the decline in the power and influence of Congress. The representative government as it was conceived two hundred years ago dissipated and became more remote from the people partly because of the rise of paid lobbyists and partly because the press arrogated to itself the right to be the people's spokesman. The fourth estate, instead of bringing the government to the people, made it distant and inaccessible.

During the 1988 election, the media, in order to appear objective, turned themselves into mere eunuchs and transcribers of the presidential candidates. For fear of appearing biased under attacks from right-wing Republicans that journalists were a bunch of liberals, they frequently assumed neutral postures and gave up incisive and adversarial reporting, which has been the glory of American journalism. Instead of showing unmanageable toxic waste dumps and devastated wilderness, the media showed the candidates touring lake fronts and harbors. The media surrendered to the message control system originally designed by James Baker for the Ronald Reagan presidential elections: create pre-fabricated photo-opportunities to capture television coverage to strengthen the theme of the day, and script your candidate so efficiently that he wards off reporters' questions like a robot. Consequently both 1988 candidates, George Bush and Mike Dukakis, sounded like pre-programmed mannequins.

Although it is rash to predict that the political order of the twenty-first century will be determined by the communications structure alone, it is quite reasonable to expect that the "new communication technologies offer the opportunity for citizen information and participation undreamed of by our Founding Fathers."[4] Public opinion may not become "the law of the land," as Ted Becker hastily predicted,[5] but public opinion polls might play an increasing role in determining the will of the people. Public opinion polls in tandem with computer-based marketing research and surveys will be the fifth estate of the future.

Opinion Polls: The Emerging Fifth Estate

Pollsters, Nielsen, Harris, Gallup et al. are emerging as a great political influence in the American political process ranging from elections to decision making. They seem to be replacing anchormen in national visibility and are taking over the function of agenda-setting – a role played by the press for such a long time.

The role of the media in agenda setting was first explored by two communications researchers, McComb and Shaw, in 1972,[6] and since then it has yielded extremely rich results in communications research. No society or organization, howsoever primitive, can exist without an agenda – a plan to discuss and decide priorities to distribute the available funds and allocate the limited resources, or to take decisive measures in regard to issues of great public interest. The agenda-setting practices of a society invariably reveal the hidden power structure. Because no society can ever match its resources with the needs of its people, the prioritizing of needs reflected politically as an agenda, becomes inevitable and worth fighting for.

By its very nature agenda-setting is a political act. Before the press began to exercise a dominant influence in the social and political lives of the people, there were power brokers who influenced the agenda-setting practices of the executive and the legislature. As communications technologies gave the press a dominant role in social and political life, the press began to play a crucial role in all branches of government. Its functions ranged from surveillance to influencing the public to think and talk about certain issues and candidates as if they were their own agendas. This central concept, that press coverage has an impact on the emerging salience of issues as perceived by the public, has guided researchers for about two decades.

Researchers have compared the press coverage of the issues of the time with the importance in ranking as given by the voters to those issues. They have also observed that the press agenda does not have a very strong causal relation with the public agenda. "As a hypothesis regarding effects of the news media," comments Prof. Chaffee, "agenda-setting has had limited success. On the other hand, as a general functional requirement of society, agenda-setting is practically indispensable. We should be evaluating the news media in terms of fulfilling that kind of function, and not falling into the old persuasional trap of looking for media influence and directional effects. The societal function of the press is not to direct and channel people's behaviors and perceptions in specific ways, but to help us to organize our activities and knowledge so that we can work in a coherent way on problems that are common to many people, communities, etc."[7] That is more of a prescription than an analysis of press behavior. The press is a private and powerful institution in America.

But communications technology, which is giving rise to another private and powerful institution, the opinion poll, is lessening the agenda-setting role of the press. The press has a rival in its role as a surrogate of the public and interpreter of the public opinion.

It is unfortunate that the dramatic rise, growth and development of public opinion polls has gone unnoticed by researchers. What started as a mere instrument to gauge public opinion in quantum terms is growing into an independent institution – the fifth estate. With the increasing use of home computers and cable TV, opinion polls will play a very significant role in the political and social life of the American people in the coming century. It is, however, the severance of public opinion polls from the mass media which is of crucial significance because this will reduce the official and the public's dependency on the media as a go-between, a mediator or surrogate of the public interest. The rise of the independent pollster is a phenomenon of great political significance.

What is public opinion? One might simplify and say that what is not measurable and verifiable is not public opinion.[8] The question which social scientists have to answer is: How does the public opinion as reflected in polls influence the news coverage in the media and the decision-making in the government? So far the question has been about the impact of the news media on public opinion which is still relevant.

There are many problems with the study and measurement of public opinion at present, but it is certainly not a pursuit of the Holy Ghost, as some scholars have made it out to be.[9]

The development of the technology of the "peoplemeter" and its application outside television program ratings and marketing research, further sophistication of survey research methodologies, and the forces of the free marketplace of goods and ideas are certainly shaping a new institution with unfathomable political consequences. A perceptive scholar has observed:

> The growth in sophistication and pervasiveness of surveys allows for a condition of 'technological democracy.' Surveys interacting with the mass media provide a fundamental link between leaders and the public: Polls transmit (both informed and uninformed) opinion to decision

makers via the media, and the public's evaluations of leaders' actions are recorded by more opinion polls. Polls allow citizens to compete with interest groups by eliminating the cost of organizing. By organizing the voice of citizens and consumer, polls allow the public to compete in defining the issues (or setting the agenda) that the government chooses to deal with.[10]

Good Questions and Right Questions

The crucial question, however, is whether polls organize public opinion or simply measure the expression of it in quantitative terms. A right question may organize responses and bring about clarity in thought and feelings, and in fact may give rise to some new consciousness. A good question, on the other hand, may reveal a non-opinion or a non-attitude and may measure something which does not exist or is irrelevant. Even variations in questions may elicit different responses. As Cliff Zukin, a political scientist and director of The Eagleton Poll, observes, "While there are technical procedures for asking good survey questions, there is no procedure for asking the right questions. It is possible to ask many good questions on the same topic, all of which will yield a different and valid reading of public opinion."[11] Zukin mentions that pollsters ask "costless" questions and the respondents answer favoring increased services and lower taxes, which eventually trap politicians into making irresponsible public statements during election times ("Read my lips: No new taxes").

No one disagrees that a policy decision is invariably about some choice among contending values and that a good question, not necessarily a right one, might ignore unpleasant economic and political questions about existing actualities. Such wrong but good questions might rally public opinion instead of measuring it objectively. As the fifth estate, the public opinion poll, begins to exercise political influence, the same ethical questions which have relentlessly dogged the press will also have to be addressed by the new mode of public communication.

New technology creates new ethical problems. It is never value-free, although its demands to be used are relentless. A well-known pollster, George Gallup, admitting that polls are far from perfect, says that no other method has been developed to assess and measure public opinion with the same degree of reliability and validity. But the value of a poll depends upon who pays the piper and whether he wants to discover the truth or he wants to prove a case. Millions of dollars are spent to prove the superiority of a particular product over its competitor in order to beguile the consumer into buying it. If political candidates also begin to indulge in this dubious kind of poll, opinion polls will also lose their credibility and fall into eventual disrepute. Since the people expect objective truth from a poll, the pollster has to choose and word his questions in a manner which should exclude bias because a slight change of wording might create an unintended shade of meaning, inject bias, and distort responses. Says George Gallup, "The best of all safeguards is to make certain that all shades of political beliefs – from extreme right to extreme left – are represented in the staff of the research organization; and these persons be given the right and responsibility to examine the questions selected for polling, the wording of questions, and the interpretation of results. Any question or criticism must not go unheeded; it must be carefully weighed."[12]

The National Council on Published Polls and the American Association for Public Opinion Research established some standards and codes for pollsters according to which all poll reports should be accompanied by description and size of the sample, how the sample was reached, the exact wording of the questions, and the time of the survey. Researchers have yet to evaluate the effect of unscientific, quick overnight polls on public opinion or the media's selection of stories after such repeated polls. These unscientific, overnight polls are not different from private polls which interested parties conduct and then leak to the press. A communication scholar, Alex S. Edelstein, asks some interesting questions:

> The question about the polls today is not what has been done but what needs to be accomplished... The polls are not reflecting a real sense of what the country is thinking *about*, *what* we are thinking, and *if* and *when* we are thinking... Because the polls do not represent, or even seek to provide, an overview of the thinking (so called options) of individuals in society, we are lacking that vital data about ourselves that a society needs to communicate and, perchance, depending upon our skills, to communicate effectively... Citizens participation (and repertories) in polls need to be increased: not in answering questions but in asking them... The new information technology, as one example, may become a means by which publics will be able to ask questions as well as answer them. The pollsters will become a part of the search for ways of organizing information that is amenable to technology, thus permitting technology to become more amenable to society.[13]

For instance, public opinion polls in 1988 might have asked what kind of questions people would have liked to ask George Bush about his role in the Iran-contra affair. With the availability of computer-telecommunications interactive technology it wouldn't have been difficult. But his political commercials diverted the public mind in another direction. And political commercials structure their messages based on findings of public opinion polls.

Negative Political Commercials? Why Not?

There is nothing more important in American political life than the civilized transfer of power from one party to another, and political advertising is a crucial vehicle in bringing about this change.

Like any other cultural form bred by modern technology, the political commercial as a method of political communication and persuasion has been very controversial and has been condemned as a modern evil. Senator Barry Goldwater (R-Ariz.) called it "The most disgusting development of my life." Senator John Danforth (R-Mo) bemoaned, "They demean the candidate. They disgust the public. They destroy our sense of fairness. They transform the democratic process into guerrilla warfare... It's a sickening ... revolting mess."[14] Comparative or negative advertising may sound rather uncivil to us but is essential for the self-renewal of a society. It is very democratic and helps a society to maintain its homeostasis. Negative advertising aids in exposing the evil deeds or the fatal flaws of political candidates; besides, it prevents hero-worship or the cult of personality from developing and thus keeps the people at a reasonable emotional and psychological distance from the emerging leaders. Because of negative campaigns people learned what not to expect from George Bush or Michael Dukakis in the 1988 campaign; their opponents exposed their soft underbellies or Achilles heels, and warned us of the dangers inherent in their leadership.

But negative campaigning is not new; it has always been a part of American political culture, and America has been strengthened because of it. John Quincy Adams called Andrew Jackson "a barbarian and savage who could scarcely spell his name." Theodore Roosevelt condemned his political opponent William McKinley as "a white-livered cur with no more backbone than a chocolate eclair."[15] American democracy was never the worse for it. If someone had exposed the seamy sides of Joe McCarthy and Richard Nixon, the nation could have been spared much humiliation and pain. John F. Kennedy's campaign was the first to initiate negative television commercials when it showed newsreel footage of Eisenhower's answer to a question as to which of his major policy decisions Nixon had made a substantial contribution: "If you give me a week, I might think of one."

A week before the "Super Tuesday" of 1988 when thousands of delegates were to be elected by Democratic and Republican voters for the national conventions, political commercials had become very dramatic and informative. They engaged the viewers totally. Through negative commercials candidates highlighted political issues more effectively. For instance, during the 1988 Republican primary, Sen. Bob Dole (R-Kan) in his "waffles" commercial accused Vice President George Bush of not defending the American textile worker from foreign competition, of not being certain about taxation, and of not clearing his conscience about the Iran-contra affair. It did not help Sen. Dole, but it certainly helped the people to know that the vice president had something to hide – an attempt which he had unsuccessfully made in an interview with Dan Rather, the CBS anchorman. George Bush was shown as a man walking on snow and leaving not a trace on the functioning of the Reagan government.

During the Iowa primary, it seemed that Dole's negative commercial calling George Bush a vanishing species seemed to work; in New Hampshire Bush's commercial calling Dole an unprincipled straddler of the important issues facing the nation worked so well that the senator never recovered from it. Rep. Richard A. Gephardt (D-Mo) made fun of Gov. Dukakis for asking American farmers to grow Belgian endive to solve the farming crisis in the country. The ad brought him a rich harvest in South Dakota. Sen. Al Gore of Tennessee raised the prison furlough argument against Mike Dukakis, which ultimately proved a decisive factor in the governor's defeat.

Scholars like J. G. Blumler and D. McQuail found that in the 1964 British elections, gaining information about candidates and issues was the main motive for watching political programs and their research was subsequently replicated in the U.S.A. The American voter gains substantial information from political commercials because the cost of gaining information from commercials is very low; moreover, it demands low commitment and involvement from the voter.[16]

The presidential election of 1952 coincided with the rise of television in the political and cultural life of the country, and since then television technology has played a dramatic role in changing people's perceptions of their political leaders. One of the most notable television commercials during the 1964 election was President Lyndon Johnson's attack against Barry Goldwater, which showed a child plucking petals from a flower as a countdown to Sen. Goldwater's nuclear doomsday. From the audience's point of view the issue was nuclear war and the total annihilation of mankind rather than an attack upon Barry Goldwater. The attack commercial was politically very healthy.

Direct Impact of TV Commercials

The dramatic nature of television, the low involvement and commitment it demands from the audience are factors which make political commercials very effective – something which advertisers and political campaign professionals learned from extensive and intensive experience while academic researchers are now catching up with new explanations and theoretical perspectives.[17] The pervasiveness of the media (98 percent of American homes, seven hours a day), the growth of television news programming and cable that offer political advertisers a ready time slot in which to reach voters, and the increased sophistication of research as a tool for developing political messages are some of the factors for the impact of the commercial.

A skilled researcher, through polling and focus group research, can analyze the electorate to a precise degree. Armed with extraordinarily detailed information about what arguments will move the well-targeted voters, the media managers reach the voters directly. The repetitive nature of sandwiched commercials nullifies what psychologists call selective exposure. Television, it is argued, has increased the tendency toward a star system in politics, and very often Ronald Reagan as president is cited as an example. Tom Shales of *The Washington Post* commented that President Reagan projected himself as "a masterful characterization of Grandpa Walton, Douglas MacArthur and George Gipp, with a little folksy Fred MacMurray in 'The Absent Minded Professor.'"[18]

A communication scholar has pointed out, "The accusation that political advertising, particularly on television, concentrates on candidate image rather than issues has generated tremendous popular controversy over advertising in campaigns at all level. Yet content analyses of television ads do not indicate that their overall content warrants such concern."[19] Studies of content analyses[20] of television ads done in 1972, 1976, 1979, and 1980 found the issue content of the television political commercials to range from 42 percent to 85 percent; and comparing the issue content of political commercials with the issue content of television news, the researchers found broadcast news to be an inferior medium for conveying issue-related information.

Researchers may be tip-toeing on a startling discovery that probably the best way to communicate issue-related information is through repetitive commercial spots of shorter duration. Also, it can be theorized that it is neither the image projected by the candidate nor the one perceived by the public that determines the outcome; it is how the two images – the projected and the perceived – coalesce to form a unified sensibility in the public that is of importance. During eighteen months of grueling primaries and caucuses, the emergence of the president of the United States is a phenomenon of great significance – something which never happened in any civilization of the past.

Can a spot do as good a job as a debate?

Political Debates in the Age of Television

In the 1988 election, before the two presidential nominees met in Wake Forest University in Winston-Salem, North Carolina on September 25 in the first of the two television debates, political spots had already raised important issues facing the nation. On issues like abortion, the death penalty, the ERA, gun control, and school prayer, they expressed totally different positions, and voters had a clear choice. On other issues of great importance, farming, AIDS, childcare, defense, drug-trafficking, trade, education, the environment, foreign relations, and nuclear power, the two candidates differed in degrees of emphasis and solutions proposed rather than substantively. What was not forthcoming from the candidates through campaigns and commercials was expected to be clarified through debates. Debates assumed crucial importance in the 1988 election because, according to The New York Times/CBS News Poll taken a week before the first debate, 37 percent respondents voiced no preference while 4 percent said that they might switch preference.[21] This indecision persisted until the end.

Have political commercials caused the demise of a fine American institution, the political debate, the glory of Greece and Rome, Great Britain, Yale, and Harvard? In spite of doubts, political debates in America seem to be establishing themselves as a respectable political institution, and those candidates who want to reach the voters directly, unfiltered by the mass media controllers feel reassured. Although most of us think of the famous Lincoln-Douglas debate of the 1858 U.S. Senate election in Illinois (not the Kennedy-Nixon presidential election of 1960) as the beginning of political debating in America, the televised debates of the 1960s were the first of their kinds, and they almost died until they were revived in 1976. President Johnson in 1964, and President Nixon in 1968 and 1972, refused to debate their opponents. They did not want their opponents to look presidential. But debates did help John F. Kennedy and Ronald Reagan to look presidential, with tremendous charisma and enhanced source credibility.

The format is simple: a panel of reporters cross-examine the candidates on various issues; and the candidates' responses and rebuttals, which are invariably re-assertions of their campaign platform and paraphrasing of the negative commercials against their rivals, are telecast directly without comments to millions of voters in their living rooms. The 1976, 1980, and 1984 debates were sponsored by The League of Women Voters, while the 1988 debates were conducted on behalf of the committee on the presidential election. Although a panel of highly respected newsmen questioned the candidates, the candidate campaigns had veto powers over the selection of media representatives. A syndicated columnist, David S. Broder, suggested that candidates should question each other rather than be questioned by a panel of reporters.[22] This would leave journalists as observers and critics of the electoral process rather than become participants and sympathizers of political fortune-seekers.

From the self-renewing paradigm, political debates via television, in spite of the possibility of raising the barrier of selective exposure of the audience, are one more means of direct transaction between leaders and the public. It is a step away from the elitist party politics of an earlier era when party bosses, churches, and other institutions mediated between voters and political leaders. The best bet for democracy is to bring the leaders and the masses into a direct transactional relationship.

Modern communications technology has taken over the role of the power broker in election campaigns.[23] Party loyalty has been replaced partly by issues and partly by images. As S. Kraus and D. Davis state, "Debates offer no magical cure for knowledge gaps in our society, but, along with other developments in political institutions, they could lessen rather than aggravate these differences... However, as currently structured, the parties and candidates retain much greater control over the content of the debates than they do over most other forms of mass communication. Only advertising allows them more control."[24]

In a 1987 survey, based on a scientifically selected cross-section of 1000 adult Americans, 84 percent said that their choice would certainly be influenced by how the candidates performed in the televised debates. The respondents were equally divided about reporters getting involved in the televised debates.[25]

Direct Transaction via Satellite

It was Southern politicians' gambit to have a decisive voice in the presidential election of 1988 which prompted them to use satellite technology to initiate the political phenomenon of multiple primaries and caucuses on Tuesday March 8, 1988. But satellite technology had been used much before anyone thought of Super Tuesday.

In 1985, RCA launched the Satcom K-2 satellite, which uses the Ku-band to transmit signals in more efficient and affordable ways. In order to encourage the use of the new technology, RCA distributed gratis several dozens portable uplink-downlink dishes to local stations, which led them to transmit and receive news from anywhere in the country. The technology not only modified the dependency relations between local stations and the networks, but also made it possible for politicians to have unmediated access to their constituents via satellite. The networks, fearing further erosion of relations with their local affiliates, hastened to provide them with Ku-band trucks and other necessary equipment. The stage was set for high-tech political campaigns of 1988 and the future, replacing the flyover tarmac-to-tarmac campaigns of the 1984 Reagan-Mondale era.

From whistle stop to tarmac to satellite, the medium, the message, the organization, the target marketing, the demographic research, and the instant feedback from computerized opinion polls have interacted to transform the political campaigns of modern times into a direct electronic democracy. Political candidates have never hesitated to use any communication means, from billboard to broadcasting, to reach the voters. In politics when everyone has equal access to the same medium, it is the message that counts.

The Big Eye is Watching

In many ways the 1988 presidential election was extremely grueling and nerve-wracking. The candidates' private lives and their public statements were subject to thorough scrutiny. In an election-related survey, respondents were asked: "If a television reporter uncovers something negative about a candidate's (a) financial affairs, (b) sexual behavior or (c) personal background, what should the reporter do? ...Put information on the air right away? Keep the information off the air? Or wait until after the election to make it known?" With a margin of error of plus or minus three points, 60 percent of the respondents said that a candidate's financial affairs should be aired right away; 62 percent said that a candidate's personal background should be revealed immediately; however, only 38 percent wanted a candidate's sexual behavior to be exposed promptly.[26] Considering the sexual follies of Gary Hart, the plagiarism of Sen. Joe Biden, and the planned evasion by Vice President George Bush about his role in the Iran-contra affair, the presidential election of 1988 became a test of one's character. From the major premises of this study – that is, the role of communications technology in the self-renewal of American society – these opinion polls and exposés are the most important developments in the political life of the nation.

Communications technology and the mass media as the nervous system of a society should help the system to undergo self-scrutiny. America does not belong to Americans only; it is a globalized country in which the rest of world is keenly interested. The American president is the leader of the free world. He bears a heavy burden and his private and public life must endure thorough dissection. "But the sad truth," as Walter Shapiro of *Time* ably observed, "is that the candidates have ceased learning firsthand anything about the nation they aspire to govern...Such are the inevitable consequences of the too much, too fast primary season. Whether he knows it or not, the man who will be the next president has already slipped the last bonds that once connected him to everyday existence. The images that he will use in the White House to try to put a human face on abstract policy issues are by this time cemented in place."[27] That is all the more reason that the presidential candidates should be subjected to a steady, hard gaze for a long time. Invention of primaries and caucuses and prolonged debates is an ingenious process of public scrutiny and is a tribute to the political genius of the American people.

The Weeding Process

Since presidential nominations are made only by primary electorates, it is very important that they must know everything about the candidates, and the only way they can know is through the society's nervous system, the mass media. The media use all kinds of technological tools to find out whether a candidate is ill-tempered, alcoholic, petty, manic-depressive, duplicitous, slow-witted, maritally unfaithful or crooked because his words and deeds have repercussions beyond America.

If the media had done their job and discovered that Spiro T. Agnew had a history of accepting bribes, the country could have been saved much embarrassment. Were the people unfair to Sen. Gary Hart? Did the nation lose a great president in him? Probably not; a vast nation of 250 million should be able to find another capable person, and it did. The strength of America emanates from its controlling center: the free marketplace of goods and ideas, decentralized freedoms, and 'we the people.'

When Gary Hart resurrected his candidacy on December 15, 1987, he issued a slogan: "Let the people decide." He lamented the media filter which obstructed the passage of sophisticated solutions to tough problems. In the age of television, he argued, sound bites produced bite-sized policies. His resurrected campaign refused to use commercials and relied on the candidate's television interviews and speeches to high school students. During his appearance on ABC's "Nightline," PBS's "MacNeil/Lehrer News Hour," CBS's "60 Minutes," and CNN's "Newsmakers Saturday," he had some control over the interview process, and he refused to answer questions about his affair with Dona Rice, his girlfriend on the boat "Monkey Business." But the electorate on the way to Iowa had found that Gary Hart had no substance in him. As Hal Bruno, the political director of the ABC News in Washington, said, "For voters to listen to any candidate, that candidate must in the beginning establish his credentials, including his character, his intelligence and his common sense."[28]

Pollsters revealed the same information about the changing expectations of the people and the new emerging mode of consciousness. For instance, a 1988 poll revealed that 85 percent people expected their president to be very honest, 84 percent said that the president should be very intelligent, and 74 percent believed that the president should have a thorough command of facts.[29]

The expectations of the electorate in the 1988 elections were very high. Character had become so important because, as R. W. Apple Jr. of *The New York Times*, commenting about the fall of Sen. Joe Biden, said that the 1988 campaign took place against a background of disillusionment. "Two decades ago, Mr. Hart's indiscretion might well have been ignored by the press and television. A decade ago, Mr. Biden's misrepresentations could not have been dramatized as they were. It was not so much the original newspaper articles that cost him dear; it was television, the tapes pulled from vast libraries showing him aping Neil Kinnock, the leader of the Labor Party in Britain, without credit, and making misstatements about his educational accomplishments in an exchange in a New Hampshire living room. The Big Eye is everywhere."[30] In an age when the party system has almost collapsed and the bosses no longer can mediate and vouch for a candidate's worth, the media, particularly television, have taken over the role of the prosecutor and the jury.

Ambushing Politicians

On January 25, 1988 Vice President Bush got into a dispute with CBS's anchorman Dan Rather over the issue of the Iran-contra affair. In a shouting match, the vice president seemed to emerge victorious and his sagging campaign became energized. However, the confrontation revived a debate about the media's role in the presidential election, and whether a news organization like CBS, which should report events dispassionately, should get involved in a public debate with politicians. The media's role now is not only to observe but also to participate in events of such momentous significance as the election of the president. It is the duty of reporters to ask politicians and public officials tough questions in public. That's the only way American society can prevent the rise of Nixons, Agnews, and Hitlers of the future. Joel Brinkley of *The New York Times* asked a series of questions which the Vice President did not answer to anyone's satisfaction, and the public had a right to know before he was allowed to enter the White House: "What role did Mr. Bush play in forming the policy? What advice did he give to the president? Was Mr. Bush or anyone in his office involved in or aware of the covert program run by Lieut. Col. Oliver North, an aide with the National Security Council, to resupply the contras with some of the proceeds from the arms sales?" [31] These are the questions which a healthy society in search of perpetual self-renewal should be asking public officials all the time.

It became clear from this ambush encounter that live TV coverage of an event can not only be dramatic but can also bring out the hidden truth. Vice President Bush did not succeed in allaying the suspicion that he knew a lot more about the Iran-contra affair than he had admitted to the public. In a telephone poll of 612 adults taken for *Time* by Yankelovich Clancy Shulman two days after the Bush-Rather interview, 79 percent respondents said that Vice President Bush knew more about the arms-for-hostages deal than he had told the public. Said the *Time* reporter perceptively, "Such moments supposedly provide insight into a hidden reality. In a flash they divulge the inner self, the man behind the mask. They are video epiphanies, what media wizards call a defining 'moment.' The viewer does not so much receive information as he does an impression. From that impression an opinion may be formed, and based on that opinion, a voter may be cast."[32]

But as the vice president progressed from the Iowa and New Hampshire primaries to Super Tuesday and beyond, it seemed that the interview had helped him to cast away his wimpish image. But the Iran-contra affair dogged him persistently... for the good of the people.

It might seem that a candidate in the future might get away with his past record, and by using subtle marketing and advertising techniques buy his way to the presidency. But just as television technology has given some advantages to political candidates in communicating directly with the electorate, it has created some haunting nightmares for them. Television in tandem with computer technology has made instant computerized retrieval of images possible, thus giving them on-the-spot historical memory. This has enabled reporters to juxtapose and preface the comments of the candidates now with what they said and did in the past, making them accountable for their total behavior. In television, time past is time present. Candidates wrapped in national flags and entombed in military tanks do create visual impacts, but they do not obliterate their pasts.

Agenda-setting by the People

It is the emerging role of opinion polls, political commercials, television debates, direct transactions with the the electorate via satellite, and television's big eye probing the private lives of political candidates that has reduced the network news program as well as the television stars, Dan Rather, Sam Donaldson et al., to a mere factor rather than a force. The converging communications technologies – that is, television, computers and satellites – are giving rise to more and more sophisticated research methodologies capable of assessing the people's pulse, and, thus, letting them decide what agenda their leader should pursue. A unique example of this agenda-setting by the people was the emergence in the 1988 election of the issue of child care for working mothers, which was wholeheartedly embraced both by Republican George Bush and Democrat Mike Dukakis. Before the presidential nominees took the issue of child care seriously, repeated opinion polls had indicated that women's votes would weigh heavily in the 1988 elections and child care was upper most on their minds.

Although communications technology is not the sole determinant of political change, one cannot but observe that American political culture is changing; that is, representative democracy is being modified by plebiscitory and a direct form of democracy. It will be a saner America, and the world will be safe from the mistakes of a superpower if all the major executive and congressional decisions are subject to public opinion polls.

Decentralized freedoms and power to the people rather than the media- and Madison Avenue-created great leaders are necessary to the process of continuous self-renewal in American society.

Chapter Eight

The American President in the Age of 'We the Media'

I am an image whose time has come.
    —Max Headroom, the TV Cartoon

My fellow Americans, I am pleased to tell you today that I've signed legislation that will outlaw Russia forever. We begin bombing in five minutes.
    —President Ronald Reagan while testing his mike.

One of the seemingly irreversible currents I have observed during 32 years of covering Washington politics is the hankering of our leaders to transform themselves from servants to sovereigns, to replace Abraham Lincoln's 'government of the people' with a government of privilege, majesty and omnipotence...the common practice has been to pursue aggrandizement and usurpation, often with mock humility.[1]
    —Jack Anderson

Although the original intention of the founders of the American polity based on the Madisonian idea of decentralized freedoms was to prevent the recurrence of the tyrannies to which Europeans had been subjected for millennia, it had the seeds of a perpetually self-renewing society in it. The delegates to the 1787 Philadelphia convention were "wary of any system that gives the reins of power to one person – a monarchy – or one group – a parliamentary system. They preferred a government with three distinct branches: a legislature to create the laws, an executive to administer and enforce them and a judiciary to resolve disputes over their meaning and application."[2] In order to harness the power of each branch of the government so that the balance of power remained in the hands of the people, the delegates disputed over the exact form of intra-branch regulatory controls to be instituted; for instance, after long deliberations the convention decided to give the president a veto subject to override by a two-thirds vote in Congress.

An interesting proposal which was partially rejected by the convention was to give the judiciary a definite share in the executive veto over unwise and unconstitutional laws. Although the proposal to give the judiciary a veto was rejected, its power today to interpret the Constitution remains the most fecund source of self-renewal in American society. In a mood of bicentennial celebration of the Constitution, Chief Justice Warren E. Burger spoke as if time had stood still over the original triumvirate power structure. The system of 'harnessed government', according to him, has worked well since 1789, in spite of two centuries of change and strife. "Throughout our history, the three separate, coequal branches have generally 'stayed in their backyards,' even though the lines that separate them are not always sharp or clear. The delegates' accomplishment is even more when one considers that they were writing on a clean slate: a government of separate powers had never before been attempted on a national scale."[3]

Communications technology has, however, upset the delicate balance between Congress, the judiciary and the executive, and has made the president seem omnipotent. The autopoietic, self-renewing system predicated upon a system of checks and balances has dissipated to an everlasting see-saw game between the president and the media. Beginning with Theodore Roosevelt, American presidents have tried to control the other two coequals, Congress and the judiciary, by reaching the people directly through the media. Politics is tantamount to media control in America today.

When the president cannot control the media, he turns himself into an entertainer: "You'd be surprised how much being a good actor pays off in politics."[4] But acting and good entertainment do not always make sensible news, nor do they solve problems when a superpower is involved in worldwide politics. The United States of America has ceased to be exclusively for Americans; its globalized economy has given every country in the world, including Iran and Nicaragua, a stake in what happens here politically.

The idea of media management – turning the media into the running dogs of the administration – sprang up when Theodore Roosevelt initiated his "reporters cabinet" and put into practice a modern political communication convention, the press conference; and he used it for his own political aggrandizement to the detriment of the other two coequals in the political power structure. Since then, by sharing limited information with the media through many devices, American presidents have made the media almost a coequal in power; Congress and the judiciary have been reduced to secondary roles. Nothing succeeds in America unless the president and the media are on the same side – and this success can be a terrible hallucination, as was seen in the early days of Vietnam.

Fortunately, few presidents have succeeded in domesticating the media;

after Theodore Roosevelt, only Franklin D. Roosevelt, John F. Kennedy, and to some extent Ronald Reagan succeeded with the media. Roosevelt and Kennedy disarmed reporters by creating the illusion that they were power brokers and people's true representatives. Franklin D. Roosevelt "packed" the Supreme Court, and tried to purge some of the unwanted members of Congress in 1938. He allowed the navy to be crippled at Pearl Harbor. Yet he survived because of his rapprochement with the media, and his fireside chats.

John F. Kennedy's excellent media relations helped to absorb the shock of the Bay of Pigs misadventure. Dwight Eisenhower came out bruised but unbroken from the U-2 spy crisis. Harry Truman's pathetic desire to prove himself strong, as he tried to do by dropping atom bombs over Japan, made him irascible and abrasive. Gerald Ford never had the credibility of a president; he was tumbling and fumbling all over the country. The media never accepted Richard Nixon and dragged him through the hell of Watergate and threatened impeachment in spite of his historic efforts in establishing political relations with China and ending the Vietnam War. Jimmy Carter could not get out of the labyrinth which developed due to the hostage situation in Khomeini's Iran. But Reagan has survived the worst embarrassment of any 20th century president: the loss of 218 marines in Lebanon, the Iran-contra affair, and decisions by astrology. In fact, with his success in summitry with General Secretary Gorbachev, he might have found a place in history; but that is not the goal of the presidency.

The historical development of the American presidency illustrates the paradigm of dissipative structures and the need to heed the warning that all open societies tend toward authoritarianism unless its members re-assert their autonomy.

Televisual Presidency

Although television, beginning with the 1952 election, had begun to assert its pre-eminent role in American politics,[5] it was Ronald Reagan in the 1980 campaign who turned the presidency into televisual theatrics. Theodore Roosevelt harnessed the print media to effect a great shift in political power from Congress to the president; Reagan neglected the press conference but harnessed television successfully and consequently turned the presidency into a daily exercise in image-building. The Reagan media managers decided "to reduce the pronouncements of [television] medium's news stars to mere dugout chatter... They don't listen to you if you're contradicting great pictures...They don't hear what you are saying if the pictures are saying something different."[6] Since television is an action-oriented dramatic medium, the carefully planned televisuals by the Reagan public relations operators reduced the critical edge of the prestige press into nothing but sound and fury.

Although television did not change the nature of the American presidency until Ronald Reagan showed up in the White House in 1981, it had begun to cast its glimmering shadow on the fortunes of political candidates in the early 1950s. It was the era of Dwight Eisenhower and Adlai Stevenson when the American voter for the first time was blasted with commercials, documentaries, and election specials – the handiwork of political consultants and public relations wizards from Madison Avenue. Eisenhower's television announcement about his decision to challenge Sen. Robert A. Taft for the Republican Party's nomination grew in crescendo as the summer of 1952 conventions zeroed in on the political consciousness of the voters.[7]

For the first time the people saw how the young medium of television was creating new heroes and destroying old reputations. The political manipulations which in the previous era used to be held behind the scenes came out into the open when Eisenhower's backers cried foul play and challenged the accreditation of delegates from several states. Taft lost his grip on the 1952 Republican convention when his political managers banned television cameras from the accreditation hearing, which made them look like old boys used to backroom politics and gave "Ike" an image of a fair and free candidate. The political momentum changed when the audience saw Eisenhower managers persuading the delegates to defeat a Taft-sponsored amendment about the credentials. Television played its decisive role in that convention when it picked up the official Minnesota delegation switching its vote to Eisenhower, ensuring his nomination.[8] At the same time television viewers saw Sen. Joseph McCarthy of Wisconsin denouncing Secretary of State Dean Acheson as the "Red Dean," and calling everyone who he did not like "Commie loving."

The Democrats, on the other hand, after a brief bout between Sen. Estes Kefauver of Tennessee and the "egghead" Adlai Stevenson had settled on the latter to lead them against "I like Ike." Stevenson reminded the nation of "an hour of history haunted with those gaunt, grim specters of strife, dissension and materialism at home, and ruthless, inscrutable, and hostile power abroad." While the hectoring gestures, long sweeping arms, and hearty grin of Eisenhower – the soldier of war and peace – won the hearts of viewers, television portrayed Adlai Stevenson as a mighty Ivy League American intellectual, the kind of politician who lost China and pushed the East European countries into the Russian empire. Stevenson's television speeches seemed ad infinitum; Eisenhower's had "intros" and "outros" in a compact 30-minute format which cried slogans like "Korea, Crime, Communism, Corruption" against the Roosevelt-Truman era. And finally when Richard Nixon, Eisenhower's running mate, was accused of benefiting from slush funds, he used a nationwide radio-television hookup to explain his position to the people. Sixty-four NBC television stations, 194 CBS radio stations and 560 radio stations of the Mutual

Radio Network broadcast Nixon's speech now known as the "Checkers speech" and rehabilitated him with Republican leaders.[9] Communications technology created a new political style.

The electronic media, as Eisenhower's victory demonstrated, began to edge out the old print media from the center stage it had occupied since the days of Teddy Roosevelt's first press conference in the White House. This era also was a witness to television's potential for societal self-renewal and its battle against the growing intestinal political cancer – McCarthyism. Ed Murrow, the conscience of American journalism, said:

> As a nation we have come into our full inheritance at a tender age. We proclaim ourselves – as indeed we are – defenders of freedom abroad, what's left of it, but we cannot defend freedom by deserting it at home. The actions of the junior Senator from Wisconsin have caused alarm and dismay amongst our allies abroad and given considerable comfort to our enemies, and whose fault is that? Not really his. He did not create this situation of fear; he merely exploited it, and rather successfully. Cassius was right: 'The fault dear Brutus, is not in our stars but in our selves'...[10]

The turbulent sixties in America began with 43-year-old John F. Kennedy's 118,550 vote victory over Richard Nixon. But the electoral victory was preceded by the unprecedented television debates which have now become a recurrent political ritual. More than 85 million people watched at least one of the four debates, in which the candidates exchanged facts and opinions about the nation's economic health and foreign relations. It was not a clash of ideas, however, which mattered to the viewers but the telegenic face, poise, and self-confidence – the presidential look, in short – which swayed the audience. John F. Kennedy won.

After entering the White House, Kennedy harnessed television technology to broadcast presidential press conferences live to the people; and he changed not only the presidency but also American political culture. Television as a mode of public communication severed itself from the comparatively slow print medium because before anyone could read a paper, he saw the event on television. The mystique of the White House press conference in the Oval Office disappeared and histrionics took over; the press reporter and the president both turned themselves into actors for the invisible stage. Opinion polls and reactions of the people in streets, not the analysis and opinions of editorial writers, became important modes of agenda-setting in America.

Kennedy held his press conferences in the evening so that the visual highlights could find a time slot in the newscast by Walter Cronkite and Huntley-Brinkley. Kennedy, humorous and imperial, turned himself into a star, and played the role impeccably; he seemed to be beckoning the future Ronald

Reagan. The age of direct audio-visual communication with the people, bypassing the printed word which had dominated politics for such a long time, had begun. It was this endearing image in the collective consciousness of the American people which enabled him to get away with the Bay of Pigs of 1961, the Cuban missile crisis of 1962, and the country's unacknowledged involvement in the Vietnam War (including the U.S. hand in the assassination of South Vietnam's President Diem), a lesson Ronald Reagan was to learn in the 1980s. During the missile crisis, Kennedy made his 17-minute fateful televisual address to the nation, throwing his ultimatum before Russia's General Secretary Nikita Khrushchev who, to worldwide relief, backed down from brinkmanship. Television was very fond of John F. Kennedy and the drama surrounding him; it forgave him his trespasses, which lesser politicians and poor imitators like Gary Hart could not get away with.

Just as in life JFK transformed, through television, the way American presidents do their political business, in his death, too, he changed the way television functioned as a medium. From November 22, when JFK was assassinated in Dallas, through November 25, when transition to the new president Lyndon Johnson was complete, Americans saw the maturity of the new medium and its central place in their daily lives. They also saw, live on television, Jack Ruby take out his handgun and pump a bullet into Lee Harvey Oswald, the president's alleged assassin. And these live newscasts became more frequent as President Johnson led the country deeper into the Vietnam quagmire.

LBJ was not fond of Kennedy-style television press conferences. The only time he used television effectively was when he stunned the television audience by announcing that he was withdrawing from the 1968 presidential race. During his presidency, television cameras turned outward to the Vietnam War and inside toward the police brutalities against protest movements to show a nation dying of its own excesses. During the 1960s and early 1970s, the nation witnessed the Bay of Pigs, the Berlin Wall, the assassination of a president, racial riots, campus riots, the assassinations of Senator Robert Kennedy and Martin Luther King, Jr., long hair, mainstreaming of cunt language, Kent State, My Lai, a tragic exit from Vietnam and Watergate. It was an age of disbelief, and television, to an extent, was responsible for it.

During the Vietnam era both Lyndon Johnson and Richard Nixon became shy of the media. President Johnson, for instance, innovated an interesting technique of avoiding the press and reaching out to the people directly: he asked network television for the privilege of a brief appearance. Apparently this gave him the advantage of broadcasting his message to the people before the written word or electronic comments were out. But in the age of disbelief, being first in announcement meant nothing, as Nixon discovered: he used this direct approach thirty-seven times while in Oval Office.[11]

When the Nixon-Agnew team in the White House failed to manage the media, they used veiled threats of censorship; for instance, Vice President Agnew reminded the broadcasting media in a speech in Des Moines in 1969 that the industry depended upon license renewal. Although the administration could not do anything against the media at that time, it did get a chance to impose prior restraint in 1971 on the publication of *The Pentagon Papers*. For fifteen days the nation regressed to its colonial days; the federal district judge, a Nixon appointee, had issued a temporary restraining order. Later, in a 5-3 per curium decision, the Supreme Court of the United States, basing its arguments on a 1931 case, Near v. Minnesota, said that the government had failed to justify the enforcement of prior restraint, which violated the constitutional guarantees of freedom of speech and expression. The case neither involved clear-and-present danger nor the balancing of opposite interests. In the meantime, the nation waited for television to open the doors to the Watergate affair.

Watergate and Television

Few events have spiritually traumatized a nation as Watergate in America; the journey through a collective purgatory consummated in autopoietic self-renewal, making the nation flush with new ideas to govern itself with dignity and self-respect for the individual. This kind of collective mass ritual, leaving no one out of its painful rites, has become a necessary condition for sociopoiesis or self-renewal of a civilization; and Americans are the first to practice it on such a universal scale, thanks to their religious commitment to the First Amendment, the right to know manifested in investigative journalism, and their pragmatic faith in technology. Civilizations in the past have perished not because of their over-extended military commitments abroad, as some scholars have pointed out, but because of the absence of a periodic internal purgation process when a society critically re-examines its roots and begins from the beginning. It happened in the Watergate affair and has happened again recently in the Iran-contra affair when the nation watched Congress exercise its authority as a coequal in power.

Watergate was a desperate fight by President Nixon to salvage his presidency from abuses of the public trust and power, but its roots extended deep into previous administrations. President Nixon and his advisers were able to use totalitarian methods wedded to electronic technology to manage their political enemies because these methods had been used by the previous administrations. There is a persistent belief in some political quarters in America that secrecy is the only key to success in domestic and foreign affair. This need for excessive secrecy in the government arose partly because the triumvirate political structure of coequals in power – the executive, Congress, and the judiciary –

as envisaged by the founding fathers dissipated due to the rise of the newspaper, which saw in the president the focus of political action.

Before Nixon began his "plumbing" operations on his domestic foes, he had secretly ordered bombing against neutral Cambodia in March 1969. Congress showed its growing distrust of the White House by twice rejecting its nominations to the Supreme Court. Then came an open invasion of Cambodia, the killing of students at Kent State University, and massive demonstrations against Nixon's totalitarian methods.

In June 1970, Nixon approved a plan by one of his aides to form a secret group consisting of representatives from the White House, FBI, and CIA to do illegal wiretappings of White House enemies – a plan which was unacceptable to J. Edgar Hoover because he would not share his turf with anyone. Nixon, then, authorized the FBI to wiretap four journalists and thirteen government officials. The administration became panicky when *The Pentagon Papers* began to be published by *The New York Times* and *The Washington Post* in 1971 because, apart from revealing the wide-scale involvement of the previous administration of LBJ and JFK in the Vietnam War, it exposed the secret bombings of Cambodia and other underhanded maneuverings of the Nixon administration. The president established a team of "plumbers" who would not only plug leaks of classified information but would also act as a surveillance team to gather intelligence on all the suspected malcontents and political opponents. Their first task was to find some discrediting information on Daniel Ellsberg, the ex-CIA employee who had handed over *The Pentagon Papers* to *The New York Times*; and therefore, the "plumbers" broke into the office of Daniel Ellesbrg's psychiatrist. A list of more than twenty political enemies of the president grew daily to include journalists, politicians, movie stars, and other prominent intellectuals.

One of the goals of this "dirty trick" campaign was to cripple the Democratic Party machine and to demoralize Senator Edmond Muskie's candidacy so that a lesser candidate, Senator George McGovern, might emerge to challenge Richard Nixon, thus ensuring his victory in the 1972 elections. On June 18, 1972, the "plumbers" financed by the Committee to Re-elect the President (called CREEP), were caught red-handed in planting listening devices in the office of the chairman of the Democratic Party, Lawrence F. O'Brien. The news media linked the burglars with the CIA and the White House; and two investigative journalists, aided by a hidden contact called "Deep Throat," started to unravel the Watergate story. The White House called it a "third-rate burglary attempt" and pooh-poohed any attempt to blow it out of proportion. From then it was an inglorious and pathetic attempt by Nixon and his "dirty trick" campaign to cover up their tracks, and the more they did, the deeper they sank into the quagmire.

In spite of the disclosures made by Woodward and Bernstein on October 10, 1972 that the White House had engaged in widespread internal political espionage, and the growing credibility gap, people had not lost their faith totally in Richard Nixon, whom they re-elected president in 1972. In the October Gallup Poll, only 52 percent of Americans recognized the word "Watergate." Part of the reason was inadequate coverage of the Watergate affair by television. Most of the print media were not extremely hostile to him; *The Los Angeles Times*, for instance, supported Richard Nixon in the 1972 elections.

It was only when Richard Nixon was installed in the White House again in 1973 that Watergate unfolded into a big story and the media intensified their investigative reporting, putting some of their most seasoned journalists onto the task. But the collective consciousness of the people began to change when they viewed hundreds of hours of television testimony conducted by the Senate Select Committee on Presidential Campaign Activities. Once the president's aide, Alexander Butterfield, testified before the Senate committee that Nixon had secretly taped all conversations since 1970, there was no way out of a downhill journey toward impeachment and disgrace. The people learned to their shock how their president could use gutter language and was capable of deranged behavior in the White House. The June 23, 1972 tape of conversation with a chief burglar, Robert Haldeman, finally convinced the public that Nixon had lied all along and that he knew about the break-ins. And then there was no stopping of the August 8, 1972 announcement that the president would resign the following day, expecting pardon from his chosen successor, Gerald Ford who accurately said: "Our long nightmare is over."[12] After Watergate, the nation emerged self-renewed because television bared the nation's soul to itself in self-examination.

The long nightmare was not only the Watergate affair but also the Vietnam War which the French had passed on as their European colonial heritage to the gullible Americans who hugged the imperial opportunity in a sensuous fatal embrace without understanding the full significance of the French experience. Although the media, particularly television, brought the war to the homes and hearths of the people, the tragic import was understood only by the marginal underground media. There was a constant flow of information, and graphic television images flooded living rooms daily ; but the very profusion seemed to drown the understanding and dull the senses of the people. David Halberstam said in the beginning of America's involvement that "to an incredible degree in Vietnam I think we were haunted and indeed imprisoned by the past."[13] If in the initial stages of involvement, 1962-1964, the media had not created a hallucination about American invincibility and had been critical and analytical, probably the war would have ended soon. But critics forget that the Americans went into Vietnam primarily to stop Chinese expansionism and the Vietnam war brought that to an end.[14] Chinese adventurism halted in its tracks and Chairman Mao's worldwide revolution wilted in Vietnam.

President Ford lost his credibility a month after he entered the White House when, on September 8, 1974, he announced a full pardon to Richard Nixon for any offenses he might have committed during his presidency, thus pre-empting all investigations in progress. By this time the television camera had begun to occupy more and more of center stage, and the viewers saw their president fumbling and tumbling, and ultimately losing to a no less inept peanut farmer from Georgia.

President Carter's attempt to establish direct relations with the people by holding frequent press conferences as well as an experimental two-hour phone-in program from the Oval Office were not successful in dispelling cynicism created by his predecessors. Today this kind of cynicism about the honesty of the president's assertions has become an ingrained mass belief: the president seldom tells the truth. What President Reagan said about Russia is equally true of the American president: Trust but verify. President Carter's historic achievement, however, was when he succeeded in bringing together President Anwar Sadat of Egypt and Prime Minister Menachem Begin of Israel in the Camp David accord of 1979. But the ayatollah Khomeini's hordes sent to American homes via television pictures of blind-folded hostages paraded helplessly in the streets of Tehran. A bold, dramatic attempt to rescue the hostages by helicopter proved a tragic disaster; Jimmy Carter never recovered from it and lost the 1980 election to a deceptively pleasant actor-governor of California, Ronald Reagan.

Why Can't the President Hear?

Reagan and his advisors, realizing that television had finally replaced the print media and Hollywood as the main source of news and entertainment in America in the 1980s, abandoned the earlier presidential communications technique of "cooperation and conflict" with the media. They changed to a new style of political communication which might be called "tele-public relations" – bypassing the media to reach the public directly through images rather than rational, logical arguments. Just as the innovation of the press conference by Teddy Roosevelt made him and the presidency more powerful, television has made American society "more presidential, more political, more volatile, and more cynical than we were in the era of traditional print, or even traditional radio."[15]

In the beginning of his presidency, President Reagan's press secretary James Brady and deputy press secretary Larry Speakes decided that each day a major idea should be presented in televisual images. But they found the president going off the planned track and indulging in off-the-cuff remarks.

Their problem was how not to let the president talk directly to reporters rather than communicate well with them. Soon reporters began to perceive that a deliberate effort was being made to keep them away from the president. Helicopter's motors were revved up knowingly to shut out reporters: "I can't hear you," the president seemed to be saying all the time. This was a part of the media strategy of Reagan's advisors.

In a recent book, Hedrick Smith repeats a story about CBS's Lesley Stahl which has become a part of today's media lore. The spokesman said the White House loved a story of the CBS correspondent during the presidential campaign of 1984 because of the great pictures, even though the report itself was very critical of Ronald Reagan: "Lesley, when you are showing four and a half minute of great pictures of Ronald Reagan, no one listens to what you say."[16] Of course the spokesman for the White House was indulging in false propaganda to denounce a brilliant television reporter and tell her that her reporting and commentaries were ineffectual. There is no empirical evidence to give conclusive proof that in the event of contradiction between words and pictures, viewers do not pay attention to words. Historical experience, especially from the field of the theater, shows that when words and images contradict each other, viewers feel disturbed, which is a necessary condition for thinking afresh. In fact Lesley Stahl may have discovered something for the television that modern playwrights have been using for a long time: that a message rigged with internal contradictions makes people think.

Reagan's media advisors attempted to portray him as a trusting mediator, not a contestant; a loyal friend rather than an executive; a president more interested in initiating overall policies than in pursuing their detailed execution. Hence, the oft-repeated statement which the cartoonist loved: "I don't remember," or "I can't hear you."

In spite of his successful attempts to stonewall reporters, Reagan seemed to be coming closer to the people; he achieved this objective by reaching the people directly through carefully crafted televisual stories and repeated public opinion polls rather than through the mediation of reporters. Martin Schram observed: "People can tell pollsters what issues concern them often because those are the issues that have already been brought to their attention by television; and television then looks at the poll results and concludes that these are the issues that should be aired because they are on the minds of the people."[17]

Reagan successfully broke through the traditional adversarial relations between the press and the White House until the Iran-contra affair erupted in the American psyche in full force, convincing Americans that no American president should ever be fully trusted; that government secrecy, in essence the denial of the right to know, may become the cause of decay and decline of American civilization as it has been for other societies.

Since television's action-oriented dramatic visuals are very effective, the White House press secretary caters more to the needs of television than to those of the prestigious newspapers. No wonder viewers in America know more about Sam Donaldson and Bill Plante than what they have been saying. In television the messenger sometimes usurps the message with terrible consequences: instead of explanation, viewers get hallucination; society becomes less self-critical, the process of self-renewal or autopoiesis is retarded and decline and fall becomes inevitable.

White House journalists, whether print or broadcast, frequently find themselves turning into the president's megaphone or reporting trivia served on a platter by the White House press secretary. Most of the press corps members feel constantly euphoric because of their prestigious assignments; a few conscientious reporters do feel grieved and cheated of their calling. Ed Bradley of CBS, while covering Jimmy Carter's presidency, commented after being subjected to routine photo opportunities and trivia briefings: "This is the sort of thing that eats up our time. Photo opportunities, briefings, releases, more photo opportunities. Most of it doesn't mean a damn thing. But the White House grinds it out and we eat it up. The network wants everything we can give them on the President. It's like jaws over there. The jaws are always open."[18]

While Nixon's White House intimidated the press corps into submission so that they could not report boldly about the Watergate, Reagan media advisors resorted to one-liners.[19] What Soviet society achieves through fear and intimidation American society achieves by the management of what is news. The land of the free is shrouded in silence, occasionally; noise in America is mistaken for freedom, sometimes.

The nature of the White House press conference has changed radically since television began to occupy center stage. It becomes a contest, a hide-and-seek game, between reporters and the president before a national audience; or, it becomes a theatrical extravaganza, a battle of wits for its own sake, mostly concealing rather revealing. Nowadays the president prefers to reveal his policies to the nation through direct television speeches rather than through a ping-pong game of a press conference which sometimes is destructive of his image.

In earlier times, the president tried to bypass the authority of Congress by embracing the press; now when he finds the press too powerful, he scuttles it by reaching the people directly via television speeches and opinion polls. The result is a distracting noise drowning the right to know and consequently damaging the self-corrective process. News becomes make-believe, a collective self-hallucination. But the ideological core, the controlling center that radiates energy throughout American society, is the free marketplace of goods and ideas. It demands measurement of performance and it belittles heroics.

The president's standing as reflected in opinion polls, economic indicators about foreign trade, unemployment and inflation, the crime rate, and inflow of drugs or secret operations like the Iran-contra arms-for-hostages deal cannot be hidden by co-opting the White House press corps or by direct television addresses to the people. An autopoietic, self-renewing society needs no heroes. It demands accountability of the individuals and institutions wielding power.

Press conferences are a way of making the president accountable to the people. Scholars and journalists at the Joan Shorenstein Barone Center on the Press, Politics, and Public Policy at Harvard in a 1988 report said:

> To some extent, our press conferences serve the same function as the British tradition of regular questioning of the Prime Minister by Members of Parliament... And it is almost inevitable that when access is denied, the press will become suspicious that something is being withheld, a suspicion that can degenerate into cold cynicism... Many public purposes would be served by resuscitating the Presidential press conference: providing more and better information about the President's agenda and thinking, enhancing a sense of public accountability of the President – and the press to the people... When Presidents must explain their policies to the public, they are forced to ask question of those who work for them. Regular meetings with the press, therefore, impose a useful discipline on the operation of an administration... The right of citizens to question those who seek and hold public office is fundamental to American participatory democracy.[20]

One of the Commission's members, David Gergen, editor-at-large of *U.S. News and World Report*, opined that "If Reagan had held more press conferences in his second term there might have been no Iran-Contra affair."[21] However, by avoiding news conferences, President Reagan escaped public scrutiny and maintained high popularity although damaging American democracy and political culture.

Television puts two kinds of pressures on the president: to hide information or work in secrecy, and to perform or constantly give an illusion of performance . Since no one in the White House can perform incessantly and produce results to influence opinion polls continuously, the president takes recourse to a PR style, leaving the implementation of the policy content to others – mostly bureaucrats. But what does Congress do, then? Has the third coequal in power been equally affected by the age of television? How has Congress been exercising its control over the president and his actions?

Chapter Nine

The Electronic Age Congress

Don't get the impression that you arouse my anger. You see, one can only be angry with those he respects.
 —Richard Nixon, October 26, 1973

Since the times of Theodore Roosevelt the American media has revolved around the presidency with a tremendous loss of prestige and power for Congress, and the situation has become progressively aggravated since television began to push out the print media from center stage.[1] Today Congress has nothing to report to the nation except its deliberations and vote counts, which become newsworthy only when a bill of great significance like the Graham-Rudmann budget-balancing bill is passed or the Senate sub-committee hearings (like those of the McCarthy era) or Watergate or the Iran-contra affair are held.

The only way Congress can recover its political power and restore the checks-and-balances system is by turning itself collectively into a permanent critic and opponent of the president, regardless of the party affiliations of the members. Media technology may be helping Congress to achieve that objective, which would serve the nation in its efforts toward self-renewal. The government of separate powers, as originally conceived, must be re-established.

Of the two branches of Congress, the Senate has more power and prestige than the House. A senator's tenure is for six years as opposed to two years for a member of the House; the Senate has 100 members, while the House has 435. The Senate confirms all presidential political appointees, including the justices of the Supreme Court; it also ratifies treaties. The House has no such power; it only takes care of the nuts-and-bolts of legislation, and sometimes this enables its members develop great expertise in their chosen areas. It serves as an echo chamber of political processes in the nation. The media, because of these differences in roles and power, pay differential attention to the two bodies, their actors, and their activities.

In the 19th century, debates in Congress were a very important source of news, and consequently the press gallery established in 1838 was always full.

But as congressional debates declined in importance at the beginning of the 20th century, the task of gathering news from Congress was left increasingly to the wire services, which provide to their subscribers matter-of-fact reports; the interpretation and analysis are left to the syndicated columnists, the Washington Post-Los Angeles Times news Service and the New York Times Service. The three prestigious newspapers, *The New York Times*, *The Wall Street Journal,* and *The Washington Post,* once virtually the opinion leaders and the national agenda-setters, seem to dictate what becomes news for the regional newspapers, which in turn become important to senators and congressmen in their home states for their re-election. Although accreditation to Congress is considered to be prestigious, the beat itself is perceived as of lesser significance by reporters.[2]

The advent of television in the House and the Senate has made a marked difference to the behavior of congressmen and has begun to restore to Congress, to some extent, the power it had lost with the rise of the print media. Communications technology may redress the balance of power between the president, Congress and the judiciary and, thus, save the nation from self-destructive wars such as in Vietnam and Nicaragua. The more newsworthy Congress becomes the greater would be its political power to control the president and save the nation.

Gavel-to-gavel coverage of the House, which began in 1979, has created new recognizable faces in the pantheon of images with which American viewers communicate daily. Just as stories about congressmen being recognized in public places began to receive wide circulation, the Senate, too, realized the time had come to open its chamber more fearlessly. Both chambers have yet to realize that exposure to the electronic media means more power to Congress and greater control over the destiny of the nation. This is because the unique medium of television, which is dramatic and visually intense, turns everyone into an actor and every utterance into a potentially newsworthy event. A soundbite is a televisual slice of life. It could be a sign of the times; a collective Freudian slip, an epiphany.

The power of Congress is nothing if not the right to know what the president is doing and who is making and implementing policies on his behalf; and, thus, become instrumental in the process of self-renewal – autopoiesis. One way Congress exercises its power as a coequal in the tripartite power structure is through televised hearings.

Televised Hearings

The potential of television hearing was first realized in 1947 when George C. Marshall presented to Congress his Marshall Plan to re-build war-ravaged Europe in order to save it from communism and Russia. In the 1950s American viewers watched the Kefauver hearing on organized crime and the Army/McCarthy hearing on the communist conspiracy. But it was the televised Watergate hearings of 1973 and the impeachment hearings of 1974 following the investigations of the Ervin panel which opened the possibility of Congress seizing the political initiative and correcting executive excesses.

The House opened its door to C-SPAN television in 1979; the Senate took another seven years to televise its sessions to the people via C-SPAN II. In 1988 there were more than 31 million subscribers to the public affairs cable coverage of Congress's activities. Norman J. Ornstein, a political scientist at the American Enterprise Institute, observed that not only rank and file members received the unexpected recognition but the House also clearly felt the effects of television. Floor debate has become lively and lightens up more often now. Because they have an audience, members want to score points with millions of potential viewers. "Now-a-days more and more members populate the floor and participate in the 'one minute,' the brief speeches usually allowed at the beginning of each session which, if topical and timely, can (and often do) end up as pithy sound bites on the evening news. Members have also become adept at using visual aids to punctuate their points. Rep. Bud Shuster (R-Pa) waved a rubber duck on the House floor in 1980 to symbolize the lame duck Democratic administration; colorful Silvio Conte (R-Mass) wore a rubber pig snout to protest a particularly outrageous piece of pork-barrel legislation."[3]

At the end of the day when the regular legislative agenda is over, some members take advantage of free debate time and reach a larger audience to express their views on vital issues like Nicaragua. In a situation like this a member does not need the presence of other House members; he needs only television cameras to face him so that he can have access to million of viewers. Never in the history of the House was it ever so important and possible for minority voices to reach the voters in their living rooms as now. The criticism that television cameras have turned the House into a spectator sport and entertainment is misplaced; on the contrary, it has made the members more responsible in their speeches and conscious of a larger audience.

The Senate, learning from the experience of the House and "by evidence that television in the House had improved the quality and crispness of floor debate, by giving lawmakers a powerful incentive to learn their subjects and communicate their messages well," decided to allow the presence of television cameras permanently in 1986. The tax reform debate in that year had a potential audience of 11.7 million viewers. "Attendance on the floor is better; debate is sharper, with fewer endless quorum calls and fewer interminable speeches. Senate procedures have been streamlined to accommodate television, but not so excessively that they have changed the essential nature of the institution."[4] And as the networks and local stations begin to use sound bites and snippets, particularly when they are dramatic and adversarial, from the Senate and House floors, the president and his policymakers will begin to listen to Congress.

The congressmen who have made the best use of television opportunities are those who know their substance, are direct in response to specific questions, understand the restraints of the television medium, and use up-front declaratory, terse, and quotable statements. "The sound bite is the crucial communications format of our time."[5]

Without the ability to videocommunicate, neither political power nor influence is possible in America today. The only way Congress can regain its lost political status as a coequal in power is to videocommunicate directly with the the people.

Media researchers confirm congressmen's complaints that the public has negative feelings about Congress. David Brinkley not only showed contempt for the slow-moving Congress but asserted its inferior status vis-a-vis the Supreme Court when he remarked: "The Supreme Court has given Congress thirty days to straighten out the problem. It is widely believed in Washington that it would take Congress thirty days to make instant coffee."[6] Congress is perceived not only as slow but also as merely reactionary to what the president does. Americans by temperament are action-oriented and believe in quick-fixes rather than in long deliberate processes. Yet the founders conceived Congress not only as a legislative body but also as an arena for contest, a platform for conflict, dissent, and righteous obstruction where presidential actions and policies could be tested and tested again. The testing and verification of presidential actions and policies are done through the congressional committees, whose investigative activities have always cleaned up the political mess created by the president and thus rejuvenated the nation. Committee reports, committee actions, committee votes and committee hearings are newsworthy stuff of great dramatic conflict amply suited for the medium of television. Now when television can create congressional celebrities and new power centers, the investigative aspect of congressional committees has drawn increasingly greater attention. There is some hope that Congress might retrieve its prestige, regain its status as a coequal in political power, and participate in policy-making processes.

Policymaking in a Partyless Democracy

The United States of America is virtually a partyless democracy. Only a generation ago, political parties and their leaders acted as a link between the government and the public. Today the media, according to Gary R. Orren, perform an important task of "scrutinizing and evaluating government performance, even setting the standards of success and failure. The roles of communicator, recruiter, and scorekeeper which political parties once shared are more and more the responsibilities of the media alone. The media have become the forum for policy discussion and debate, both inside and outside the government."[7] Orren argues that in the American system responsibility far exceeds control and a public official is accountable to multiple sources of supervision and authority. "In this kind of setting, the media are one of the few available levers for building and sustaining political support inside and outside the government."[8]

It is true that government officials try to cop-out with some reporters. But the reporter, in order to do his job, "must grow close to politicians and win their trust, but his job is also to publicly expose them. To do his job he must develop confidential relations with sources and protect those sources, but his job is also to strip the veil of privacy from everyone else's businesses."[9] It is the latter function, "to strip the veil of privacy from everyone else's businesses," which is a crucial societal function because that leads to self-criticism and course correction. In the Soviet system the officials demand cooperation from the media and they get it; in the U.S.A., this cooperation meets more than half the expectations of the policymakers, and, sometimes, creates hallucination and euphoria of self-righteousness. Successful management of the media, rather than correctness of a given policy, in itself becomes a worthy goal.

In a research on "How the Press Affects Federal Policymaking,"[10] a very large number of respondents involved in federal policymaking agreed that the media had a significant impact on all phases of policy: identification of the problem, formulation of solution, adoption of policy, implementation, and evaluation. This is a role which is normally played by the Communist Party in Russia and China, and should be played by Congress in the U.S.A. But the role has been taken over by the media in America, particularly television. Unfortunately, the report authored by Martin Linsky[11] ends in a cookbook recipe as to how policymakers should handle the press and turn it into a friendly dog.

Although there is a "crucial distinction between managing the news – for example, trying to put the best possible face on an issue or setting the agenda – and lying or deliberate misrepresentation," it is naive to say that "having more policymakers who are skilled at managing the media will make for better government."[12] You can't manage something which you don't control. It is not universally true to say that "most reporters have no stake in a particular policy result, but have a huge interest in the continuing story ... and in the story continuing."[13] Responsible journalists do pursue policy results. Media constitute the nervous system of a society; the more limited they are, the more attenuated is their capacity to describe reality on which depend the decision making processes of the policymakers.

The economic failures of communist countries can be traced to the fact that by controlling the media the party rulers no doubt achieve non-critical acceptance of their policies, but they fail to realize that their policy decisions are based upon limited data, a limited understanding of reality which leads to disastrous consequences. Dean Rusk, a former secretary of state, was misinformed when he suggested that "the press operates in a field of opinion."[14] The press, mostly, bases its opinion on well-researched and verifiable facts. James McCartney of Knight-Ridder said, "I believe in the adversary relationship between the press and the government. I believe it's my job to assume that they may very well be lying and misrepresenting because all of my experience suggests they probably are."[15]

A complex and vast nation with a globalized economy whose presence is felt from Chad to China cannot be left to its elected and appointed officials; it must be made accountable not only to its own people but to the rest of mankind, which has an equally great stake in its functioning in a healthy and internationally responsible manner. The only way this overall goal of continuous self-renewal – of not only the American economy but also of human ideals enshrined in the Constitution – can be achieved is through an adversarial strategy of the press and Congress toward the government.

The Necessity of Adversarial Relations

An adversarial relation is not necessarily hostile or antagonistic. It does not mean that the press regards the government as its enemy, or the enemy of the people, though it could become totally alienated from the people as happened during Watergate. The adversarial relation is tantamount to contesting and testing government's description of reality and the policies based upon it – a function which by and large should be performed by Congress. Congress can perform this function by forging an alliance with the press, particularly with television.

When government policymakers attempt to develop friendly relations with the press, their motives, in the words of CBS's Robert Pierpoint, are suspect: "They don't like the process of being examined by reporters. They want the policy process to be final and finished before it is exposed. Then they can trot out the policy and say 'here it is, it's wonderful, and here's why it is wonderful' and the agonies of how they reached that and what they left out of the policy, or what they neglected, or what they're ignoring or what they're hiding is something they don't want to discuss with the press."[16]

Policymakers are afraid of sharing information about a policy in the formative stages because they don't want it to become a public issue; they don't want their actions to be scrutinized. It is much easier to find scapegoats later on if a policy goes wrong rather than be stopped in one's tracks; and hence policymakers' obsessive urge for secrecy and Congress's and the media's social duty to develop adversarial relations.

Television offers a great temptation to policymakers who think that they can reach millions of people directly at the same time and with the same message, bypassing the criticism of Congress and the media. It will be tragic for the nation if policymakers get away with providing excellent visuals, believing that unfriendly words will be drowned out by friendly pictures.

Just as television globalizes a national issue, similarly it nationalizes a regional and a local issue and puts it on the national agenda. Martin Linsky recounts how in 1980 the Carter administration reached a decision about relocating 710 families who were living close to an abandoned toxic waste dump called Love Canal located near Niagara Falls, New York. An investigation showed a surprisingly high rate of chromosomal damage among some residents. Television coverage turned a local story into national one. "Policies in which there is a high level of public interest and, better yet, a high level of public support, are easy policies to support. Television creates the interest, and sometimes, as in the Love Canal case, it generates sympathy and support as well. The relocation decision that seemed so far away at one point was much easier to make a couple of days later after the steady drumbeat on the nightly news."[17].

Hastening the Process

Television's ability to hasten policymakers' agendas lies not so much in its repetitive, drumbeating capacity or its quick information transmission power simultaneously to millions, "but in the transmission of experience"[18] in dramatic, conflictual, good, and evil terms. The medium fascinates the viewer by naming names and fixing the blame. All problems and their solutions are seen in human terms, perpetrators and their victims. H.A. Simon observed that "human thinking powers are very modest when compared with the complexities of the environments in which human beings live. Faced with complexity, uncertainty, lacking the wits to optimize, they must be content to satisfy – to find 'good enough' solutions to their problems and 'good enough' courses of action."[19] Television fulfills the need to simplify complex issues and hence its tremendous power.

Congress must understand that television along with the prestigious newspapers shapes the public's political and social priorities by "priming certain aspects of national life while ignoring others," and thereby "sets the terms by which political judgments are rendered and political choices made."[20] Iyenger and Kinder explain in their path-breaking study that the "agenda-setting and priming constitute related but distinct manifestations of the political power of television news," and priming "presumes that when evaluating complex political phenomena, people do not take into account all that they know – they cannot, even if they are motivated to do so. Instead, they consider what comes to mind, those bits and pieces of political memory that are accessible."[21] Each evening television draws attention to some problems and ignores others – that is, it primes or prioritizes events – and by its repetitive, drumbeating tendency, it sets the agenda and the standards by which the president, his policymakers and Congress might be evaluated.

Early in the century the print media, by paying undue attention to the chief executive as the most important source of political power from which emanated all that was fit to print as news, began to upset the triumvirate power structure consisting of the judiciary, Congress and the president as coequals. The American president stepped forth as an imperial sovereign destroying the cherished ideal of a government of the people, by the people, and for the people. But no American president has ever succeeded in domesticating the press, which has gradually transformed itself into a loyal, permanent opponent, pushing the other two equals in power, Congress and the judiciary, into the background.

The press's schizophrenic attitude – to lionize the president as well as to oppose him – has been a source of dynamic tension in the political life of the nation for the past century. If there is a two party system in America, it is not created by the Republicans and the Democrats but by the press and the president. When the press and the president are at peace with each other, America hallucinates, and the world beware. Congress must correct this hallucination.

In the 1950s when television was struggling in the marketplace and in homes, it seemed that the new media technology would re-inforce the political centralization initiated by the print media. But television's tremendous power for good and evil was discovered when television cameras turned their focus on the jungles of Vietnam and the street demonstrators at home. Television made the startling discovery during the Vietnam era that it could cause a shift in political power by just turning its roaming eye to anyone capable of dramatics, aphorism, and sensible sound bites. No wonder everyone, from prostitutes and plumbers to policemen and presidents, wants access to television.

It has been a source of revival of power for Congress vis-a-vis the president since the days of the televised McCarthy hearings. Although empirical research has yet to confirm it, it seems that subsequent televised hearings like the Watergate and Iran-contra hearings have restored some political power to Congress. All that Congress has to do to regain its constitutionally designed status as a coequal in political power is to discover scams like the Pentagon procurement scandal of the 1988 and subject it to a televised inquiry – a method of exercising the people's collective right to know, which triggers the process of self-renewal.

Chapter Ten

Programming the American Mind

I mourn because I left all of my heart and much of my youth at a network. I mourn what's happening there, but every time I read a story, or see the demise of the documentary and special events, you don't have much hope anymore. That situation seems to degrade day by day.
    –Fred Friendly

Television programmers, along with anchormen and admen articulate the collective consciousness and aspirations of the American people by engineering symbolic convergence of meaning. Driven by market forces and ratings wars, they shop around for dramatized fantasies created by independent producers; or, relying upon their intuitive judgment about the changing tastes and preferences of their audiences, demand from their creative sources that certain programs be created. Over a period of time they build a unified sensibility, a rhetorical vision which holds people together in description and narration. Take away the tales, legends, dramas, myths, stories, descriptions, and narratives of a culture and you have a total reversion to barbarism, or a fertile ground for colonization of that culture. One might venture to say that a culture is nothing but a set of arguments and stories constituting the symbolic core or the controlling center of that society.

The cognitive domain of a society – its power of understanding the phenomenal world from the AIDS virus to Islamic fundamentalism – is its linguistic and audiovisual narrative and description. To expand its cognitive domain – that is, its knowledge base – society needs newer technology, of heart transplants, of star wars, of perpetual youthfulness and needs to test its possibilities through Prometheus, Frankenstein, G.I Joe, Rambo, Superman, Star Trek, etc. New technology is the stuff of dreams and fantasies which, once realized and accepted in the marketplace, enhances the cognitive domain, the phenomenal world as linguistic and televisual description. Thus technology, collective fantasies, and the cognitive domain of a society may constitute a closed circle or an ever widening spiral of limitless possibilities. Television programmers of America, by their choice of narratives, descriptions, dramatizations, and fantasies, act either as eunuchs of the collective consciousness or the unrecognized legislators of America. Theirs is the harem, theirs is the kingdom of the future.

This unique view of television programming and programmers is based upon the concept of humans as "homo narrans" who share fantasies. According to a leading communications scholar, Ernest G. Bormann, they provide "group members with comprehensible forms for explaining their past and thinking about their future – a basis for communication and group consciousness."[1] The sharing of fantasies and collective consciousness produced by televisual culture is explained by the symbolic convergence theory of communication. The theory explains the "recurring communicative forms and patterns that indicate the evolution and presence of a shared group consciousness." This group consciousness could be in the form of a collective fear, for instance, about the American family and its dissipation, or about another depression. It describes the forces and dynamic tendencies within a cultural group that explain "why group consciousnesses arise, continue, decline, and disappear and the effects such group consciousnesses have in terms of meanings, motives, and communication within the group." The memories of the holocaust, for instance, among the Jews and other victims of Nazism bind them together and continue to create new interpretations.

Why do people share fantasies, narratives, myths, legends and descriptions as they do? Bormann gives a functional explanation:

> Used as a technical term in symbolic convergence theory, 'fantasy' refers to the creative and imaginative shared interpretation of events that fulfills a group psychological or rhetorical need. Rhetorical fantasies are the result of homo narrans in collective sharing narratives that account for their experiences and their hopes and fears. Rhetorical fantasies may include fanciful and fictional scripts of imaginary characters, but they often deal with the things that have actually happened to members of the group or that are reported in authenticated works of history, in the news media, or in the oral history and folklore of other groups and communities.[2]

But what saves a group or a society from collective hallucination is its constant testing of reality through the technology it deploys to solve its problems. Technology and the collective narrative of a society co-exist in dynamic and creative tension, each trying to nullify the other's rationale for existence. Yet both are indispensable to the homeostasis-morphogenesis spiral which an autopoietic self-renewing society undergoes. The storyteller's narratives, however, could take a society away from technological advances and chain it to its self-created superstitions as happened in Tibet, which made it a victim of its brute neighbor.

The American mass media, the collective storyteller, have only two choices: to program the American mind for autopoiesis – that is, perpetual self-renewal and rejuvenation – or toward sovietization of American society. A society could be sovietized without becoming communist.

Sovietization is not collectivization of property; it is nothing if not the collective colonization of the mind of the people by the ruling elite. It could happen anywhere. Television programmers conjure up audiences through narrative and dramatized fantasies which have psychological correspondence with the mode of consciousness of the time. Understanding of programming practices gives us a qualitative view of social reality; opinion polls, ratings, and surveys provide us with a quantitative measure of the same reality. Both are mirror images and sum up the narrative- and technology-determined knowledge base of a society at a given point in its history. Reality is what our technology and narrative permit us to perceive.

Television programming has long-term social and cultural consequences. Every institution and civilized activity, universities, churches, courts, clubs, reading, sports, games etc. – has some entrance requirements, but not television: from Supreme Court justices and university dons to dropouts and drunkards, everyone is welcome to television. It is this easy accessibility along with its capacity for continuous unfolding of the reality of the outside world through special bulletins and newsbreaks which makes the medium a special institution. Because of its perceived and documented social impact, it is constantly being regulated and deregulated and constantly traded in the marketplace. Whatever the case, television programmers are not America's keepers. They are Nielsen's slaves.

So it is not the quality of programs or cultural responsibility of programmers or producers which is of central concern; rather, it is how the marketplace is driving programmers and producers to produce certain cultural products, but not others. The network's chief interest is audience flow from hour to hour, from one program segment to another. What happens to the minds of the people should be the concern of the television critic – the critic as a social prophet, as discussed elsewhere.[3]

Communications technologies cannot hasten the creative processes – art, theater, music, literature – of a society. There is always a cultural lag between what technology can do and what its users can make of it. There is only a trickle of originality; the rest is cloning, recycling, packaging and repackaging, and redressing of leftovers. Narrative culture of a society does not change overnight.

Television is essentially a dramatic medium and does not accept sermonizing or anything else unless presented in the dramatic mode. Programmers are aware of television's tremendous appetite for drama, from Challenger's debacle to Ollie North's theatrics. But millions of dollars invested by the industry in programming do not ensure program survival.

Although the networks program most of the scheduled hours of television stations and cover a vast number of households, they originate little programming except news, documentaries, and public affairs programming. The dramatic and fictional programming – sit-coms, dramas, movies, mini-series, soaps – are provided by a select group of production companies, mostly in Hollywood. They are the storytellers, myth-makers and legend creators of America who, together with science and technology, determine Americans' perception of reality through linguistic and audiovisual description. For any society, reality is a captive of its collective fantasies and its state of science and technology. Since the development of technology is faster than the growth of the collective narrative, there is always a cultural drag in a society.

Programming is more or less a group activity, with the programmer playing a lead role in negotiating various constraints and responding to different constituencies of interests. It is a resultant of many variables and constants which a programmer has to manipulate to survive in the marketplace – of goods and ideas.

In the marketplace, measurement is all. Technology is also dependent upon measurement. Advancement of science and technology necessitates a search for greater precision in measurement because without reliable measurement neither explanation nor prediction, which is the function of scientific research, is possible.

Since the advent of television in the U.S.A. as a cultural force and a marketplace in the early 1950s, market research companies like Arbitron and Nielsen have been recording its eerie glow in our living rooms. They have sold that information to advertisers as ratings which have constituted the basis for the selling of television time in segments of 15 seconds, 30 seconds, and 60 seconds. Television measurement has been a factor of great importance in the development of the form and shape of television drama, movies, mini-series, and other genres as much as poetic meter has been responsible for the footfall, rhyme, and rhythm of poetry.

But Nielsen's ratings business is not limited to providing advertising agencies better and more accurate information about television audiences; it aims at correlating the audiences' viewing behavior with their buying behavior in the marketplace and selling this lucrative information to packaged goods companies like General Foods, Bristol-Myers, Pepsico, etc.

According to Nielsen's chief executive and chairman, John C. Holt, "Our future will lie in customizing single-source systems that integrate TV and product data bases for consumer packaged goods companies."[4] The direction that the TV ratings business, which is a small component of a much larger information business, takes will have a tremendous effect upon the kind and quality of television programming. General Foods Corp., for instance, might find from correlated data that certain programs with particular themes have a very great appeal to their Jell-O-buying customers, or that they will have a persuasive impact upon the non-buyers of Jell-O. It may demand their advertising agencies to tutor the programming executive how to develop programs.

Consumer industries might in the long run become the real programmers of television in America. A consumer research company, R.D. Percy, has developed a system which uses a heat-sensitive device to record television watching behavior in the house. It provides information to clients about channel-switching during commercials, and it is developing a method of evaluating the holding power of commercials during a show. The whole thrust of consumer and television research today is toward developing compatibility between programs, commercials and the buying behavior of the audience. A crude example of this compatibility is that immediately after a segment of "The Cosby Show," Bill Cosby appears in a Jell-O commercial urging moms to give their kids nutritious and tasty Jell-O. But consumer product companies could find better and more sophisticated ways of programming people's minds to make them go to supermarkets in a buying frenzy. As the television creature Max Headroom would have it: "I am an image whose time has come." But commercial filibustering is keeping political and social issues from being debated in the public interest, and the collective mind of the people is being gradually atrophied through non-use. No wonder Ollie North, Poindexter, and McFarlane could pre-empt political decision-making during Ronald Reagan's presidency.

Diversity of programming, which in reality means breaking the monopoly of the three networks and a handful of Hollywood producers under their tutelage, would produce diversity of thinking about some of the grim problems – drugs, street violence, teen-age pregnancies, corruption, the environment, AIDS which the nation is facing today. A nation which is forced to read the same text again and again falls asleep and is overtaken by others.

Communications technology holds the potential of transforming America, as it is doing in some East European countries like Poland and others.

Technology and Narrative

The humanizing and socializing effect of storytelling cannot be denied or underestimated in any culture. It is through storytelling that technology is finally domesticated and humanized and loses its monstrous aspect. The primary function of storytelling is to entertain the listener, but it does more than tell how the queen died of grief after the king died. Stories, through commentaries, descriptions, anecdotes, and selective arrangements of facts or plotting of events, explain what things are, how they work, and the values and choices they offer to the listener.[5] Their truth is accepted if it corresponds with the reality created by the state of technology; if it doesn't, then stories remain in the realm of fantasy, entertaining but meaningless. The story of biblical creation is still very entertaining but ceased to be meaningful once Darwinism was widely accepted. But Darwinism itself is a great story which, through explanations of what life is and how it works, has imposed certain values and choices upon people. Every storyteller, from Buddha and Jesus to Newton and Einstein, has imposed his values and choices through his stories. Because of the medium, their stories spread at differentiated rates of diffusion, but with the advent of television as the quickest mode of storytelling reaching massive audiences around the globe simultaneously, the storyteller of today has assumed a sinister significance.

Television the storyteller has created so much fear in certain quarters that some scholars demand:

> It is important, therefore, to learn publicly warrantable ways of discovering what our collective stories are and do, and, most of all, how and on whose behalf they reflect, express, and shape our world... [P]eople engage in long and costly struggles – some still going on – to tell stories and thus shape reality from their own point of view. The struggle is necessary for the formation of new identities and interests as the industrial age breaks the community into different and conflicting classes, mixes together religious and ethnic groups, and restructures the process of humanization heretofore confined by geography and relative stability.... The industrialization of story-telling makes socialization and public-formation a product of the system of the symbol mass-production... Citizenship in the television age involves the struggle for access and real participation in institutional decision-making affecting the humanization of the species and the shaping of its world.[6]

But who should have access to our minds, particularly our children's mind? What stories should they be told? What toys should they play with – militaristic or educational?

Children Made For Television

The violent entertainment forms affect children in other ways. If they are not becoming actively delinquent – our "good" middle-class children, yours and mine – they are becoming passively jaded. As a kind of self-protection, they develop thick skins to avoid being upset by gouging, smashing and stomping they see on television. As the voice of reason is shown to be a swift uppercut to the chin, child viewers cannot afford to get involved, for if they did, their emotions would be shredded. So they keep "cool," distantly unaffected. Boredom sets in, and the cycle starts over again. Bring on another show with even more bone-crushing and teeth-smashing so the viewers still react.

— Eve Merriam in *Ladies Home Journal*[7]

Television as the major storyteller brings about quick maturing of children's minds by exposing them to a barrage of fictional characters during their tender, formative years. It has a syncopating effect upon children's social learning by saturating their sensibilities with audiovisual descriptions. Without television a child is left to the resources of his imagination and the maturing process keeps pace with biological growth.

But there is no going back on television now; an American child, on average, watches television for more hours a day than he spends in school. Does television violence cultivate violent and aggressive behavior in children? Does it desensitize children to brutalities and eventually dehumanize them? Should children be protected from advertisers? Or, by controlling children's programming, could we produce a new generation of nonviolent, compassionate, caring people? Should we, if we could?

The suspicion persists that television is an unappointed teacher and an unreliable entertainer who is always home and, like the fabled pied piper, may take the children away. A close watch, it is suggested, be kept over what is portrayed in television because on "a typical Saturday morning a child will see no ads for fruit, vegetables, cheese, eggs or other valuable nutritional foods but instead will be cajoled to buy a new sugared cereal with a toy premium or to put syrup into his milk to make it 'fun'."[8]

The increasing concern of people in the 1960s about the unknown effects of television upon impressionable kids led to a collective anxiety situation which prompted Senator John O. Pastore, chairman of the Subcommittee on Communications of the Senate Commerce Committee in 1972 to ask for a surgeon general's report about television and social behavior. The Surgeon General's Scientific Advisory Committee On Television And Social Behavior worked around five themes: Media Content and Control; Television and Social Learning; Television and Adolescent Aggressiveness; Television in Day-to-Day Life: Patterns of Use; and Television's Effects: Further Explorations. These five themes were explored in 60 research reports undertaken by some of the most celebrated research scholars in the country; they were published in five volumes.

Like any other government sponsored report, the surgeon general's report too raised heated controversies, not only about its conclusions but also about its formation and the selection of researchers. In spite of the differences between what the researchers investigated and how those investigations were interpreted by the press and the government, no one questioned the existence of violence in American television. For instance, George Gerbner observed in his report:

> The average cartoon hour in 1967 contained more than three times as many violent episodes as the average adult dramatic hour. The trend toward shorter plays sandwiched between frequent commercials on fast-moving cartoon programs further increased the saturation. By 1969, with a violent episode at least every two minutes in all Saturday morning cartoon programming (including the least violent and including commercial time), and with adult drama becoming less saturated with violence, the average cartoon hour had six times the violence rate of the average adult drama hour, and nearly 12 times the violence rate of the average movie hour.[9]

Gerbner's report scientifically confirmed what the concerned citizens and politicians had been complaining about for a long time: that children's television programming contained an unacceptable level of violence. Does television violence trigger violent behavior in children in real life?

Many researchers working on the surgeon general report discovered a significant correlation between actual behavior and what children viewed on television. For instance, J. R. Dominick and B. S. Greenberg found that exposure to violence made children conclude that violence could be a solution to many conflicting situations and should be used in real life. They concluded that for "relatively average children from average environments... continued exposure to violence is positively related to acceptance of aggression as a mode of behavior. When the home environment also tends to ignore the child's development of aggressive attitudes, this relationship is even more substantial and perhaps more critical..."[10] Research data also suggested that there may be a long-term effect of television violence on children and that excessive viewing of violent programs has a tendency to desensitize children toward violence and aggressive behavior.[11] The researchers also concluded that television violence did not uniformly affect all children and that there were many other factors which modified such effects. Aristotle's age-old theory of catharsis – that tragedy, by arousing pity, fear, and terror purges the viewers of such emotions – was not demonstrable scientifically.

Controversies about the surgeon general's report continued and provoked fierce reactions in many responsible quarters. For instance, the American

Medical Association developed a messianic zeal to check violence and one of its members wrote in the *New England Journal of Medicine*: "... shall we medicos and our spouses and friend sit back, as we have been doing, and fold our hands over contented bellies, while the after-dinner entertainment of our children shows that nothing can be accomplished in this world without brass knucks, kicks in the groin, switch blades or Saturday Night Specials?"[12]

The voice of dissent, however, was not unheard. Robert Kaplan and Robert Singer raised issues so fundamental and complex that there is no simple answer: "It is unlikely that war, murder, suicide, the battered child syndrome, other violent crimes, and man's inhumanity to man stem to any marked degree from television viewing. Many social scientists may have become victims of 'the bearer of bad news' syndrome. Like the Persian emperor beheading messengers who brought bad news, we berate television, which it is true, shows us ad nauseam and out of all proportion the aggression which man commits against man."[13]

Would television violence have the same effect upon children if they came from well-integrated families, where the specter of joblessness and hopelessness was never known? Kaplan and Singer suggest: "... investigation into the connection between violence and unemployment, racial prejudice, poor housing and lack of medical care, the prevalence of guns and the ease of obtaining alcohol, the high mobility of the population, the prevalence of broken families, the role of age, the still partly subservient role of women, the lack of public school courses in child rearing, and possibly declining faith in the just nature of our political and judicial system."[14] Doing research with complex and multiple variables is expensive and time consuming, and most of the researchers end up by doing simplistic research, albeit in good faith.

Although the last word on television violence and children's behavior has not been said, the public perception persists that children are being exploited by the commercial media, who are more interested in making enormous profits rather than serving the children's interest. Welfare of the child would occupy a central place in a society committed to rejuvenation.

Trashing the Child
Saturday Morning TV Programs as Commercials

> Research has demonstrated that children attend to and learn from commercials, and advertising is at least moderately successful in creating positive attitude toward and the desire for products advertised. The variable that emerges most clearly across numerous studies as a strong determinant of children's perception of television advertising is the child's age. Existing research clearly establishes that children become

more skilled in evaluating television advertising as they grow older, and that to treat all children from 2 to 12 as a homogeneous group masks important, perhaps crucial differences. These findings suggest that both researchers and policymakers give greater attention to the problem of younger viewers, since they appear to be the most vulnerable...[15]
— National Science Foundation

After four decades of protests and promises, network "kidvid" remains a national embarrassment — a brain rotting assault of animated comic books and shrieking commercials that border on child abuse.[16]
— Harry F. Waters in *Newsweek*

Peggy Charren, the president of Action for Children's Television, along with many others, laments that children's TV shows are program-length commercials based on toys and they are designed to sell products. The idea is working so well that more and more companies are coordinating their toy lines with television shows and are entering into profit-sharing deals with television stations in order to get their program-commercials on the air. The situation, according to her, is so bad that "if you want to produce a program on the life of Helen Keller, you have first to talk Mattel into making a Helen Keller doll... Toy-based programs keep everything else of the air."[17] Instead of 30-second commercials, the children programs today are nothing but 30-minute commercials which have become a barrier to market entry for non-fiction programming, live drama, music shows and good educational cartoons.

Peggy Charren's concerns and views about children's television have widespread support even at the highest level. Deploring the thoughtless actions of the FCC which in 1984, under the influence of Reaganism, repealed its 1974 guidelines for children programming, Representative Edward J. Markey, D-Mass., chairman of the House Telecommunications Subcommittee said: "Recently, a broadcasting executive of one of the three networks was quoted as saying that 'broadcast is just a business, like any other. He got it wrong. Broadcasting is a business unlike any other, and we must constantly ensure that it uses the precious public resources, the air waves, to fulfill its responsibilities to the American public — particularly to America's children."[18]

The ingenious, though socially disastrous, idea of starting a children's program to showcase animated version of toys was initiated in 1983 by Mattel, Inc., which turned its toys He-Man and the Masters of the Universe into successful television cartoon programs. He-Man became a top-selling toy in the country within a year and transformed children's television programming forever. Today a toy manufacturer not only thinks of a new line of toys but also about the possibility of turning it into a television show in order to stimulate sales. In 1988 there were more than 40 children's cartoon shows which supported toy lines directly.[19]

Apart from the fact that toy companies subsidize the animated programs, they also offer financial interests to the entertainment companies which own and control television stations. A case in point is the Tribune Entertainment Co., which is "a 50-percent partner in the "Ghostbuster" program and receives royalties on every Ghostbuster lunch box, comic book or toy sold."[20] This makes the broadcaster a peddler of toys who would work not in the public interest but for the toy manufacturer. Apart from keeping good children programs off the air, the practice, fueled by the $12.5 billion[21] toy industry, involves serious ethical issues. What has worried ACT's Peggy Charren and others is the entry of interactive shows like "Captain Power and the Soldiers of the Future," where kids use guns to shoot high-frequency sounds or infra-red rays to interact with what is happening on the television screen. This gives them a tremendous sense of power over the artificially created video environment and produces in them a craze to buy more interactive toys – a kind of commercial manipulation, hitherto unknown.

The psychological impact of these highly involving and exciting toys upon the growth and development of children has not yet been fully investigated; nor is it known if such toys could be used for the socially constructive purpose of educating children and hastening the learning process. For instance, can "Sesame Street" use these interactive toys to teach better mathematics, geography, and language skills to kids? It is, however, indisputable that children's attention span and their available time after school are limited; so is the television time society can afford to set aside for children.

It is difficult to trust the commercial interests with the children's mind. Would He-Man, the Masters of the Universe, She-Ra, Princess of Power, G.I Joe, the Transformers, the Ghostbusters, Captain Power, the Soldiers of the Future, California Raisins – creatures which mostly inhabit the imaginative landscape of our children today – toughen our children in a world where terrorists lurk everywhere? Probably this diet should be balanced with more of "Mister Rogers' Neighborhood" and "Sesame Street," the "Cosby Kids," "Fat Albert," etc. so that children cultivate prosocial behavior as the surgeon general's report expected.

Surgeon General William Stewart said before a U.S. Senate subcommittee: "If television can have a negative effect on children, it can also be a positive stimulus. Although television may have power to incite, it also has the power to enlighten and educate. We must learn more about how to promote this latter capability while we learn how to avoid the hazard of the former."[22] The researchers so far have paid attention to the negative effects of television. Very little attention has been paid to what constitutes good television for children and how to create it. Nor has any viable alternative been suggested to commercial television.

Communications technology, which promises to open up closed societies, liberalize old orthodoxies and dull ideological fanaticism, has the potential of desensitizing and dehumanizing the youth of America and ultimately rendering the classroom ineffectual. If the human nervous system is extended by communications technology, and mass media constitute the collective nervous system of the society, the question is whether the profits of the marketplace should control it or some higher set of values leading to intellectual growth of the child should guide the programmers. Self-renewal is not pre-ordained; it can be a consequence of policymaking.

A landmark bill (1990) requiring television stations to upgrade the quality of children's programming may rescue the American child from the clutches of toy and cereal manufacturers. Good television, and universal health insurance (as proposed by Governor Mario Cuomo of New York) should be the birthright of every American child.

Chapter Eleven
Communications Technology and the Human Nervous System

> ... the biggest of Big Brothers is helpless against the technology of the Information Age.
> –Ronald Reagan

> The enemy of the people stands on the roof.[1]
> –East German Communist boss Walter Ulbright (1961)

Many scholars see communications technologies as expanding choices for interpersonal relations and execution of work both at home and in business places; expansion of choices implies more freedom for the individual and enhanced profits for business. Essentially, this uses and gratification approach, according to some scholars,[2] fuels the adaptation and diffusion of new communications technologies which seem to liberate us from the limitations of older technologies. For instance, coaxial cable and fiber optics make possible the simultaneous transmission of several messages; mobile telephones and teleconferencing free man from space-bound two-way interpersonal and group communication; computers and video disks make random search of information possible; video tapes free the user from the tyranny of programmers; video and teletext annihilate the need for printing and distribution of textual material; and communications satellites globalize information flow. The multi-port global access to information and entertainment has unchained humans from the 9-to-5, temporal and spatial clockwork; technology has changed them from passive receivers to active gratification-seekers.

Although the feeling of control over one's sources of information and entertainment in itself gives a sense of gratification, what happens during the process of reception and after its use is equally important. A user may succumb to what is being offered rather than react and retain his autonomy; he may yield to the mass media agenda or seek to set up his own agenda by pursuing certain information in depth, depending upon his level of education and involvement in the topic.[3] For example, a travel video about Las Vegas might arouse the interest of a viewer, but before he makes up his mind to take his family on a vacation, he might access another source to find the state of street prostitution, the incidence of rape and drug-addiction in the gambling capital of the world, and further seek their correlations with violent crime in the city. He may further seek to investigate whether it would be a family vacation or an Indiana Jones-type of adventure in the heart of America; this might lead to trade-offs and alternative uses of time and financial resources.

Interactivity with the media during and after its use depends upon the user's education and training. Similarly, management information systems, fax machines, word processing, electronic mail, CD (for read-only memory, interactive and video), computer and tele-conferencing have changed the organizational environment, but their uses and perceived gratifications depend upon training. "The opportunities promised by new electronic media are equaled only by their amorphousness and their complexity,"[4] and the mutually cannibalizing technologies might create anxiety rather than newer uses and enhanced gratifications.

But if the anxiety syndrome about the ever-changing technology is overcome, or if it is perceived as nothing but a change of models as consumers see in the case of annual car models, the use of newer technologies could be facilitated and gratification could be sought in diversified areas. For instance, satellite communications technology, in the popular imagination, is associated with broadcasting, international data transfer, and telecommunications. But when accounts of the technology being used by small businesses and educational institutions began to appear frequently in the trade press in the mid-1980s, the technology lost its remoteness and became domesticated.

In 1988 there were 8000 corporate receive-sites for 42 private satellite networks in the U.S. and another 16 business-oriented satellite program services. Educational institutions accounted for an additional 5000 receive-sites in the country. According to industry sources, more than 10,000 hours of business video were telecast in 1987, which is expected to increase to 66,000 hours on 300 networks.[5] Most of the telecasts deal with the continuing training needs of the highly skilled professionals in various fields. Some are sponsored while others are advertising supported.

It seems that in the future each profession or trade would be covered by a regional or national network telecast. Some of them may become specialized satellite feeds for cable and commercial networks, thus finding wider audiences. Others, like American Law Network, American Rehabilitation Education Network for health-care professionals, Bankers TV, Biznet and Financial News Network, Food Business Network, 24-hour Hospital Satellite Network, Institutional Research Network for the financial industry, and Satellite Conference Network[6] show some of the ways by which communications technology is slowly being domesticated. Not far in the future, even the American housewife will be able to access any of these services to make decisions.

Implosion of communications technologies means integrated technologies from fax on auto-receive and erasable interactive CDs to satellite networks on one console. The implosion of technologies will change our environment with a consequent behavioral impact. What worries Americans is not so much the fear of falling behind the Japanese and the Germans in industrial production as a pervasive feeling that their children may not be ready for a world replete with push-button information technologies. This altered perception about the environment will change attitudes toward school education which in the course of time will change behavior. Change in behavior is facilitated, as social-psychologists state, by value expectancy or the rewards which a person anticipates.

Perception, attitude, and behavior do not constitute a sequence in time; but they are situated in the same plane, and a change in any of one of them holds the possibility of bringing about a change in the other. Today communications technology plays a significant role in changing perception-attitude-behavior. It is thus that communications technology and the human nervous system become co-extensive. Since the human nervous system captures reality through description, any change in communications technology, by altering the human nervous system, would consequently alter the perception of reality. As developments in communications technology change our perceptions, forcing us to create new descriptions, we move from one model of revelation to another, from Newton to Einstein, from Einstein to Stephen Hawke, from Stalin to Gorbachev.

While each communications technology gives a sense of liberation, it also attenuates our senses in some other aspects. For instance, the invention of writing revolutionized society by liberating people from the tradition of passing social heritage from one generation to another by word-of-mouth. Writing made permanent records possible; but it also forced the linear and sequential nature of the printed word upon individuals, which was a retreat from the multidimensional sensory world of the pre-print era, as Marshall McLuhan reminded us. It gave rise to a vast illiterate class tied to an educated power elite who monopolized information and created sacred orthodoxies to perpetuate itself in power.

The electronic media, by restoring the multi-sensory environment, trivializes the pretensions of the printed word and challenges the existing power structure. The very fact of television's being a trivial medium, an idiot box not to be taken seriously, poses the greatest threat to people in power. Like the fool in the king's court, television packs the truth in trivialities and mockeries, which is a source of its power.

But communications technologies are more than television; each has its own unique impact either in the workplace, or in social and political life. For instance, computer- and satellite-based conferencing frees users from the constraints of time and space. In computer-conferencing, users can interact with messages according to their own time schedules in any part of the world; all they need is a personal computer, and a telephone modem. Teleconferencing brings individuals in large or small groups located far away, even in different countries, into a dialogue. Ted Koppel of ABC, in 1987, held a four-hour-long nationwide town-hall type teleconference on AIDS, connecting several communities and individuals. In the same year ABC's anchorman Peter Jennings in "Capital-to-Capital," a Moscow-Washington teleconference lasting for more than thirteen hours, brought the lawmakers and politicians of the two countries together in a dialogue. The consequences of technology bringing different peoples face-to-face on the future of international relations and world peace were seen in 1989 when dictators fell like hobby horses.

It is this awareness of togetherness, of being in touch and in control (or what a communications scholar, Frederick Williams, calls "connectivity") which is giving rise to new communities isolated from their geophysical moorings. "A person living in a dense urban environment may not sense any greater degree of connectivity than a person in an isolated rural area if there is no active interaction with other individuals or groups. This is where the role of communications technology emerges importantly, because it is the technology that tends to be the growth factor for connectivity – not transportation, not urban change, not the traditional physical factor."[7] Of course this does not satisfy the psychological need, the urge to be physically together, of being close to a group for emotional reasons.

Electronic connectivity gives rise to a newer kind of mobility which, although, it does not replace traditional transportation-dependent mobility, can add a new dimension to human freedom. But communications technology which is developed for commercial purposes may have unpredicted political consequences. It can sometimes create a revolutionary agenda, as we see in the case of the video cassette recorder.

Political Consequences of the Video Cassette Recorder

As a consumer item, the public uses the VCR for time-shifting – that is, to record a program for use at a more convenient time (however, data about how many people actually use such programs at a later date is still not available); to build a home library of pre-recorded and taped off-the-air broadcast programs; to play rented or purchased exercise tapes, movies, music videos, etc.

Since cable and broadcast programs in America are available twenty-four hours a day, the American consumer uses the VCR for alternative sources of entertainment and information as well as to have a greater control over his own time and resources. In a country where broadcasting is limited to a few channels and is government controlled, the VCR owner might use it to watch foreign cultural programs, or even politically subversive revolutionary programs. It may be used for educational and training purposes or to have access to intellectual resources of a European or an American University. But the American user who is accustomed to plenty, may trivialize it as merely an extension of television.

Just as technology to a great extent determines our culture, the use of technology is similarly determined by culture. A Kuwaiti Arab may like to watch a "playboy" tape, having the feeling that, like the fabled chieftains and sultans of his country, he, too, has a harem or a seraglio; but an Egyptian Arab might watch a revolutionary tape from Iran or an English language lesson.

The uses and gratifications of technology, to some extent, are limited by one's culture. With inexpensive camcorder and video-editing equipment available and within the easy reach of most consumers, the VCR takes on a new meaning depending upon one's culture. Theoretically there is no reason why the monolithic Chinese Communist society, as the spring of 1989 showed, or any dictatorial regime, could not be sabotaged from within with the help of the VCR and other communications technology. During the brief interregnum when the prime minister of India, Indira Gandhi, suspended her country's constitution, imposed press censorship, and ruled as a dictator, the opposition spread the message of the revolutionary leader, J.P. Narayan, through audio and video cassettes. Feeling confident that she had castrated her opposition, she held general elections in the country; but to her shock, she was uprooted at the hustings. Although television is state-controlled in India, the people now have a choice of video news-documentary cassettes produced by independent producers. For instance, the popular newsmagazine, *India Today* produces a 90-minute video tape once a month. The video news-magazine, "Newstrack," similar to "60-Minutes," consists of investigative reporting on current topics. "Insight" is another independently produced, advertisement supported video news-magazine which presents an alternative view of reality to viewers in India. The political consequences of the VCR in India are unfathomable and immeasurable by present empirical methodology. The shah of Iran was overthrown by the VCR; the ayatollah's video tapes were smuggled into Iran to build and keep up the opposition to the shah.

The VCR is a people's technology, and its use cannot be determined by any central authority, public or private. Books, newspapers, radio, television, etc. are controlled by large organizations; but a video tape of Michael Jackson or Madonna can be easily reassembled, re-edited, and interspersed with revolutionary commercials or subliminal messages and sent to China, Russia, or any other closed society. The VCR cannot be jammed. Its contents, not being linear and sequential as in the print media, can be re-arranged and re-formulated in the host country in any manner to create developmental or revolutionary messages.

In the U.S.A. researchers have focused their attention upon the behavioral aspects of the VCR, asking industry-inspired questions as to the frequency, type, and origins of program recorded, replayed, rented, or bought. There is a broad consensus that VCR use in the United States and Western Europe has led to a slight diminution of 'live' broadcast viewing. VCRs are used primarily for time-shifting purposes; the rental or purchase of prerecorded cassettes is an important but secondary use. "By contrast, patterns of video use in other national settings – the Middle East or Third World, for example – reportedly involve much higher level of prerecorded tape replay and virtually no time shifting... These cross-national differences in VCR-use patterns are generally thought to be the result of variations in national media systems."[8] But it is naive to believe that time-shifting takes place in America because of "a seeming multiplicity of high quality program options."[9]

Time-shifting takes place because the user wants to re-schedule broadcasting programming; he doesn't have to do this in the case of cable because cable programming is repetitive. Soap viewers tape afternoon soaps in order to watch when they return from the office; sports fans may record an event broadcast at an inconvenient time.[10] It is a method of making a transient event into a semi-permanent event – subject to further uses like frame-by-frame analysis, slow motion, replay of a scene, freeze frame, fast forward or zipping, pausing to cut out commercials or zapping, etc., which are all manifestation of control over the medium. The VCR combines the pleasure of a book and a broadcast. Greater control means greater involvement in the selection of the material to be watched and in its optimum use (conversing with friends and lending tapes and the decision to erase or keep the tape for home library.

Whether the VCR is an evolutionary technology amounting to nothing but an extension of traditional media behavior or it is a machine with a revolutionary and developmental potential depends upon the kind of society (open or closed) a person lives in. In India and Iran its use was revolutionary; similar uses have been seen in China and Russia.

In an affluent society like the U.S.A., the VCR is one more communications technology which creates the convenience of time-shifting, the viewing of theatrical movies at home, and enriching interpersonal relations, extending and complementing motives with which American viewers watch television. It could be "surveillance or information seeking; diversion or seeking exciting entertainment; social utility or seeking interpersonal connection with others; and habit of viewing out of ritual to fill time or to relieve boredom."[11] All these uses in varying degrees are also available to the users in non-Western countries.

Smuggling of video tapes or video piracy is a form of unregulated international trade, and all unregulated trade activities have a destablizing impact upon society. The VCR, in short, has the capacity to re-inforce the internal fluctuations in a society, to lead it away from the status quo and equilibrium toward a new threshold of self-organization.

Change through the VCR

The video cassette recorder poses a great threat to an authoritarian society. Douglas A. Boyd, a communications research scholar, has pointed out:

> In the developing world – more specifically in the Arabian Gulf – VCRs are the visual equivalent of short-wave radios. Tuned to foreign broadcasts, the radio provides a means of gaining an alternative view to that provided by local government stations. The video recorder puts the owner in control of what he or she sees. The VCR is the automobile and broadcast television is the mass transit. VCRs provide the ultimate in visual freedom ... The Arab Gulf states did become increasingly concerned about VCRs as 1970s drew to a close. They did not object to machines per se, but it became increasingly clear that various ministries of information had lost control over what their citizens were watching at home. Three particular aspects of the VCR bothered Gulf governments: the increasing wide-spread use particularly by women and adolescents of imported Western and Egyptian material, pornography, and potentially revolutionary-oriented material.[12]

Since the subservient position of women has deep roots in the Arab Gulf society, the governments of the region have forbidden women to enter video parlors.

Communist countries may have banned tapes for use by students in order to keep their minds undefiled. What will eventually happen to Russian, Chinese, and Cuban societies if the emigrants from those countries continue sending videotapes to their relatives back home? Has the VCR played any part in perestroika and glasnost? One can only speculate on the impact that the smuggling of videotaped movies from the West is having upon the Eastern Bloc countries. But tapes do provide access to different sources of information and also show possibilities of different social structures. Once technology alters perceptions, people begin to demand changes.

Even in America the cultural revolution brought about by the VCR is not limited to a complementary role – an extension of broadcasting/cable – as observed by communications scholars. For instance, the VCR has had an impact upon the film industry, which sells film rights not only to commercial broadcasters and cable companies but also to video rental stores. Vincent

Canby observed in *The New York Times*: "Today movies that haven't been smash hits in their theatrical engagements turn up less than a year, in video rental shops, side by side with the latest masterpieces of John Avildsen, John Hughes and Joe Dante, and golden oldies by Michael Cutiz and Irving Rapper. On the shelf of video shop, every movie is the same size. Every movie is equal..."[13] The VCR by changing the viewing context demands a different kind activity from the audience.

But it is the combination of technologies, the combination of the video cassette recorder with low-cost consumer-grade portable camcorders and desktop computerized equipment that can edit, title, and add special effects, that is changing the use of VCRs. By the end of 1990, industry sources estimate, the home video hobby industry could grow into a $600-million business.

Traditionally, video editing has been done by using two decks and dubbing selected parts of one tape on to the other. Apart from being a time-consuming process, this kind of editing, in the hands of a layman, produces jerky and uneven scenes. Computerized editing equipment, costing as little as $400 can produce smooth professional looking "wipes" and "fades." Computer software programs like Electronic Arts' Deluxe Video create futuristic graphics for the home camcorder user. A smart videophile can shoot parties and weddings, rock-video boutiques, and high-priced real estate video brochures. Future developments in video computers would give the VCR owner still greater control over what he rents or tapes off the air. For instance, Videonic's DirectED, a video computer, allows the user to lay a track on the entire tape and mark desired scenes which can be experimentally rearranged, and the computer can make a new tape of selected scenes, all done by hand-held remote control.[14]

Some people, particularly those with a sense of pride in their family achievements, are turning to making family documentaries from old film footage and stills. Andy Meisler, a TV journalist, recounts how Carla Howard, a former theater director, began producing family documentaries when she started a Los Angeles based firm, Nostalgia Productions. The heart of the matter is that old family movies shot by amateur hands contain some precious moments. "What Howard does (for customers including Mary Tyler Moore, who commissioned and narrated a tribute to her parents on their 50th wedding anniversary) is to transfer the old movies to videotape. Then, working closely with her clients, she uses sound, voice-overs, still pictures and professional editing techniques to create – voila! – a "TV program" for the narrowest of audiences."[15] Apart from the fun of it, the past is resurrected. This is a cultural revolution in the making which may have a far greater impact upon the less the developed societies than in America.

No other culture emphasizes self-learning, do-it-yourself and self-improvement as America does. It is a part of American individualism, and along with free speech and free market it reveals a secret source of America's undiminished energy. Dale Carnegie and Jane Fonda will always be part of the American daily lore, and people will never get tired of them. Apart from myriads of self-improvement books, now the VCR age has brought into the market the instructional video – another example of how an old technology, the book, gets wedded to a new one, the video recorder – to create new uses.

The instructional cassette market is flourishing, and the number and variety of cassettes is growing fast. Today there are 8 million instructional tapes which are indexed according to subjects, from "The Art of Meeting Men" and "20 Minutes to the Perfect Buttocks" to "Zucchini Soup" in such video outlets like VideoSchoolHouse (California), Videotakes (New Jersey) etc. Golf, topped by "Golf My way with Jack Nicklaus," alone has 200 tape titles, for instance. And the appetite for instructional tape is growing as more and more experts, some fakes, enter their chosen fields. This is a kind of return to an electronic age version of pre-industrial apprenticeship, or individual tutoring which the rich in the past provided to their children.

What Happened in Poland?

Communications scholars like Mark Levy and Barrie Gunter have concluded from their research that the use of video cassettes tends to be individualistic or in twosomes rather than in family- or group-oriented settings. "Even more so than exposure to off-air television, VCR use occurs in a social context that appears to be individualized media exposure, a kind of communications separateness, a privatized media experience, often unshared even between members of the same house hold."[16] They conjecture that this may be due to differences in content preferences between men and women. But their research, like most of communications research done in Europe and America, is based upon American and Western European society and has little reference to East European societies.

In family-oriented societies the use of video cassettes will be family-oriented. Levy and Gunter also forget that the idea of family is different in the West and the East. Family in America is thinly glued and fragile. Men and women cannot stand each other for long. Men find it easier to develop working relations with their co-workers and bosses rather than with their wives. It is this peculiar social context which probably explains why the use of VCRs is so individualistic and privatized in America, Britain, and other western countries. An eyewitness report from Eastern European countries said that before the 1989 revolution in Poland communal viewing of videotapes was "not only a welcome social occasion for Poles but one more way, along with sanctioned television, for them to forget their problems."[17]

The use of video cassette technology, in combination with satellite and other technologies, was a contributory cause of the political and social upheaval which occurred in the entire Eastern bloc in 1989. The governments found it difficult to keep people disinformed because of a unique combination of dissident voices supported by VCRs and satellite television. Control of information and censorship without which authoritarian societies cannot exist for long, was made impossible by the widespread use of the VCR.

The battle in Poland was between the official version of the truth and the existing actualities as lived by the people and presented by the dissidents via the underground transmission of video-recorded messages which interrupted and burst into party-controlled television.

Until the formation of the coalition government in 1989, party television covered mostly the activities of the Communist Party; it avoided mentioning Solidarity and the Catholic Church, refused to explain chronic shortages of food and consumer goods and, through a selective use of television images, attempted to penetrate the minds of the people in order to control them. The Chernobyl nuclear catastrophe was not mentioned even after everyone else in Europe knew about it. Pope John Paul (of Polish origin) was shown on a visit to his homeland as a priest surrounded by nuns and other priests, not as a universally admired spiritual leader of the masses.

The obvious manipulation of television by the authorities created a cynical attitude toward official information, according to dissident leaders. This turned the people to alternative sources of information like the smuggled video tapes from the free world. The underground publications of the Solidarity printed articles about the availability of illegal videocassettes and dish antennas. Neil Hickey, a TV journalist reported that the Polish underground frequently interrupted the prime-time TV schedule with audio newscasts broadcast from secret transmitters, which, of course, the police quickly located and destroyed. Occasionally, signals in the form of a text "crawl" carrying anti-government messages would appear on the screen. Leaflets announced the appearance of the next underground broadcast.[18]

The real information revolution began because satellite-dish antennas became a window to the uncensorable fresher ideas from the West. The authorities weren't able to control the inflow of free information, via USIA's Worldnet and Murdoch's Skywatch, and the collective mind of the Eastern Europeans became free. Once the collective mind was liberated, what could the Soviet Red Army do?

While satellites hold a future threat to the communist monopoly of information, VCRs constituted a clear and present danger. In 1988, more than a million of them were in private hands in Eastern Europe, and bootlegged tapes were smuggled daily. A Radio Free Europe research paper noted that the communist regimes concluded that the video revolution could no longer be controlled.

Nonetheless several countries tried to stem the tide. Bulgaria decided "to adopt effective measures restricting and overcoming the inordinate circulation of videotapes of poor ideological and artistic quality." The most active video underground was in Poland where freedom pirates did a roaring business, offering cheap access to screenings of Western movies forbidden in Polish theater or on television.[19] Moreover USIA offered free tapes through its lending libraries, which were used extensively by the Polish people. The Catholic Church was not far behind in encouraging the use of its video tapes by the faithfuls.

Satellite television and VCRs constitute the cutting edge of the information revolution in the Soviet bloc. Since they want to have the standard of living of Japan and Western Europe, the communist authorities have to allow the free flow of ideas, which in turn may dissipate, if not destroy, communism. Unfortunately, the media research being done in the ivory towers of America and Western Europe does not measure the revolutionary impact of communications technology upon communist countries and what it might do for and against the dictatorial regimes of Asia and Africa.

The West is fighting its battles against the authoritarian regimes of the Eastern bloc with communications technology. But in Afghanistan, the same battle is being fought with lethal weapons which have dehumanized and brutalized the people of the region. The Stinger missiles which America has been giving to the Afghanistan freedom fighters have been used against Americans in the Gulf region and Lebanon. But no one can say that the transmitter and satellite dish antenna technology and video tapes which America provides to Eastern European dissidents can ever be used against the West. The Stinger missile is a two-way weapon; the video cassette recorder or the satellite dish is a one-way weapon.

The sound of a gun destroys and mutilates humans; the sound of a television drama penetrates the mind and soul. The ultimate test of communism is freedom, not star wars. The question is whether communism will survive the communication revolution. Without the benefits of communication technology, the living standards of Japan, Germany, and America will remain for them only pipe dreams. Freedom and technology go together. No sooner had Mikhail Gorbachev realized that the technology of economic progress and the technology of dissent go together, than he began to loosen the reins. The Chinese realized too late that the fax machine was a technology of freedom also.

While America saves the rest of the world, who will save America from the subtle tyrannies of the conglomerated mass media hell-bent on profit and power? What would happen to America if its collective nervous system were to be controlled by defense contractors? Authoritarianism in America may look different, but it will be no less destructive of individual autonomy and local initiative, without which rejuvenation cannot occur.

The Liberation of America
Mass Communication as the Collective Nervous System

The human nervous system realizes itself through linguistic description. It articulates itself through language which captures physical reality for humans. What we call facts, truth or reality in fact describes the limitations of our nervous system. If we knew some way of extending the nervous system, the nature of reality would change because the nervous system would produce a different linguistic description of that reality. For instance, when the ancient Hindus discovered the zero, which led to the development of the decimal system and algebra, they ushered in a revolutionary change in the perception of reality; the universe came under the control of mathematics, as it were.

Before Galileo's telescope changed the linguistic description of the firmament, the human nervous system described the reality of the earth as a stationary planet. If satellite pictures had not shown the existence of the Russian missiles in Cuba in the 1960s when JFK was the president of the United States, the Americans would have accepted the fact that there was no threat to the country.

If satellite technology becomes extremely sophisticated and, in combination with electronics and miniaturized computers, picks up sights and sounds of humans through remote sensing operations, it may become possible for the outside world to know how the Chinese communists have been systematically destroying the Tibetans. The Tibetan genocide, like the Nazi Holocaust, would cease to be an internal affair.

The human nervous system alone is inadequate in the description of reality; but with technology it extends itself and gives an improved or a different description of reality. Without technology humans become prisoners of their own nervous system. Each new communications technology, therefore, gives a feeling of liberation from the bounds of an earlier linguistic description of reality and demands the development of new ethics, social relations, and lifestyles until the humans as observers again begin to feel imprisoned by their extended nervous system.

Each new technology brings in some unknown aspect of the previously known reality, or bursts open something never suspected before, pressuring language to change to capture the new phenomenon. Thus, freedom manifests itself as technology. Technology is the promise of freedom. All knowing is predicated upon technology, which is the extension of the human nervous system. Doesn't this mean that anyone who controls our technology limits our freedom? As soon as the East German police pulled down television antennas from the rooftops, they sprang up again. The enemy was always on the rooftop, as the communist chief Ulbright helplessly bemoaned.

Domination

Communications technology extends linguistic description. Those in power want to control linguistic descriptions, explanations, stories, narratives, and historical accounts. It is through the control of linguistic description that the powerful impose their own ideology upon the powerless.

Britain ruled successfully as a colonial power for two hundred years by denying the colonies the right to know their own stories, or by supplanting the local stories with their own literature and legends. By systematic denial of the right to learn their own language, narratives, stories, and explanations as well as exclusion from science and technology, Britain succeeded where, in contradistinction, the Nazis had to resort to holocaust; the Nazis did not have two hundred years with them.

Communist China is successfully decimating Tibet by transplanting its stories upon the young Tibetans so that by the time they grow up, their reality will be different from that of their parents, unless modern communications technology – Sky Channel, audio and video tapes, short-wave broadcast – keep them alive as Tibetans. But by denying them technology and their own stories – in short, by controlling the Tibetans' collective nervous system – China will succeed where Hitler failed.

The Jewish intellectuals told so many stories after WWII that it was impossible to deny them the truth of the Holocaust. The Tibetans have no storytellers left; their rooftops have no antennas. Without communications technology, the Dalai Lama is "an ineffectual angel beating his luminous wings in the void." And America, under the misguided influence of Henry Kissinger, is too busy selling Kentucky Fried Chicken, Coke, and defense technology rather than human rights to the Chinese.

What is the recipe for domination and power? In other words, how does a nation control the collective nervous system of another society or its own people? Obviously through linguistic descriptions and communications technology. As Herbert Schiller observed:

> From the time of Gutenberg, and even before, information production has been controlled and has led to social stratification based on unequal access. What is of special significance about the current situation, is the centrality of information in all spheres of material production, as well as its increasing prominence throughout the economy. Today, information increasingly serves as a primary factor in production, distribution, administration, work and leisure. For these reasons, how information itself is produced and made available become crucial determinants

affecting the organization of the overall system.[20]

Since the human nervous system in tandem with communications technology creates human consciousness and defines reality, it becomes important that "the investigation and public demonstration of industrial behavior in the cultural field – both policy formation and concept-cultivation –" be taken seriously; and a disciplined, publicly demonstrable attempt be made "to understand and expose the dynamics of myth-making in society, and to discover what happens when that process touches the lives of millions of people."[21]

The crucial question is whether the collective audio-visual stories, narratives and descriptions produced by the mass media – society's nervous system – serve the public interest of self-renewal, autopoiesis; or, are they methods of hegemonial control over public consciousness?

Chapter Twelve

Essentials of a Self-Renewing Society

The quack, the charlatan, the jingo, and the terrorist can flourish only where the audience is deprived of independent access to information.[1]
—Walter Lippmann

Some Theoretical Conclusions

Left to itself – that is, to its ruling classes – the natural course of historical evolution of human society is toward authoritarian and dictatorial control because those in power have vested interest more in the stabilization of the existing relations than in the growth and self-renewal of human beings as observers and critics. In the name of efficiency, probably born out of a misplaced philosophical belief in the general system theory that all structures must maintain their equilibrium, they attempt to smother the noise and chaos of democracy by shutting out the people from vital information. Secrecy, secret deals, secret diplomatic flights, secret exchanges, etc. are some of the outward symptoms of this collapsing society. Monsters masquerade as heroes – sometimes in mock-operas and docu-dramas.

One way of keeping the people in a numbed state is to control the collective nervous system of the society – that is, its mass communications system. This way authorities control or dampen any fluctuation in the system's equilibrium and thus prevent its re-organization. Iraq, for instance, could get away with the genocide of the Kurds by sealing its own people and the outside world from any news about it. Israel, on the other hand, by allowing television cameras to record its troops' atrocities against the Arabs, turned its own people into critics and thereby kindled some hope of change and self-renewal and an internationally acceptable solution. If Israel had followed the advice of Henry Kissinger not to allow television cameras in the occupied territories, it might have succeeded in its short-term goals but would have taken a firm step toward authoritarianism, stagnation and self-destruction.

Television and other mass media constituting the collective nervous system of a society can be controlled and drugged. They can be controlled very crudely as is done in Russia, China, and other authoritarian societies. We see their space satellites and rockets going up successfully, but we do not see their Chernobyls, their Tibets, and their psychiatric wards. In an open society like the Unites States of America, the collective nervous system can be drugged by trashing it with sex, violence, and euphoric commercials leaving the nation like an etherized patient on a surgical table waiting to be operated upon by some quack.

The collective nervous system of a healthy society, undrugged and untrammeled, expands its cognitive domain or knowledge base by enabling it to interact with existing outside realities and saves it from collective hallucination – of invincibility, of "Britannia Rules the Waves," of a thousand years of the Third Reich, of the white man's burden. Great civilizations of the past declined not because of their overseas expansions beyond their economic and military means but because of their collective self-hallucination arising out of a benumbed, uncritical state created by self-perpetuating interests. Therefore, the consequences of conceptualizing television and other mass media in America as its collective nervous system are very serious and they demand a nationwide debate.

American society, like any other human society, lives in a domain of discourse – stories, narratives, descriptions, arguments. They are disseminated by the mass media and communications technology, which are the product of the the free marketplace of goods and ideas. America originated in the free marketplace of goods and ideas, with the least control by the government or the private sector, and the essential, inherent dignity of man, which is the definition of an autopoietic, self-renewing society. The American domain of discourse, therefore, is nothing but the product of the interaction between communications technology and the symbolic core – that is, the free marketplace of goods and ideas.

The American mass media, including television, can describe only what its free market- and free speech-driven communications technology permits it ... to perceive or to hallucinate. H.R. Maturana says:

> But what was still more fundamental was the discovery that one had to close off the nervous system to account for its operation, and the perception should not be viewed as a grasping of an external reality, but rather as the specification of one, because no distinction was possible between perception and hallucination in the operation of the nervous system as a closed network.[2]

In the 1960s, Chairman Mao of China perceived the United States of America as a paper tiger and wanted to start a nuclear war even on his own territory while the Soviet Union's general secretary Khrushchev viewed it as a paper tiger with nuclear teeth and wisely retreated from nuclear brinkmanship. China's hallucination could have been disastrous for mankind. Similarly, it was America's collective hallucination created by its nervous system, the mass media, about its invincibility which led to its deeper involvement in the Vietnam War, or its involvement in the Iran-contra affair.

Since it is difficult to distinguish between collective perception and collective hallucination, the only way a society can save itself from self-destruction through hallucination is to encourage social creativity and criticism – activities which are potentially anti-social. The critic as a social prophet is basically out of step with the people on Main Street, but it is his dissenting vision which leads to self-correction. It is the critic who, through the mass media, turns a society into a self-observing system which creates a collective self-consciousness of the American way, to be preserved and replenished.

The choice before us is either to make the mass media an instrument of self-renewal through the generation and encouragement of those modes of behavior which support and satisfy the autopoietic conditions of the society, or let corporate America turn the mass media into another profit-making venture. In the 1950s, Joe McCarthy used the mass media for a campaign of character assassination to capture power, but he damaged the nation's psyche. McCarthyism and fascism lie dormant in every society, and through the manipulation of the collective nervous system of the society they could be conjured up and allowed to take control of the collective mind.

No society is totally sane and rational; it could revert to barbarism. In the 1988 presidential campaign, the George Bush campaign smeared Mike Dukakis by repeated use of the image of a black murderer, Willie Horton, who raped a white woman while on a furlough from a prison in Massachusetts. The sinister voice-over of "gave weekend furloughs to first-degree murderers: 268 escaped," suggested that Governor Dukakis was soft on crime that he was an unreliable stranger who did not understand America. It played on the subconscious fear of the American people about blacks, minorities, and outsiders and tried to undo historical gains made since the 1960s civil rights movement. This is the kind of self-poisoning of the collective nervous system of a society which gradually closes the minds of the people and leads them toward authoritarian control.

George Bush, who promised "a gentler and kinder nation," attained the American presidency only after wounding the nation's soul. Political observers and critics were so dumbfounded by this evil strategy of winning elections at any cost that their feeble protests were not heard. The media stayed neutral.

The terrible truth about the mass media is that they are a self-inferential and self-referential system, and they work as if something happened once will happen again. They believe in their own truth. The next presidential candidates might use the same tactics of bypassing the normal media channels of news conferences, debates, and discussions and use sinister, fear-arousing commercials to capture the minds of the people. The latter-day Hitlers will use commercials to seize and herd a free nation into a mass unless the critic assumes his mantle of the social prophet and keeps the society free from fear.

Therefore, the question of who controls the collective nervous system of a society, its mass media and communications technology, is crucial to the society's self-renewal. Commercial interests which control the media and communications technology in America are more likely to form mergers and conglomerates to maximize profits and market power even if they have to castrate and blind the watchdog. The right to know can disappear in the sound and fury of the television commercial in a free society. The critic is laid to rest and the media consultant and the image builder take over; the nation hurtles through spirals of alternating commercials and opinion polls, thus forming a closed system where the people hallucinate. When political and business interests unite, the sounds of free society are muted. This will be the sovietization of American society... though its shape may be gentler and kinder; the American people may not feel the decline and fall of their civilization because they will think this is the law of nature.

What Can be Done?

Let's recapitulate, in the words of Erich Jantsch, Ilya Prigogine et al., the essential principle of a self-renewing society as an open state of order, far from equilibrium, subject to internal re-inforcement of fluctuations or autocatalysis which drive the society from one creative threshold to another. A self-renewing society is an ethical society, where a critic is more honored than a hero. America needs no more heroes: George Washington and Abraham Lincoln are enough. In operational terms, we can take the following practical steps:

(1) In a self-renewing society, the mass media and communications technology would be held in trust with the right of access regulated by some fairness doctrine. It is through the diversity and plurality of voices that the elected officials can be made accountable to the people. It is through the trusteeship idea of the collective nervous system of the society that the growing might of the private sector can be made to serve the public interest. Thomas S. Rogers, a senior counsel of the U.S. House of Representatives Subcommittee on Telecommunications, Consumer Protection, and Finance, once remarked that he would like to develop the theme of "all power to the audience ... by searching for new ways in which the public can shape the media.... In terms of helping us understand the world we live in, our television environment is as important a part of our environment as air and water are in our physical environment. But though we have moved in many ways to protect our natural environment – for

example, by working to control toxic waste and acid rain – we have done very little as involved citizens in a concerted effort to try to shape the television environment."[3]

(2) Equally important is the fact that an autopoietic society is basically an ethical society because "all actions, however individual as expressions of preferences or rejections, constitutively affect the lives of other human beings and hence, have ethical significance... That is why in a human society a social change takes place as a permanent phenomenon only to the extent that it is a cultural change: a revolution is a revolution only if it is an ethical revolution."[4]

Historians regard the Watergate era in American history as a long dark night, a nightmare. But on closer inspection, from the autopoietic point of view, it was the most creative interregnum in American history because the people asserted their right to ask accountability of their rulers. Having elected Richard Nixon for a second term as president, they asked him, "Mr. President, now that you are in the White House, tell us how you got there." They should be asking the same question of George Bush: "What kind of campaign did you run, Mr. President? Will this lead us to a gentler and kinder nation? Or, is victory all that matters in the polls?" The end of every election in America should be the beginning of soul-searching. In the White House, along with the president of the United States, Banco's Ghost should be a permanent resident. In an autopoietic, perpetually self-renewing society, a mother should ask her child not only "Go and get it," but also ask, "How did you get it, child?" A self-renewing society needs political activists and critics.

(3) Historians have argued that civilizations in the past declined because they failed to respond to the challenges from superior outside forces; that they collapsed because of internal corruption; that they overextended themselves militarily, chewing much of the domestic product which could have been otherwise used for growth-oriented reinvestment; that decline and fall of a civilization is inevitable because it is the law of nature that every human activity must correspond to the shape of a normal statistical curve; that every civilization peaks and then pukes.

The consequences of this defeatist ideology are that people become resigned to what is not necessarily inevitable. Getting out of this mode of thinking in itself requires tremendous moral courage. If the collective nervous system of society, its communications technology and mass media, has become used to spewing images of entropy, decay, and death, it might regenerate them continuously, thus conditioning the collective mind that it is a matter of time that Japan will take control of American economic and political life. Or, the mass media might hallucinate and chant mantras as the medieval Hindus did when a handful of Arab horsemen confronted them and began their conquest. For centuries, Britons failed to do anything responsible in their own backyard, Ireland, except for the brutalization of the population through starvation and neglect, but they did hallucinate that "the sun never sets on the British Empire."

All the ancient and modern civilizations which have now become a part of the dustbin of history had two things in common: (a) absence of the people's right to know – the most dangerous of human rights which makes the ruling classes tremble and accountable for all their deeds and misdeeds to the people; (b) decentralized freedoms, which enable an individual to surrender as much of his autonomy as is absolutely essential for the maintenance and self-renewal of the society. Were these rights available to their people, the excesses and overindulgences of their ruling classes might have been corrected and self-renewal would have been possible. Britain, for instance, succeeded in getting out of India but failed to do so in Ireland. But the solution offered to both the countries was the same: divide them. Division of Ireland brought a daily crop of murders; division of India brought Russia into Afghanistan and China into Tibet.

(4) Assuming that technology did not permit past civilizations to allow their people to exercise their right to know and enjoy a wider base of freedom, the modern technology of mass communications and the media have certainly created such a possibility. Controls can be handed back to the people through debates, discussions, responsible political commercials, and direct satellite communication of messages not only between the president and the people but also between various groups of people. But the same technology could be used for entering into the personal and private lives of the people to chill their creative thoughts, to degrade their minds with titillating narratives of sex and violence, and to program them to buy more. In other words, there is a "pressing societal need for closing the gap between technological intelligence and socio-cultural intelligence. Societal self-renewal is possible only if we develop the kind of collective consciousness, wisdom and social cultural intelligence that will empower us to guide science and technology so that they can serve all mankind."[5]

Communications technology and the way mass media are structurally organized (bound to the First Amendment and free market) do extend the cognitive domain of American society, and along with cultural diversity and plurality, give America a unique destiny of self-renewal.

Like any other society, America is bounded, but through the right to know and decentralized freedoms it has created the hope of becoming unlimited. That's the meaning of Prometheus Unbound.

(5) Equilibrium is stagnation and death, as Erich Jantsch says. Society must be kept in permanent internal turmoil so that vested interests created by politicians, corporations, the mafia, gangs, drug-lords, police, and other organized groups are eliminated. This can be done through social activism in the form of protest marches, hunger strikes, and various acts of civil disobedience as preached and practiced by Thoreau, Tolstoy, Gandhi and Martin Luther King, Jr.

A free press is not enough to keep a society free. A nation can have a free press and yet a closed mind. A nation can be well-versed in the classics and yet be a bigot. Let's not forget that Nazis were great lovers of music, painting, and the arts. Pol Pot of Cambodia had drunk deep of French culture.

Periodically, the life of the nation must be paralyzed so that corruption is drained off from its festering wounds and the healing and self-renewing process quickens. Events like Watergate and the Iran-contra affair test a nation's soul and eventually make it strong. They must be periodically invented or devised so that those in power tremble and obey 'we the people.'

Chapter Thirteen

Propositional Summary

Chapter One

ALL social systems are power systems and communications in the system would reflect the power dynamics.

REALITY is what the state of our communications technology, which is our collective nervous system, permits us to describe. To describe is to realize, potentially.

A SOCIETY is held together by a centralizing symbol, a core, which is the sum total of all its values, a set of constants, a radiating center that suffuses the entire society with its energy.

LEFT to historical forces or unimpeded technological processes, there is no reason why America should not degenerate into a totalitarian society, or become a grotesque giant by overextending itself overseas.

Chapter Two

THE essential logic and thrust, the bias of technology is to solve problems by providing its users with choices and alternative modes of actions – a way out of a maze. But each technological solution creates newer problems and the need for better technology.

TECHNOLOGY is Janus-faced: it creates self-confidence as well as anxiety, a sense of power and powerlessness, a promise of stability and a threat of destabilization; benefits some sections and hurts others; extends man's senses and imprisons his mind; enlarges his freedom and puts shackles on him. Not the least, each new technology creates a cultural lag and ethical issues.

IN the United States, the people in distress do not pray God for succor, they call an 800 number.

TECHNOLOGY, like art and literature, is criticism of society because it questions the assumptions on which the society is based by suggesting alternatives.

Chapter Three

PRIVACY is the cradle of creativity.

A NATION whose people don't talk back is a slave nation.

IT is not big brother but the corporate brother who threatens the privacy, autonomy and potential for autopoietic self-renewal of the individual in America.

IT is the pattern-making capabilities of modern computers which have given so much power to corporations and wealthy groups and have left the common man in America so helpless.

IT is the pressure to feed the hungry media machine which makes journalists blind to what is the public interest and what is the domain of privacy.

THE assault on privacy does not matter so long one gets paid for it; nor does any one mind being naked in a naked society so long one's topless act is paid for. When the cash register rings in America, most of the people forget their privacy.

THE fate of the earth may depend upon how the ordinary people organize themselves and exercise their right to know.

FOR every individual there is someone who is undesirable and unfit to live and roam freely and should be subjected to surveillance.

THE temptations of technology are so great and sometimes so evil that the very freedom and privacy which led to the resurgence of technological innovations are threatened by technology itself.

AMERICAN society, which rests on the twin foundation of free speech and a free market economy and has the potential of eternal self-renewal may become a victim of not only the uncontrolled excesses of communications and computer technologies but also the unholy alliance between the mass media and corporate America.

Chapter Four

WHEN the public mind is fed with trivia, it becomes easy to take control of it.

THE deregulation policy of the Reagan era has let loose bloodhounds on the free marketplace of ideas. The soft and quiet voice of intelligence is being

A Self-Renewing Society   Chapter Thirteen

drowned by the loudmouth ruckus of game shows and trivia.

THE process of mind control in Russia and China is crude but its refined version could be made acceptable to the American people.

THE difference between Soviet society and American society is basically who controls access to information. What the Chinese and Russian communist parties achieved – central authority over information – through violent revolution, corporate America may achieve through modern technology, mega-mergers, and conglomerates.

AS commercial speech advances in America, political and social speech retreats.

HIDDEN persuaders are taking over the arena of the free marketplace of ideas.

AS the rape of the mass media by corporate America continues, the sovietization of American society, less rigorous but more effective, will become irreversible.

SINCE humans live in descriptions and narrations, access to story time has become crucial to all segments of American society; but only corporations have the money to control that access, and consequently the collective mind of American society.

BETWEEN libel suits and commercial speech, America is being choked to death.

IT is only the outrageous speech which sets a society free and helps it to renew itself continuously.

Chapter Five

THE noblest of all human rights is the right to know, which no other civilization in the past ever thought of conferring upon its people – a right which is the key to the perpetual self-renewal, autopoiesis, of a society.

GOOD government depends upon the listener's knowledge and his right to know and it seems a dangerous right to all those in power.

IF the Fairness Doctrine is enacted into a law, safe from the meddling whims of politicians, America will have created a very important condition for self-renewal.

THE courts, too, have not understood the full significance of how the right to know can save American civilization from its touted decline and fall.

WORSE than capital punishment is the brutalization of a criminal in prison.

Chapter Six

NO jury can ever be impartial.

IN a self-renewing society, no institution is hermetically sealed.

HAVING established direct inspirational links with some ultimate source of wisdom, judges have always feared communications technology prying into their faces and making them look ordinary and fallible.

THERE is nothing more ludicrous than undressing a judge because most of the fabled wisdom of the judge is in his attire.

FEW civilizations in the past granted to its people the most subversive of human rights – the right to know, to ask questions, to challenge those in authority and power and, thus, prevent their decline and fall.

AMERICAN society is the first in the history of mankind to make a beginning toward perpetual self-renewal by granting its people the right to know about who lives in prison, and why and how; about the internal working of courts, political and executive decision-making, access to media, etc.

Chapter Seven

EACH new communications technology is an incitement to sabotage the existing patterns of political behavior because it makes information available to the dispossessed.

TECHNOLOGY subverts ideology by widening the base of knowledge, enlarging debate, and creating dissent.

ELECTRONIC democracy is not meant to supplant representative democracy but to supplement it and to provide a new form of checks and balances.

THE rise of the independent pollster is a phenomenon of great political significance.

WHAT is not measurable and verifiable is not public opinion.

NEGATIVE advertising aids in exposing the evil deeds or the fatal flaws of political candidates; besides, it prevents hero worship or the cult of personality from developing and thus keeps the people at reasonable emotional and psychological distance from the emerging leaders.

FROM the self-renewing or autopoiesis paradigm, political debates via television in spite of the possibility of raising the barrier of selective exposure of the audience, are one more means of direct transaction between the leaders and the public.

IN politics when everyone has equal access to the same medium, it is the message that counts.

IN television, time past is time present.

DECENTRALIZED freedoms and power to the people rather than great leaders are necessary to the process of continuous self-renewal in an autopoietic society.

Chapter Eight

THE judiciary's power to interpret the Constitution today remains the most fecund source of self-renewal in American society.

POLITICS is tantamount to media control in America.

NOTHING succeeds in America unless the president and the media are on the same side – and this success can be a terrible hallucination, as was seen in the early days of the Vietnam War.

CIVILIZATIONS in the past have perished not because of their overextended military commitments abroad, as some scholars have pointed out, but because of the absence of a periodic internal purgation process when a society critically re-examines its roots and begins from the beginning. It happened in the Watergate affair and has happened recently in the Iran-contra affair when the nation watched Congress exercise its authority as a coequal in power.

AFTER Watergate, the nation emerged self-renewed because television bared the nation's soul to itself in self-examination.

WHAT President Reagan said about Russia is equally true of the American president: Trust but verify.

A MESSAGE rigged with internal contradictions makes people think.

IN television the messenger sometimes usurps the message with terrible consequences: instead of explanation, viewers get hallucination; society becomes less self-critical, the process of self-renewal or autopoiesis is retarded, and decline and fall become inevitable.

THE land of the free is shrouded in silence, occasionally;noise in America is mistaken for freedom, sometimes.

AN autopoietic self-renewing society needs no heroes.

Chapter Nine

THE more newsworthy Congress becomes, the greater would be its political power to control the president and save the nation.

A SOUNDBITE is a televisual slice of life. It could be a sign of the times, a collective Freudian slip, an epiphany.

THE adversarial relation is tantamount to contesting and testing government's description of reality and policies based upon it – a function which by and large should be performed by Congress.

WHEN the press and the president are at peace with each other, America hallucinates, and the world beware.

TELEVISION could cause a shift in political power by just turning its roving eye to anyone capable of dramatics, aphorism, and soundbites. No wonder everyone, from prostitutes and plumbers to policemen and presidents, wants access to television.

Chapter Ten

TELEVISION programmers, along with anchormen and admen, articulate the collective consciousness and aspirations of the American people by engineering symbolic convergence of meaning.

ONE might venture to say that culture is nothing but a set of arguments and stories constituting the symbolic core or the controlling center of that society.

TELEVISION programmers of America, by their choice of narratives, descriptions, dramatizations, and fantasies, act either as eunuchs of the collective consciousness or the unrecognized legislators of America. Theirs is the harem, theirs is the kingdom of the future.

A SOCIETY could be sovietized without being communist.

REALITY is what our technology and narrative permit us to perceive.

WHATEVER happens to the minds of the people should be the concern of the television critic – the critic as a social prophet.

FOR any society, reality is a captive of its collective fantasies and its state of science and technology.

CONSUMER industries might in the long run become the real programmers of television in America.

COMMERCIAL filibustering is keeping political and social issues from being debated in the public interest.

WITHOUT television a child is left to the resources of his imagination, and the maturing process keeps pace with biological growth.

SELF-RENEWAL is not pre-ordained; it can be a consequence of policymaking.

Chapter Eleven

LIKE the fool in the king's court, television packs the truth in trivialities and mockeries, which is a source of its power.

WHAT would happen to America if its collective nervous system were to be controlled by defense contractors?

ALL knowing is predicated upon technology, which is the extension of human nervous system.

IT is through the control of linguistic description that the powerful impose their own ideology upon the powerless.

THE storyteller of today has assumed a sinister significance.

Chapter Twelve

THE right to know can disappear in the sound and fury of the television commercial in a free society.

WHEN political and business interests unite, the sounds of a free society are muted.

A NATION could have a free press and yet a closed mind.

IN the White House, along with the president of the United States, Banco's Ghost should be a permanent resident.

Chapter Notes

Chapter One
1. Paul M. Kennedy et al., *Lessons from the Fall and Rise of Nations: The Future of America* (Washington, D. C.: Woodrow Wilson International Center for Scholars, 1987), p. 4.
2. Ludwig von Bertalanfy, *General System Theory: Foundations, Development, Applications* (New York:Braziller, 1968), pp. 32-37.
3. Kenneth Boulding, "General Systems Theory – The Skeleton of Science," in *Modern Systems Research for the Behavior Scientist*, ed. Walter Buckley (Chicago: Aldine, 1968), p 4.
4. Stephen W. Littlejohn, *Theories of Human Communication*, 2nd ed.(Belmont, CA: Wadsworth Publishing Company, 1983), pp. 29-43.
5. Norbert Wiener, *Cybernetics or Control and Communication in the Animal and the Machine* (New York: MIT Press, 1961), pp. 1-29.
6. Stephen W. Littlejohn, p. 33.
7. Norbert Wiener, *The Human Use of Human Beings: Cybernetics and Society* (Boston: Houghton Mifflin, 1959), pp.49-50.
8. A.D. Hall and R.E. Fagen, "Definition of System," in *Modern System Research for the Behavioral Scientist*, ed. Walter Buckley (Chicago: Aldine, 1968), pp. 85-86.
9. Francisco Varela, Humberto Maturana and Richard Uribe, "Autopoiesis: The Organization of Living Systems, its Characterization and a Model," *Biosystems* 5 (1974):187-196; Klaus Krippendorff, "Paradigms for Communication and Development with Emphasis on Autopoiesis," in *Communication Theory: Eastern and Western Perspectives*, ed. D. Lawrence Kinkaid (San Diego, CA: Academic Press, 1987), pp. 189-206; James Gleick, *Chaos: Making of a New Science* (New York: Penguin Books, 1987).
10. Herberto Maturana and Francisco J. Varela, *Autopoiesis and Cognition: The Realization of the Living* (Boston: D. Reider Publishing Company, 1980), pp.xxviii-xxix, 53.
11. Ibid.
12. N.D. Batra, *The Hour of Television: Critical Approaches* (Metuchen, N.J.: Scarecrow Press, 1987).
13. Erich Jantsch, *The Self-Organizing Universe* (New York: Pergamon Press, 1980), p. 31.
14. Ilya Prigogine, "Order through Fluctuation: Self-organization and Social System" in *Evolution and Consciousness: Human Systems in Transition*, eds. Erich Jantsch and Conrad H. Waddington. (Reading, Mass.: Addison-Wesley, 1976).
15. Jantsch, p. 43.

Chapter Two

1. M. Blute, "Sociocultural Evolutionism: An Untried Theory, *Behavioral Science* 24 (1979), pp. 47-48.
2. Woody Allen, "The Colorization of Films Insults Artists and Society," *New York Times*, 28 June 1987, sec. 4, p. 25.
3. Keith Schneider, "Services Hurt by Technology: Productivity is Declining," *The New York Times*, 29 June 1987, sec. D 1.
4. Ibid.
5. Ibid.
6. Philip Elmer-DeWitt, "Can a System Keep a Secret?," *Time*, 6 April 1987, pp. 68-69.
7. "After the Baby M Case", *Newsweek*, 13 April 1987, pp. 22-23.
8. Ibid.
9. "Kids and Contraceptive," *Newsweek*, 16 February 1987, pp. 54-55.
10. Everett M. Rogers, *Communication Technology: The New Media in Society* (New York: The Free Press, 1986), p. 2.
11. Andrew L. Yarrow, "The Revolution Wrought by Toll-Free Calls," *The New York Times*, 13 Feb. 1987, sec. C, p. 1.
12. Ibid.
13. Lisa Belkin, "The 900 Number as Audience Pollster," *The New York Times*, 6 July 1987, p. 50.
14. John Rockwell, "Taking Advantage Of Musical Technology," *The New York Times*, 25 June 1987, sec. H, p. 28.
15. Walter Shapiro, "What's Wrong," *Time*, 25 May 1987, p. 15.
16. Ezra Brown, "Looking to Its Roots" *Time*, 25 May 1987, p. 29.
17. Ibid.
18. Quoted in the Preface to the special issue "Ethical Issues in New Media Technologies," *Communication*, vol. 9, no. 2 (1986), p. i.
19. H. Arendt, *Totalitarianism*, ed. C. J. Friedrich (Cambridge, Mass.: Harvard University Press, 1954), p. 133.
20. J. Gould, "Ideology," *A Dictionary of the Social Sciences*, eds. Julius Gould and William L. Kolb (Glencoe, NJ: The Free Press, 1964), p. 315.
21. A. L. Kroeber and C. Kluckhohn, "Culture," in *Dictionary of Social Sciences*, p. 165.

Chapter Three

1. Arthur Miller, *Assault on Privacy* (Ann Arbor: University of Michigan Press, 1971), p. 8.
2. *Black's Law Dictionary*, 5th ed. (St. Paul, Minn.: West Publishing Co., 1979), p. 1075.
3. Le Mistral, Inc. v. Columbia Broadcasting System, 61 A.D.2d 492, 402 N.Y. S.2d 815 (1st Dept. 1978).
4. Samuel Warren and Louis D. Brandeis, "The Right to Privacy," *Harvard Law Review* 4 (1890): 196.
5. Brisco v. Reader's Digest Association, 4 Cal.3d 529. 93 Cal. Rpt. 866, 483 P. 2d 34 (1971): 36-37.
6. Arthur Miller, "The Right to be Let Alone" in *Mass Media Issues*, ed. George Rodman, 2nd ed. (Chicago: Science Research Associates, 1984), p. 298.

7. J. Ellul, *The Technological Society*, tans. J. Wikerson (NY: Alfred A. Knopf, 1964), pp. 373-374.
8. L. Harris and A. Westin, *The Dimension of Privacy* (New York: Garland Publishing, 1981).
9. J. Pointdexter, "Shaping the Consumer," *Psychology Today*, May 1983, pp. 64-68; F. Schumer, "The New Magicians of Market Research," *Fortune*, July 1983, pp. 72-74.
10. N.D. Batra, *The Hour of Television: Critical Approaches*, pp. 228-231.
11. V. Mosco, *Push-button Fantasies* (Norwood, NJ: Ablex, 1982).
12. D. Burnham, *The Rise of Computer State* (NY: Random House, 1983), p. 242.
13. David H. Flaherty, *Protected Privacy in Two-Way Electronic Services* (White Plains, NY: Knowledge Industry Publications, Inc., 1985), p. 6; Louis Harris & Associates and Dr. Alan F. Westin, *The Dimension of Privacy: A Natural Opinion Research Survey of Attitudes Toward Privacy* (New York: Garland Publishing, Inc. 1981), p. 8.
14. Marshall McLuhan and Bruce Powers, "Electronic Banking and the Death of Privacy," *Journal of Communications* 31 (Winter 1981): 167-68.
15. Wayne Walley, "Mailers plug into cable, TV spots tell viewers what's coming," *Advertising Age*, 4 May 1987, p. 36.
16. D. Burnham, p. 242.
17. S. Boorman and P. Levitt, "Block Models and Self- Defense, *The New York Times*, sec. F, p. 3.
18. Dietmann v. Time, Inc. 449 F.2d 245, 246 (9th Cir. 1971); Harold L. Nelson and Dwight L. Teeter, Jr., *Law of Mass Communications*, 5th ed.(Mineola, NY: The Foundation Press, 1986) p. 214.
19. Restatement quoted in Virgil v. Time, Inc. 527 F. 2d 1122, 1124 (9th Cir. 1975), pp. 1129, 1129n.
20. "Darts and Laurels," *Columbia Journalism Review*," March/April 1986, p. 25.
21. Land Remote-Sensing Commercialization Act of 1984, Pub. L. 98-365, 98 Stat. 451 (1984), 15 U.S.C.A. 4201.
22. California v. Ciraolo, 106 S. Ct. 1809 (1986), 54 USLW 4471, No. 84-1513.
23. Dow Chemicals Co. v. United States, 106 S. Ct. 1819 (1986), 54 USLW 4464, No. 84-153.
24. Ibid.
25. Flora Lewis, "Little Brother Watches," *The New York Times*, 5 October 1988, sec. A, p. 33.
26. Manfred Stanley,*The Technological Conscience: Survival and Dignity in an Age of Expertise* (New York: Free Press, 1978), p. 70.
27. Alvin Gouldner, *The Dialectic of Ideology and Technology: The Origins, Grammar and Future of Ideology*. (New York: Seabury Press, 1976), pp. 101-102.
28. Office of Technology Assessment, Congress of the United States, *Computer Based Information Systems: Technology and Public Issues*, 97th Congress (Washington: United States Government Printing Office, 1981), pp. 23-24.
29. Paulo Feriere, *Pedagogy of the Oppressed*, trans. Myra Bergman Ramos (NY: Seabury Press, 1970), p. 73.

Chapter Four

1. John Stuart Mill, *On Liberty*, ed. David Spitz (NY: Norton, 1975), p. 44.
2. Zachariah Chafee, Jr., *Free Speech in the United States* (Cambridge, MA: Harvard University Press, 1941), p. 36.
3. 249 U.S. 47 (1919).
4. Chafee, p. 150.
5. Alexander Meiklejohn, *Free Speech and its Relations to Self-Government*, reprinted in *Political Freedom* (NY: Harper and Row, Publishers, 1960), p. 26.
6. Ibid., p. 37.
7. Thomas I. Emerson, *The System of Freedom of Expression* (NY: Random House, 1970), pp. 6-7.
8. Whitney v. California, 274 U.S. 357 (1927).
9. Emerson, pp. 17-18.
10. John L. Hodge, "Democracy and Free Speech," in *The First Amendment Reconsidered*, eds. Bill F. Chamberlin and Charlene J. Brown (NY: Longman, 1982), p. 149.
11. Emerson, p. 728.
12. "Networks lambasted at hearing," *The Boston Globe*, 29 April 1987, p.26.
13. Ibid.
14. Ibid.
15. Toby J. McIntosh, "Why the Government Can't Stop Press Mergers," *Columbia Journalism Review*, December 1980, pp. 48-50; "America's Press: Too Much Power for Too Few?" *U.S. News & World Report*, 15 August 1977, pp. 27ff; Kevin Phillips, "Busting the Media Trusts," *Harper's Magazine*, July 1977, pp. 23ff; and Neil Hickey, "Can the Networks Survive?" *TV Guide*, 21 March 1981, pp.7ff.
16. Ben H. Bagdikian, *The Media Monopoly* (Boston: Beacon Press, 1983). p.xv.
17. Ben Bagdikian, "The Media Grab," *Channels of Communication*, May/June 1985, p. 18.
18. *Editor & Publisher*, 3 January 1981, pp. 9ff.
19. Alex S. Jones, "And Now the Media Mega-Mergers," *The New York Times*, 24 March 1985, sec. 3, p. 11; "When the junketing has to stop," *The Economist*, 27 April 1985, p. 91; Fred R. Bleakley, "The Power and Perils of Junk Bonds," *The New York Times*, 14 April 1985, sec, 3, p. 1.
20. Albert Scardino, "On the Road to Monopoly," *The New York Times*, 18 September 1988, sec. 3, p. 1.
21. The figures are from the 1986 *Guinness Book of World Records*.
22. Bagdikian, *The Media Monopoly*, p. 37.
23. Jerome A. Barron, *Freedom of the Press for Whom?* (Bloomington, Ind.: Indiana University Press, 1973), p.xiv.
24. Jerome A. Barron, "Access to A New First Amendment Right," *Harvard Law Review* 80 (1967), pp. 1641-1678.
25. Thomas I. Emerson, *The System of Freedom of Expression* (NY: Random House, 1970), p. 670; Thomas L. Tedford, "Freedom of Speech in the 1960s," *America in Controversy: History of American Public Address*, ed. DeWitte Holland (Dubuque, Iowa: Wm. C. Brown, 1973), pp. 403-404.
26. Miami Herald Publishing Co. v. Tornillo, 418, U.S. 241 (1974); CBS v. Democratic National Committee, 412 U.S. 94 (1973); FCC v. Midwest Video Corporation. 440 U.S. 689 (1979); and CBS v. FCC 453 U.S. 367 (1981).

27. Harold Evans, "Free Speech and Free Air," *U.S. News and World Report*, 11 May 1987, p. 82.
28. Gulf and Western Industries paid $3.2 million for insertions in the February 5 1979 U.S. and selected overseas edition of *Time* magazine; ABC charged $550,000 for a 30-second commercial on the 1985 Super Bowl broadcast.
29. Harold Evans, p. 82.
30. T. Barton Carter, Marc A. Franklin, and Jay B. Wright, *The First Amendment and the Fourth Estate* (Mineola, NY: The Foundation Press, 1985), p. 24.
31. Sec. 317. [47 U. S. C. A. 317.]
32. David Hajdu, "Why the Cheers Gang Switched to Stroh's Beer," *TV Guide*, 30 July 1988, p. 31.
33. Wilson Bryan Key, *Subliminal Seduction: Ad Media's Manipulation of a Not So Innocent America* (New York: New American Library, 1973), pp. 100-115.
34. Burnett v. National Inquirer, Inc. 144 Cal. App. 3d 991, 193 Cal. Rptr. 206 (1983).
35. Westmoreland v. CBS, 596 F. Supp. 1170 (S.D.N.Y. 1984).
36. Gertz v. Robert Welch, Inc. 418 U.S. 323, 94 S. Ct. 2997, 41 L. Ed. 2d 789.

Chapter Five

1. Whitney v. California, 274 U.S. (1927) (Brandeis, J., joined by Holmes. J., concurring), at 375-376.
2. William E. Hocking, *Freedom of the Press: A Framework Principle* (Chicago: University of Chicago Press, 1947), p. 96.
3. Alexander Meiklejohn, *Free Speech and Its Relation to Self-Government*, reprinted in *Political Freedom* (New York: Harper & Row, Publishers, 1960), p. 57.
4. Ibid., p. 26.
5. Commission on Freedom of the Press, *A Free and Responsible Press* (Chicago: University of Chicago Press, 1947), p. 81.
6. Thomas v. Collins, 323 U.S.(1944) at 545-546.
7. Rodney A. Smolla, *Suing the Press* (New York: Oxford University Press, 1986), p. 27.
8. Ibid., p. 35.
9. 376 U.S. 254 (1964), at 271.
10. Ibid. at 271-272, quoting NAACP v. Button, 371 U.S. 415, 433 (1963).
11. Ibid.
12. 376 U.S. 254 (1964); Also, Smolla, p. 51.
13. Associated Press v. United States, 326 U.S. 1, 20 (1945). Also, T. Barton Carter et al., p. 483.
14. 395, U.S. (1967); Carter, p. 384.
15. Ibid.
16. Ibid.
17. 418 U. S. 241 (1974).
18. 418 U. S. at 251. Also, "Most citizens in the United States experience monopoly newspapers, a small number of television stations that are dominated by network programming, and a large number of radio stations broadcasting interchangeable programs with a minimum of concern for public affairs." Benno C. Schmidt, Jr., *Freedom of the Press V. Public Access* (New York: Praeger, 1976), p. 39.
19. 418 U. S. at 251 n. 14.

20. Edward Karam, " The FOI Act Gets Teeth," *Freedom of Information Center Report No. 337*, (Columbia: School of Journalism, University of Missouri, May 1975). The House voted 371-31, and the Senate, 65-27 to override President Ford's veto.
21. 5 U.S.C. section 552a.
22. Kissinger v. Reporters Committee for Freedom of the Press, 445 U.S. 136, 100S.Ct. 960, 63 L. Ed.2d 267 (1980).
23. Henry Kissinger, *White House Years* (Boston: Little, Brown, 1979).
24. Chrysler Corp. v. Brown, 441 U.S. 281, 99 S.Ct. 1705, 60 L.Ed.2d 208 (1979).
25. Environmental Protection Agency v. Mink, 410 U.S. 73, 93 S.Ct. 827, 35 L.Ed,2d 119 (1973).
26. 730 F. 2d 773 (D.C.Cir.1984).
27. Consumer Product Safety Commission v. GTE Sylvania, Inc., 447 U.S.102, 100 S.Ct. 2051, 64 L.Ed.2d 766 (1980).
28. United States Department of State v. Washington Post, 456 U.S. 595, 102 S.Ct.1957, 72 L. Ed.2d 358 (1982).
29. Federal Bureau of Investigation v. Abramson, 456 U.S. 615, 102 S. Ct. 2054, 72 L.Ed.2d 376 (1982).
30. 5 U.S.C section 552b.
31. Quoted in Smolla, p. 42.
32. 417 U.S. 817 (1974).
33. 417 U.S. 843 (1974).
34. Ibid. at 2820
35. 438 U.S. I, 98 S.Ct. 2588, 57 L.Ed.2d 553.

Chapter Six
1. 384 U.S. 333, 86 S.Ct. 1507 (1966).
2. Ibid. at 337-338.
3. Ibid. at 341-342.
4. Ibid. at 358.
5. Ibid. at 349-350.
6. Nebraska Press Association v. Stuart, 427, U.S. 539, 96 S.Ct.279 (1976).
7. 448 U.S. 555. 100 S.Ct. 2814, 2833, 2837 (1980).
8. John Lofton, *Justice and the Press* (Boston: Beacon Press, 1966), pp. 103-104; p. 124.
9. American Bar Association, "Report of Special Committee on Cooperation between Press, Radio and Bar," Annual Report, Vol. 62, pp. 851-8866 (1937), p. 861; also, New Jersey v. Hauptmann, 115 N.J.L. 412, 180 A. 809 (Ct.Err. & App. 1935), certiorari denied 296 U.S. 649, 56 S.Ct. 310 (1935).
10. Rideau v. Louisiana, 373 U.S. 373 U.S. 723. 724, 83 S.Ct. 1417, 1419 (1963).
11. 381 U.S. 532, 538-539, 85 S.Ct. 1628, 1631 (1965).
12. Ibid. at 595-596.
13. Chandler v. Florida, 449 U.S. 560, 101 S.Ct. 802 (1981).
14. Commonwealth v. Corderio et al., Massachusetts Superior Court, 1984.
15. Paul M. Kennedy, *The Rise and Fall of the Great Powers: Economic Change and Military Conflict From 1500 to 2000* (New York: Random House, 1987).

Chapter Seven

1. T.L. Becker and R. Scarce, "Teledemocracy emergent: The state of art and science." Paper delivered at the APSA annual meeting, 1984, Washington, DC., p. 29, quoted in F. Christopher Arterton, *Teledemocracy: Can Technology Protect Democracy?* (Beverly Hills, CA: Sage Publications, 1987), p. 20.
2. F. Christopher Arterton, *Teledemocracy: Can Technology Protect Democracy?* p. 29.
3. J. Elstain, "Democracy and the Qube tube," *The Nation*, 7 August 1982, p. 108.
4. Frederick Williams, *The Communication Revolution* (New York: New American Library, 1982), p. 199
5. Ted Becker, "Teledemocracy: Bringing power back to the people," *Futurist*, 15(6), December 1981, p. 9.
6. M.E. McComb and D.L. Shaw, "The agenda-setting function of the mass media," *Public Opinion Quarterly*, 36 (1972), pp. 176-187; M.E. McComb, "The Agenda-Setting Approach," in *Handbook of Political Communication*, eds. Dan D. Nimmo and Keith R. Sanders (Beverly Hills, CA: Sage Publication, 1981), pp. 121-140
7. Quoted in McComb, "The Agenda-setting Approach," p. 136.
8. Dan Nimmo, *Political communication and public opinion in America* (Santa Monica, CA: Good Year, 1978), p. 10.
9. V.O. Key, *Public Opinion and American Democracy* (New York: Alfred A. Knopf, 1961), p. 8.
10. Cliff Zukin, "Mass Communication and Public Opinion," in *Handbook of Political Communication*, p. 368.
11. Ibid., p. 369.
12. George Gallup, "The Ethical Problems of Polling," in *Ethics, Morality and the Media: Reflections on American Culture*, ed. Lee Thayer (New York: Hasting House, 1980), pp. 207-213.
13. Alex S. Edelstein, *Ethics, Morality and the Media*, pp. 214-217.
14. Neil Hickey, "It's High Noon Now for Political Mudslingers – Let the Targets Beware," *TV Guide*, 18 October 1986, p. 4.
15. Ibid.
16. J.G. Blumler and D. McQuail, *Television in Politics* (Chicago: University of Chicago Press, 1965).
17. C.K. Atkin, "Political Campaigns: Mass Communication and Persuasion," in *Persuasion: New Directions in theory and research*, eds. M.E. Roloff and G. R. Miller (Beverly Hills, CA: Sage Publications, 1980).
18. *Editorial Research Reports*, 12 October 1984, p. 761.
19. Lynda Lee Kaid, "Political Advertising," in *Handbook of Political Communication*, p. 255.
20. R.A. Joslyn, "The content of political spot ads," *Journalism Quarterly*, 57 (1980), pp. 92-98; R.D. McClure and T.E. Patterson, "Television news and political advertising," *Communication Research*, 1 (1976) pp. 3-33; C.R. Hofstteter and C. Zukin, "TV network news and advertising in the Nixon and McGovern campaigns," *Journalism Quarterly*, 56 (1978), pp. 106-115.
21. *The New York Times*, 25 September 1988, p. 1.
22. David S. Broder, "Real Presidential Debates," *The Washington Post*, 5 September 1984, quoted in *Editorial Research Reports*, 12 October 1984, p. 761.

23. S. Kraus and D. Davis, *The effects of mass communication on political behavior* (University Park, PA: Pennsylvania University Press, 1976.)
24. S. Kraus and D. Davis, "Political Debates," in *Handbook of Political Communication*, p. 290.
25. Michael A. Lipton, "Exclusive TV Guide Poll: Campaign '88 and TV," *TV Guide*, 23 January 1988, pp. 2ff.
26. Ibid.
27. Walter Shapiro, "Hello, I Must Be Going," *Time*, 7 March 1988, p. 20.
28. "Straight from the Hart: Assailing the 'media filter'," *Broadcasting*, January 1988, pp. 123-124.
29. *TV Guide*, 23 January 1988, pp. 2ff.
30. R.W. Apple Jr. "Biden Flunks the 'Character' Test: Candidates' Transgressions Loom Large on Home Screen," *The New York Times*, 27 September 1987, sec. 4, p. 1.
31. Joel Brinkley, "Bush's Role in Iran Affairs: Questions and Answers," *The New York Times*, 29 January 1988, sec. A. p. 1ff.
32. Richard Stengel, "Bushwhacked!" *Time*, 8 February 1988, p. 16.

Chapter Eight

1. Jack Anderson, "Why I Tell Secrets," *Parade*, 30 November 1980, p. 12.
2. Chief Justice Warren E. Burger, "Constitutional Question: Power to Whom?" *TV Guide*, 31 October 1987, p. 37; Also with Bill Moyers, "The Constitution in Crisis," PBS, 4 November 1987.
3. Ibid.
4. Ronald Reagan, "Current Quotes," *U.S. News and World Report*, 14 May 1984.
5. Edwin Emery and Michael Emery, *The Press and America*, 5th ed. (Englewood Cliffs: N.J.: Prentice Hall, 1984), p. 502.
6. Martin Schram, *The Great American Video Game: Presidential Politics in the Television Age* (New York: William Morrow and Company, 1987); quoted in Mark Hertsgaard,"A Gadget for the Gipper," *Columbia Journalism Review*, July/August, 1987. p. 59.
7. Sig Nickelson, *The Electric Mirror: Politics in The Age of Television* (New York: Dodd, Mead, 1972).
8. William Manchester, *The Glory and the Dream* (Boston: Little Brown, 1973).
9. Eric Barnouw, *The Tube of Plenty* (New York: Oxford University Press, 1977), pp. 137-39.
10. "Senator Joseph R. McCarthy," *See it Now,* CBS News, 9 March 1954.
11. Emery and Emery, pp. 594-596.
12. *Watergate: The Chronology of a Crisis* (Washington, D.C.: Congressional Quarterly, 1975); Dan Rather and Gary Paul Gates, *The Palace Guard* (New York: Harper & Row, 1974), pp. 182-183; J. Anthony Lukas, *Nightmare: Underside of the Nixon Years* (New York: Viking Press, 1976), p. 3.
13. Cited in Philip Knightly, *The Casualty* (New York: Harcourt Brace Jovanovich, 1975), p. 423.
14. N.D. Batra, *The Hour of Television*, pp. 173-175.
15. Michael J. Robinson and Margaret A. Sheehan, *Over the Wire and On TV: CBS and UPI in Campaign '80* (New York: Russell Sage Foundation, 1983), p. 262.

16. Hedrick Smith, *The Power Game: How Washington Works* (New York: Random House, 1988); also, Martin Schram, *The Great American Video Game: Presidential Politics in the Age of Television* (New York: William Morrow and Company, 1988); Rich Jaroslovsky, "Manipulating the Media Is a Speciality for the White House's Michael Deaver," *Wall Street Journal*, 5 Jan. 1984, p. 42; Rich Jaroslovsky, "White House Trips Over Its Words: Great Communicator?" *Wall Street Journal*, 16 February 1984, p. 54.
17. Quoted in Mark Hertsgaard, "A Gadget for the Gipper," p. 62.
18. Stephen Hess, *The Washington Reporters* (Washington, D.C.: Brookings Institution, 1981), pp. 51-60; Anthony Lukas, "The White House Press 'Club,'" *The New York Times Magazine*, 15 May 1977, p. 22.
19. Jane Mayer, "How Reagan Staff Manages News," *The Wall Street Journal*, October 12, 1984, p. 50; Timothy Crouse, *The Boys on the Bus* (New York: Ballantine Books, 1972), pp. 203-256.
20. "Reviving the Presidential News Conference: Report of the Harvard Commission on the Presidential News Conference," Joan Shorenstein Barone Center on the Press, Politics, and Public Policy, 1988, pp. 11-39.
21. Ibid., p. 38.

Chapter Nine

1. Elmer E. Cornwell, Jr., "Presidential News: The Expanding Public Image," *Journalism Quarterly*, 36 (Summer 1959), pp. 275-283; Alan P. Balutis, "Congress, the President and the Press," *Journalism Quarterly*, 53 (Autumn 1976), pp. 509- 515.
2. Stephen Hess, *The Washington Reporters*, p. 49.
3. Norman J. Ornstein, "Yes, Television Has Made Congress Better," *TV Guide*, 25 July 1987, p. 6.
4. Ibid., p. 8.
5. Tom Shales, quoted by Norman J. Ornstein, "Which Lawmakers Are Best on TV – and Why," *TV Guide*, 16 August 1986, p. 4.
6. Michael J. Robinson and Kevin R. Appel, "Network News Coverage of Congress," *Political Science Quarterly*, 94, (Fall 1979), pp. 412-414.
7. Gary R. Orren, "Thinking about the Press and Government," in Martin Linsky, *Impact: How the Press Affects Federal Policymaking* (New York: W.W. Norton & Company, 1986), p. 10.
8. Ibid., p. 11.
9. Martin Linsky, *Impact*, p. 235.
10. Martin Linsky, *Impact*.
11. Ibid., pp. 203-222.
12. Ibid., pp. 203-204.
13. Ibid., p. 205.
14. Ibid., p. 206.
15. Ibid., p. 208.
16. Ibid., p. 28
17. Ibid., p. 65.
18. E. Epstein, *News from nowhere* (New York: Random House, 1973), p. 242.
19. H.A. Simon, *Models of thought* (New Haven: Yale University Press, 1979), p. 3.
20. Shanto Iyenger and Donald R. Kinder, *News That Matters* (Chicago: The University of Chicago Press, 1987), pp. 4, 33.

21. Ibid., pp. 97, 114.
22. Ibid., p. 132.

Chapter Ten
1. Ernest G. Bormann, "Symbolic Convergence Theory: A Communication Formulation," *Journal of Communication*, Vol. 35, No. 4 (Autumn 1985) pp. 128-138; Walter R. Fisher, *Human Communication as Narration: Toward a Philosophy of Reason, Value, and Action* (Columbia, SC: University of South Carolina, 1987).
2. Bormann, pp.129-130; Also see, Sydney Head, "Programming Principles," in *Broadcast Programming*, eds. Susan Tyler Eastman, Sydney W. Head and Lewis Klein (Belmont, CA: Wadsworth Publishing Company, 1981), p. 4; James T. Tiedge and Kenneth J. Ksobiech, "The 'Lead-in' Strategy for Prime-Time TV: Does It Increase the Audience?" *Journal of Communication*, Vol. 36, No. 3 (Summer 1986), p. 51; "The Man with the Golden Gut," *Time*, 5 September 1977, p.50; J.G. Webster, "Program Audience Duplication: A Study of Television Inheritance Effects," *Journal of Broadcasting & Electronic Media*, 29 (Spring 1985), pp. 121-133; J.G. Webster and Wakshlag, "A Theory of Television Program Choice," *Communication Research*, 10 (October 1983), pp. 430-446; "Leading from Strength," *Broadcasting*, 10 September, 1979, p. 76; David Diamond, "Is the Toy Business Taking Over Kids' TV?" *TV Guide*, 13 June, 1987; Robert F. Lewine, Susan Tyler Eastman and William J.Adams, "Prime-Time Network Television Programming," in *Broadcast/Cable Programming*, 2nd ed., eds. Susan Tyler Eastman, Sydney W. Head and Lewis Klein (Belmont, CA : Wadsworth Publishing Company,1985), p. 127; Jeff Kay,"Networks Mull New Tactics for Next Summer," *TV Guide*, 8 August 1987, p. A-3; Fred Friendly, "How Fred Friendly sees it now; the changing face of TV journalism," *Broadcasting*, 25 August 1986, pp. 51.
3. N.D. Batra, *The Hour of Television*, pp. 218-227.
4. Claudia H. Deutsch, "The Battle to Wire the Consumer," *The New York Times*, 26 July 1987, sec.3, pp. 1, 12-13.
5. George Gerbner, "The Challenge Before Us," in *Communication And Domination: Essays to Honor Herbert I. Schiller*, eds. Jorg Becker, Goran Hedebro and Leena Paldan (Norwood, NJ: Ablex Publishing Corp., 1986), p. 233.
6. Ibid., pp. 234-236.
7. Eve Merriam, "We're teaching our children that violence is fun," *Ladies Home Journal*, October 1964, pp. 44ff, reprinted in O. Larson, ed., *Violence in the mass media* (New York: Harper & Row, 1968), pp. 40-47.
8. Action for Children's Television, "ACT petitions Federal Trade Commission," *ACT NEWS-LETTER*, Spring/Summer 1972.
9. George Gerbner, "Violence in television drama: Trends in symbolic functions," in *Television and Social Behavior: Media Content and Control*, Vol.1, eds. G. A. Comstock and E.A. Rubenstein (Washington, D. C.: U. S. Government, 1972), p. 36.
10. J.R. Dominick and B. S. Greenberg, "Attitudes toward violence: The interaction of television exposure, family attitude, and social class," in *Television and Social Behavior: Television and Adolescent Aggressiveness*, Vol. 3, eds. G. A. Comstock and E. A. Rubenstein (Washington, D. C.: U.S. Government Printing Office, 1972), pp. 329-333.

11. Ibid., pp. 35-135.
12. Dr. F.J. Ingelfinger, "Violence On TV: An Unchecked Environmental Hazard," *New England Journal of Medicine*, 8 April 1976, p. 837-838.
13. R.M. Kaplan and R.D. Singer, "Television violence and viewers aggression: A re-examination of the evidence," *Journal of Social Issues*, 32 (1976), pp. 63-64.
14. Ibid.
15. National Science Foundation, "Research on the effects of television advertising on children: A review of the literature and recommendations for future research," (Washington, D. C.: National Science Foundation, 1977), pp.i-ii.
16. Harry F. Waters, "Watching What Kids Watch," *Newsweek*, 8 January 1990, pp. 50-51.
17. Peggy Charren, "FCC should ban these half-hour commercials," *USA Today*, 8 October 1987, sec. p. 10.
18. Rep. Edward J. Markey, "We need law to help parents regulate TV," *USA Today*, 8 October 1987, sec. A, p. 10.
19. David Diamond, "Is the Toy Business Taking Over Kids TV?," *TV Guide*, 13 June 1987, p. 5ff.
20. Ibid., p. 6.
21. Ibid.
22. United States Senate Subcommittee on Communication, *Federal Communication Commission Policy Matters and Television Programming*, Part 2 (Washington, D.C.: U.S. Government Printing Office, 1969), p. 339.

Chapter Eleven

1. Jonathan Alter, "Prime Time Revolution," *Newsweek*, 8 January, 1990, p. 25.
2. E. Katz, M. Gurevitch, and H. Haas, "On the Uses of the Mass Media for Important Things," *American Sociological Review*, 38 (1973), pp, 164-181; also, K.E. Rosengren, L.A. Wenner and P. Palmgreen, *Media Gratifications Research* (Beverly Hills, CA: Sage Publications, 1985).
3. D. McQuail and M. Gurevitch, "Explaining Audience Behavior: Three Approaches Considered.," in *The Uses of Mass Communication: Current Perspective on Gratification Research*, eds. J. Blumler and E. Katz (Beverly Hills, CA: Sage Publications, 1974), pp. 287-301; also, M.R. Levy and S. Windahl, "Audience Activity and Gratification: A Conceptual Clarification and Exploration," *Communications Research*, 11 (1984), pp. 51-78.
4. Neal Weinstock, "Business embraces high-tech media," *Advertising Age*, sec. S, p. 4ff.
5. Ibid.
6. Ibid. p. 26.
7. Frederick Williams, *Technology and Communication Behavior* (Belmont, CA: Wadsworth Publishing Company, 1987), p. 243
8. Mark R. Levy, "Some Problems of VCR Research," *American Behavioral Scientist*, (May/June 1987), p. 465.
9. Ibid.; also, Gladys D. Ganley and Oswald H. Gandy, *Global Political Fallout: The First Decade of the VCR 1976 – 1985* (Cambridge, MA: Harvard University Center for Information Policy Research, 1987).
10. M. Levy and E. Fink, "Home video recorders and the transience of television," *Journal of Communication*, 34 (1984), pp. 56-71.

11. Alan M. Rubin and Charles R. Bantz, "Utility of Videocassette Recorders," *American Behavior Scientist*, (May/June 1987), p. 483.
12. Douglas A. Boyd, "Home Video Diffusion and Utilization in Arabian Gulf States," *American Behavior Scientist* (May/June 1987), pp. 550-551. 13. Vincent Canby, "VCR's Give Movies a Fresh Start," *The New York Times*, 30 August 1987, sec. 2, p. H 17.
14. Mike Rogers, "Giving Home Movies a Hollywood Flair," *Newsweek*, 10 August 1987, pp. 60-61.
15. Andy Meisler, "Your Family History: See It Now," *TV Guide*, 22 August 1987, pp. 33-34.
16. Barrie Gunter and Mark R. Levy, "Social Context of Video Use," *American Behavioral Scientist*, (May/June 1987), p. 491.
17. Neil Hickey, "Western Ideas, Dissident Voices: TV is opening up the Soviet bloc nations – whether they like it or not," and "The Message for Poland Rulers: Beware of Fresh Ideas – Your Control of TV Is Slipping," *TV Guide*, 22 August 1987, pp.4-12 and August 29, 1987, pp. 17-23.
18. Ibid., p. 20.
19. Ibid., p. 22.
20. Herbert Schiller quoted in George Gerbner, "The Challenge Before Us," in *Communication And Domination: Essays to Honor Herbert I. Schiller*, eds. Jorg Becker, Goran Hedebro and Leena Paldan (Norwood, NJ: Ablex Publishing Corp., 1986), p. 233.
21. Gerbner, pp. 234 -235.

Chapter Twelve

1. Walter Lippmann, *Liberty and the News* (New York: Harcourt, Brace, and Howe, 1920), pp. 54-55.
2. Humberto R. Maturana and Francisco J. Varela, *Autopoiesis and Cognition:The Realization of the Living* (Boston: D. Reider Publishing Company, 1980), p. vx.
3. Thomas S. Rogers, "How Can Television Serve The Public Interest?", in *Television as a Social Issue*, ed. Stuart Oskamp (Beverly Hills: CA, Sage Publications, 1988), p. 79.
4. Maturana, pp. xxvi-xxvii.
5. Bela Banathy, Director, International Systems Institute; personal communication.

Index

ABC, 41, 126, 157; "Nightline," 86
Abramson, Howard, 62
Access, media, 16, 23, 28, 31; effect of mergers on, 40-47; and government information, 58-64
Acheson, Dean, the "Red Dean," 92
Action-oriented, television, 91, 100, 106
Activism, 143; activists, 141
Actor-governor, Ronald Reagan, of California, 98
Actual malice, 55
Adams, John Quincy, 80
Advance Publications, 41
Adversarial reporting, 75; adversarial relations, 99, 106, 108, 150
Advertising, political, 80-82; Saturday morning, 119-122; *See* Commercials
Advertising Age, 30
Afghanistan, 14, 133, 142; freedom fighters, 133
Africa, 133
Agenda-setters, 104; agenda-setting, 76, 77, 88, 93
Agnew, Vice President Spiro, 59, 86
AIDS, 11, 15, 16, 36, 80, 82, 105, 111; vaccine, 4
Alabama, 53
Alabama Supreme Court., 54. *See* New York Times v. Sullivan
Alaska, 61
Albanian guerrillas, 61. *See* CIA
Aleutian Islands, nuclear explosion under, 61
"ALF," 47
Ali, Mohammed, 48
Allen, Woody, 13, 48, 154
Alter, Jonathan, 163
American Association for Public Opinion Research, 79
American Bar Association, 70
American Enterprise Institute, 105
American Express Card, 26
American Law Network, 124
American Medical Association, 119
American prison system, 63
American Rehabilitation Education Network, 124
Anderson, Jack, 89, 160
Anti-Vietnam War social and political actions, 11
Apartheid, 9
Aphasia, political, 45
Apocalyptic, 53
Appel, Kevin R., 161
Apple, R. W., Jr., 86
Arabs, 129, 137, 142
Arabian Gulf, 129
Arbitron, 114
Arendt, H., 154
Aristotle, catharsis, 118
Army/McCarthy hearings, 105
Arterton, Christopher, 159
Asia, 133
Associated Press v. United States, 45
Associated Press v. Walker, 55
Astrology, decision by, 91. *See* Reagan
AT&T, 3
Atkin, C.K., 159
Auctioneers, free speech monopolized by, 40
Authoritarianism, 91, 133, 137
Authoritarian society, 8
Autocatalysis, 140. *See* Dissipative structures
Automotive industry, 9
Autopoiesis, paradigm of, 2, 7, 35; 137-142. *See* Maturana, Humberto. R
Avildsen, John, 130

Baby M, 6, 14; as a product of technology, 6, 12, 14
Bagdikian, Ben H., 40, 41, 43, 156
Baker, James, 75
Balutis, Alan P., 161

– 165 –

Banathy, Bela, 164
Banco's Ghost, 141
Bankers TV, 124
Bantz, Charles R., 164
Barnouw, Eric, 160
Barrone, Jerome. A., 44, 156
Bay of Pigs, 91, 94. *See* Kennedy, John F.
Becker, Jorg, 162
Becker, T. L., 76, 159
Begin, prime minister Menachem, of Israel, 98
Behaviorscan, 27
Beijing, the massacre in, 20
Belkin, Lisa, 154
Berlin Wall, 94
Bernstein, Carl, 97
Bertalanfy, Ludwig von, 2, 153
Bicentennial, 90
Biden, Sen. Joe, 85, 86
"Big Dan's" rape trial, 71
Birth control technology, 12, 14
Biznet, 124
Black, Justice Hugo, 45
Bleakley, Fred R., 156
Blythin, Herbert, 68
Boesky, Ivan, 17, 42
Blumler, J., 81, 159, 163
Blute, M., 12, 154
Bondage of virginity, 6. *See* Birth control technology
Boorman, S., 30, 155
Bormann, Ernest G., 112, 162
Boulding, Kenneth, 153
Bradley, Ed, 100
Brady, James, 98
Brandeis, Justice Louis, 24, 34, 39, 59, 154
Brennan, Justice William J., 54, 55, 64, 69
Brinkley, David, 106
Brinkley, Joel, 87, 160
Brinkmanship, 94, 138. *See,* Khrushchev, Nikita
Britain, 1, 8, 9, 83, 135; British Empire, 7, 73; imperial Britain 8; Britons, 142; "Britannia Rules the Waves," 138
Broder, David S., 83, 159
Brown, Charlene J., 156

Brown, Ezra, 18, 154
Bruno, Hal, 86
Bureaucrats, 14, 101
Burger, Chief Justice Warren E., 34, 90, 160
Burnett, Carol, 47
Burnham, D., 28, 30 155
Brutus, 93
Bulgaria, 133
Busch, 47
Bush, George, 75, 79, 85, 87, 88, 139. *See* Horton, Willie
Butterfield, Alexander, 97
"Butterfly effect," 6
Boyd, Douglas A., 129, 164

C-SPAN, 105
Cable Communications Act of 1984, 30
Cable-mail, 30
"California Raisins," 121
California, The State Board of Health of, 31
Cambodia, 96
Camcorder, 127, 130
Camp David accord, 98. *See* Carter, Jimmy
Canby, Vincent, 129, 164
Cannibalization, 124
Canons of Professional Ethics, American Bar Association's, 70
Capital Cities Communications, 41
"Captain Power," 121
"Capital-to-Capital," 126
Carnegie, Dale, 131
Carpet-baggers, 74
Carson, Johnny, 48
Carter, T. Barton, 157
Carter, Jimmy, 91, 98, 100
Cassius, 93
Catholic Church, 132; dominance of Europe by, 15; medieval, 7
Caucuses, political, 43, 82, 84, 85
CBS, 40; "60 Minutes," 86, 127; anchorman Dan Rather, 87
Censorship, 5
Census blocks, 27
Census Bureau, 27
Central Intelligence Agency, 56
Chad, 108
Chaffee, S., 76

Chaffee, Zachariah, 38, 156
Challenger, 113
Chamberlin, Bill F., 156
Chandler v. Florida, 71
Chaos, 137, 153; Chaos theory, 6
Charren, Peggy, 120, 121, 163
"Checkers Speech," Nixon's, 93
Checks and balances, 75, 90, 103, 148
"Cheers," 46, 47
Chernobyl, 14; disaster, 34; nuclear accident, 33; nuclear catastrophe, 132
Childcare, 82
Chileans, 25
China, 8, 9, 19; under Deng Xiao Ping, 20; adventurism, 98; expansionism, 97; missiles, 34
Choice-making, 28
Choreography, 17
Cronkite, Walter, 93
Chrysler Corp., 60
CIA, 59, 60, 62, 96
Citizen Kane, 13
City Light, 13
Civil disobedience, 143
Civil War, 53
Clark, Justice Tom C., 68, 70
Classroom Teachers Association, Florida, 58
Clear-and-present danger test, 38, 95
Closing of the American mind, 5
Clusters, 27; clustering, 26, 28; cluster-targeting, 31
CNN, 71; "Newsmakers Saturday," 86
Coca-Cola, 3, 135
Cognitive domain, society's, 111
Collective hallucination, America's, 139
Collectivization, free speech, 37, 44, 113
Collective self-criticism, 2. *See* Cybernetics
Colonization of mind, 111, 113
Colorization of film, 13, 48, 154
Columbia School of Journalism, 40
Commercials, 44, 46, 47; political commercials, 80-83; Saturday morning commercials, 119-122; commercial filibustering, 115. *See* Advertising
Commission on Freedom of the Press, 52

Committee to Re-elect the President (CREEP), 96
Communications Act of 1934, 46
Comparator, 4. *See* Cybernetics
Computer-conferencing, 126
Computer-networking, 73
Computer-telecommunications, interactive technology, 79
Comstock, G. A., 162
Concept cultivation, 136; conceptualizing, 138
Conglomerates, media, 37, 40-43, 49, 140, 147
Connectivity, electronic, 126
Consumer Report, 61
Conte, Rep. Silvio, 105
Cooke, Fred J., 56
Cornwell, Elmer E., Jr., 161
Cosby, Bill, 115; "The Cosby Show," 115; "Cosby Kids," 121
Count Dracula, 33
Cowles Media, 41
Creativity, 7, 8, 10, 23, 24, 35, 139, 146
Cuban missile crisis, 94
Cuisinart, 47
Cultural revolution, China's, 52
Cultural lag, 12, 13, 113, 145
Culture, definition of, 20
Cunt language, mainstreaming of, 94
Cuomo, Governor Mario, 122
Curtis Publishing Co. v. Butts, 55
Cutiz, Michael, 160
Cybernetics, 2, 4-7, 52; as collective self-criticism, 5

Darwinism, 116
Data-collecting, 23, 28, 59; database, 27, 35; datafiles, 35, 36. *See* Invasion of Privacy
Davis, D., 84, 160
Daily News, 42
Dairy Board, 47
Dalai Lama, 135. *See* Tibet
"Dallas," 47
Danforth, Sen. John, 80
Dante, Joe, 130
Debates, political, 82-84
Decentralization, 7
Decentralized freedoms, 2

De-chaining, media, 45
De-conglomerating, media, 45
"Deep Throat," 96. *See* Watergate
Defamation, 40. *See* Libel
Deregulation, 30, 146
The Des Moines Register, 41
Detroit, 42
Deutsch, Claudia H., 162
Diamond, David, 162, 163
Dietmann, A.A., 31
Diamond Information Center, 47
Disappearing Through the Skylight, 11
Digital addressability, 26; *see* Invasion of privacy
Discontinuities, 12
Dissipative structures, theory of, 10, 90, 140, 153
DNA "fingerprints, 38; DNA coding, 37; DNA technology, 38
Docu-drama, 32, 65, 67, 137
Dominick, J. R., 118, 162
Do-it-yourself temperament, Americans', 2
Donaldson, Sam, 88, 100
Dow Chemical Co., 33
Drug-addiction, 124; drug-pushing, 44, 48, 67; drug-lords, 143
Drumbeating, television's, 109, 110
Dukakis, Governor Mike, 75, 80, 81, 88, 139
"Dynasty," 47
Dyson, Freeman J., 11

Eagleton Poll, 78
Eastman, Susan Tyler, 162
Eastwood, Clint, 48
Edelstein, Alex S., 79, 159
Egypt, 1, 7, 8; Egyptian Arab, 127
Ehrlichman, John D., 62
Einstein, Albert, 116, 125
Eisenhower, Dwight, 80, 91, 92
Electronic banking, 28. *See* Invasion of privacy
Electronic Communications Privacy Act of 1986, 29
Electronic Fund Transfer Act of 1978, 29
Electronic democracy, 75
Electronic slavery, 26
Ellsberg, Daniel, 96

Ellul, J., 18, 25, 155
Elmer-DeWitt, Philip, 154
Elstain, J, 159
Emerson, Thomas I., 37, 39, 156; expression-action theory, 39
Emery, Edwin, 160
Emery, Michael, 160
Endosymbiosis, 6
Entropy, 1
Enzyme-and-nerve technology, 11
Epstein, E., 161
Equifax, 26
Equifinality, 6. *See* General system theory
Equilibrium systems, 10
"Equalizer," 47
Ervin panel, 105
Estes v. Texas, 70
Ethiopia, 17
Euripides, 37
Europe of 1992, 48
European Common Market, 6
Evolutionary models, 12
Evans, Harold, 45, 157

Fagen, R.E., 7, 153
Fairness Doctrine, 30, 55, 59
Falwell, Jerry, 48
Fantasy, role of, 112, 116
Fascism, 139; Fascist Italy, 7
"Fat Albert," 121
FBI, 60, 62, 96
FCC, 40, 42, 55, 56, 120
Feriere, Paulo, 36, 155
Financial News Network, 124
Fink, E., 163
First Amendment, 9, 26, 32
Fisher, Walter R., 162
Flaherty, David H., 155
Florida House of Representatives, 58; right-of-reply statute, 58; sunshine laws, 63
FOI, 60-62
Fonda, Jane, 131
Food Business Network, 124
Ford, Gerald, 91, 97
Fourth Amendment, 33
Fowler, Mark, 41, 42
France, 1; French Revolution, 3; French SPOT, 33

Frankenstein, 14, 111
Franklin, Marc A., 157
Free Speech in the United States, 38
Freedom of Information Act of 1966, 31
Free speech, debate model of, 58
Freudian, 104, 150
Friedrich, C.J., 154
Friendly, Fred, 40, 111, 162
Fundamentalism, 111
Futuristic, 130

"G.I Joe," 111, 121
Galbraith, John. K., 41
Galela, Ron, 24
Galileo's telescope, 134
Gallup, George, 76, 78, 159
Gallup Poll, 97
Gandhi, Mahatma, 73, 143
Gandhi, Indira, prime minister of India, 127
Gandy, Oswald H., 163
Ganley, Gladys D., 163
Gannet, 41, 42
General Accounting Office, 59
General Foods Corp., 115
General system theory, 2-3
Genetics, 2
Genocide, 137
Gephardt, Rep. Richard A., 81
Gerbner, George, 118, 162, 164
Gergen, David, 101
Gertz v. Robert Welch, 48
"Ghostbusters," 121
Gigantism, 20
Gipp, George, 82
Glasnost, 5; its impact, 129
Gleick, James, 153
Global Village, 33
GNP, 13
Goetz, Bernhard, New York vigilante, 16
Goldwater, Sen. Barry, 56, 80, 81
Goldwater — Extremist on the Right, 56
Gorbachev, Mikhail, 5, 20, 91, 125, 133; glasnost policy, 34
Gore, Sen. Al, 81
Government in the Sunshine Act, 63
Gould, J., 19, 154
Gouldner, Alvin, 35, 155

Graeco-Roman civilization, decline of, 15
Graham-Rudmann budget-balancing bill, 103
Grandpa Walton, President Reagan as, 82
Gratification-seekers, 123
Greenberg, B.S., 118, 162
Greece, 1, 83
"Growing Pains," 47
GTE Sylavania, 61
Gulf region, 133
Gurevitch, M., 163
Gunter, Barrie, 131, 164
Gutenberg, 135

Haas, H., 163
Hajdu, David, 157
Halberstam, David, 97
Hand, Justice Learned, 65
Heins, 47
Haldeman, Robert, 97
Hall, A.D. 7, 153
Hardison, O.B., Jr., 11
Hargis, Rev. Billy James, 56
Harlan, Justice John Marshall, 70
Harris, L., 155
Harris Poll, 76
Hart, Gary, 5, 85, 86, 94
Harvard Law Review, 24
Harvard University, 3, 24, 83
Hauptmann, Bruno, 69
Head, Sydney. W., 162
Headroom, Max, TV cartoon, 89, 115
Health-care, 124
"He-Man," 120, 121
Hedebro, Goran, 162
Hegemony, 3, 4, 43
Hellman, Lillian, 48
Herbert v. Lando, 55
Hershey bar, 47
Hertsgaard, Mark, 161
Hess, Stephen, 161
Hickey, Neil, 132, 156, 159, 164
Hierarchy, 3, 7, 8
Hindus, discovery of the zero by ancient, 134; priests, 61; medieval Hindus, 142
Hitler, 52
Hocking, William E., 157

Hodge, John. L., 156
Hofstteter, C.R., 159
Holland, DeWitte, 156
Holmes, Justice Oliver Wendell, 38, 51
Holocaust, 112, 135
Holt, John. C., 114
Homeostasis, 6, 7, 9, 80. See General system theory
Hoover, J. Edgar, 56, 62, 96
Horton, Willie, 139
Hospital Satellite Network, 124
House Energy and Commerce Committee, 40
House Telecommunications Subcommittee, 120
Howard, Carla, 130
Hufstedler, Judge Shirley, 32
Hughes, John, 130
Huntley-Brinkley, newscast, 93
Huxley, brave new world order, 25

IBM, 3
Ideology, 6, 19-21
Image-building, 28, 91; image-making, 4
Impartial jury, 67
Impeachment hearings, Nixon's, 105
Implosion, communications technologies', 125
Ingelfinger, F.J., 163
India, 73, 127, 128, 142
India Today, 127
Individual creativity, privacy and, 23
Infinite in All Directions, 11
Information neighborhoods, 25
Information Resources Inc., 27
Information technology, 17
Information theory, 2
Innovativeness, 2, 7, 35
Inside trading, 17
"Insight," 127. See *India Today*
Institutional Research Network, 124
Interdependence, 6, 7
Intrusive technologies, their effect on privacy, 31
Invasion of privacy, 23; obtrusive invasion, 31
Investigative journalism, 95
Iowa, 17

Iran, 90
Iran-contra affair, 5, 14, 36, 59, 91; arms-for-hostages deal, 101; Irangates, cyclical events, 28
Ireland, 142
It's A Wonderful Life, 13
Ivy League, 92
Iyenger, Shanto, 109, 161

Jackson, Andrew, 80
Jackson, Justice Robert J., 53
Jantsch, Erich, 10, 140, 143, 153
Japan, 7, 9; Japan of 2001, 48; Japan-Pacific rim countries, 6
Jaroslovsky, Rich, 161
J.C. Penny, 27
Jefferson, Thomas, 37
Jennings, Peter, 126
Jerry Lewis Labor Day Telethon, 43
Jewish intellectuals, 135
JFK, 94, 96, 134
Jim Crow laws, 54
Johnson, Lyndon, 81, 83, 94
Jones, Alex S., 156
Jones, Shirley, 48
Jorg, Becker, 162
Joslyn, R. A., 159
Jungle, 4
Jurisprudence, 67
Jury-dependent judicial system, 65

Kaid, Lynda Lee, 159
Kaplan, R. M., 119, 163
Karam, Edward, 158
Katz, E., 163
Kay, Jeff, 162
Kefauver, Sen. Estes, 92; Kefauver hearing on organized crime, 105
Keller, Helen, 120
Kennedy, John. F., 80, 83, 91, 93
Kennedy, Paul. M., 1, 71, 153, 158
Kennedy, Robert, 94
Kent State, 94, 96
Kentucky Fried Chicken, 135
Key, V. O., 159
Key, Wilson Bryan, 47, 157
Khomeini, ayatollah, 19, 91, 98; Islamic orthodoxy, 9
Khrushchev, Nikita, 84, 138

Kinder, Donald R. 110, 161
King, Martin Luther, Jr., 54, 94, 143
Kinkaid, D. Lawrence, 153
Kinnock, Neil, 86
Kissinger, Henry, 60, 135, 158
Klein, Lewis, 162
Kluckhohn, C., 20, 154
Knightly, Philip, 160
Knight-Ridder, 42, 108
Kolb, William L., 154
Koreans, 25
Koppel, Ted, 126
Krasnoff, Russ, 47
Kraus, S., 84, 160
Krippendorff, Klaus, 153
Krown Entertainment, 47
Ksobiech, Kenneth. J., 162
Kurds, 137
Kuwaiti Arab, 127

Ladies Home Journal, 117
Land Remote-Sensing Commercialization Act of 1984, 33
Larson, O., 162
Latter-day Hitlers, 140
LBJ, 94, 96
Laxalt, Sen. Paul, 45, 48
League of Women Voters, 83
Lebanon, 14, 17, 133; loss of marines in, 91
LeMistral, 23. *See* Invasion of privacy
Levitt, P., 30, 155
Levy, M.R., 131, 163, 164
Lewine, Robert F., 162
Lewis, Flora, 155
Libel, 65
Library of Congress, 59, 60
Life, 3, 31
Lincoln-Douglas debate, 83
Lindbergh Case, 69
Lindbergh, Charles, 69
Linguistic/audio-visual description, 8
Linsky, Martin, 107, 109, 161
Lippmann, Walter, 137, 164
Lipton, Michael A., 160
Listeners' right, 56, 57, 58, 147
Littlejohn, Stephen W., 4, 153
Lobbyist, rise of paid, 75
Lofton, John, 148

Look, 3
Love Canal, 109
Lugosi, Bela, 33
Lukas, Anthony, 161
Luther, 9. *See* Catholic Church
Lysol, 47

MacMurray, Fred, 82
"MacNeil/Lehrer NewsHour," 86
Madison Avenue, 25, 47, 92
Madison, James, 54
Madonna, 127
Mafia, 3
Mailer, Norman, 48
Manchester, William, 160
Manifest destiny, 7
Mannequins, politicians as, 75
Mao Tse-tung, 52, 138; Chinese Revolution, 3; Mao's thoughts, 52; worldwide revolution, 98
Marijuana, 33, 34
Market segmentation, 27
Markey, Rep. Edward J., 40, 120, 163
Marshall, George, 104; Marshall Plan, 104
Marx, Karl, 9
Mary Hitchcock Memorial Hospital, 18
"Masters of the Universe," 120, 121
Mattel, 120;
Maturana, Humberto R., 7, 8, 10, 73, 138, 153, 164
Mayer, Jane, 161
MacArthur, Douglas, 82
McCarthy, Sen. Joseph, 52, 80, 92, 139; McCarthy era, 103; McCarthyism, 90, 139
McCartney, James, 108
McComb, M.E. 76, 159
McGovern, George, 96
McIntosh, Toby J., 156
McKinley, William, 80
McLuhan, Marshall, 15, 29, 125, 155
McQuail, D., 81, 159, 163
Media Monopoly, 40
Media-created great leaders, 88; media access, 44, 58; media power, concentration of, 43
Meese, Edwin, 42
Mega-mergers, 5, 43, 147

Mega-verdicts, libel, 47
Meiklejohn, Alexander, 37, 38, 52, 54, 156, 157
Meisler, Andy, 130, 164
Mephistophelian legends, 14
Merriam, Eve, 117, 162
Merrill, Circuit Judge, 32
Metal-and-silicon technology, 11
Metcalf, Jackie, 31
Miami Herald, 58
Miami Herald Publishing Co. v. Tornillo, 44, 58
Mill, John Stuart, 37, 156
Miller, Arthur, 24, 154
Miller v. Casey,, 61
Miller, G. R., 159
Mini-series, 114
"Mister Rogers' Neighborhood," 121
Milton, John, 37
"Miranda Warning," 66
Models, evolutionary and developmental, 12
"Monkey Business," 86. *See* Hart, Gary
Monopoly, 58, 115, 132
Moore, Mary Tyler, 130
Morphogenesis, 6, 7. *See* General system theory
Mosco, V., 155
Moyers, Bill, 160
Multimedia approach, 26
Multi-sensory environment, 125
Murdoch Rupert: Skywatch, 132; News Corp., 41
Murrow, Edward R., 41
Music technology, 16
Muskie, Edmond, 96
Mutual Radio Network, 92
My Lai, 94
Myths, 11, 112; myth-making, 136; myth-makers, 114

Nader, Ralph, 9, 48
Narayan, J. P., 127
Narrans, Homo, 112
Narrative, 46-47; 111-115
Narrowcasting, 24, 26
National Commission on Electronic Fund Transfers, 29
National Council on Published Polls, 79

National Inquirer, 47
National Science Foundation, 120
National Security Council, 14, 87
Nazi Germany, 7; holocaust, 134
Near v. Minnesota, 95
Nelson, Harold L., 155
"Newstrack," 127. See *India Today*
New England Journal of Medicine, 119
New York Giants, 16
New York Times, 13, 16, 30, 53, 86, 87, 96, 104
New York Times/CBS News Poll, 83
New York Times v. Sullivan, 5
News, make-believe, collective self-hallucination, 100
Newspaper Preservation Act of 1970, 42
Newton, Isaac, 116, 125
Newton, Wayne, 48
Niagara Falls, 109
Nicaragua, 90, 104, 105
Nickelson, Sig, 160
Nielsen, 76; Nielsen's ratings, 5; Nielsen's slaves, 113
Nimmo, Dan D., 159
Nintendo, 47
Nixon, President Richard, 14, 21, 52, 60, 62, 80, 83, 91, 93, 94, 95, 141; "plumbing" operations, 96
Non-equilibrium, dynamic internal, 10
North, Lieut. Colonel Oliver, 14, 87, 115
Nostalgia, 130

O'Brien, Lawrence, 96
Obscenity, 40
Oligopoly, media, 42
"On Liberty," 37
Onassis, Jacqueline Kennedy, 24
Oneida silveware, 47
Order through fluctuation, 10. *See* Dissipative structures
Ornstein, Norman J., 105, 161
Orren, Gary R., 106, 161
Orwellian world, 25
Oswald, Lee Harvey, 94
Output-feedback-adjustment loop, 6. *See* Cybernetics

Paldan, Leena, 162

Palmgreen, P., 163
Pan-American, 43
Panama canal, 5
Parade, 43
Participatory democracy, 51, 101
Pastore, Sen. John. O., 117
Patterson, T. E., 159
Paul, Gary, 160
Pearl Harbor, 91
Pedagogy of the Oppressed, 36
Pell v. Procunier, 63
Pentagon Papers, 95, 96
Pentagon, procurement scandal of the 1988, 110
Peoplemeter, 77
Pepsico, 114
Perception-attitude-behavior continuum, 125
Percy, R. D., 115
Perestroika, 129. *See* Gorbachev
Persian emperor, 119
Persian Gulf, 14
Peters, Justice, of the California Supreme Court, 24
Phillips, Kevin, 156
Phonecian Women, 37
Photo opportunities, White House, 75
Pierpoint, Robert, 108
Plante, Bill, 100
"Playboy," 127
Plebiscitory democracy, 74
Plurality, 10, 140, 142
Poindexter, J. 155
Pol Pot, 143
Police state apparatus, 5
Political action committees, 75
Polls, opinion, 76-79
Pollsters, 76, 78, 79, 86, 99
Pope John Paul, 132
Pornography, 129
Post-Newsweek Stations, Florida, In re Petition of, 71
Powell, Justice, Louis, 48, 64
Powers, Bruce, 155
Praise The Lord, 3
Presence of the Kingdom, 18
Presley, Elvis, 33
Press conference, 90; Presidential press conference, 101

Prigogine, Ilya, 10, 140, 153
Prime-time, 46, 47, 132
"Princess of Power," 121
Prior restraint, 95. *See* Censorship
Privacy Act of 1974, 31, 60
Product placement companies, 47
Program-commercials, children's television, 120
Programming, television, 111-114
Prometheus, 111
Psychiatric wards, 5
Public-formation, the role of television in, 116

Radio Free Europe, 132
Rambo, 111
Ramos, Myra Bergman, 155
Rapper, Irving, 130
Rather, Dan, 81, 88, 160
Ray, William, 31
RCA, 84
Reader's Digest, 43
Reagan, President Ronald, 60, 75, 82, 83, 91, 94, 115, 123; Reagan as "Absent Minded Professor," 82; deregulation policy, 42; Reaganism, 120
Red Lion Broadcasting Company, 56; Red Lion Broadcasting v. FCC, 55. *See* Fairness Doctrine
Remote-sensing, 33, 34, 59; satellites, 33
Representative democracy, 74
Reproductive technology, 15
Retrievability, information, 29
Rice, Dona, 86
Rich, Lucille, 23
Richmond Newspapers v. Virginia, 69
Rise of the Computer State, 28
Right to know, 10; model, 58
Right-to-reply statute, 63
Roberts, televangelist Oral, 18
Robinson, Michael J., 160, 161
Rockwell, John, 154
Rodman, George, 154
Rogers, Everett M., 15, 154
Rogers, Mike, 164
Rogers, Thomas S., 140, 164
Rolling Rock, 47
Romania, 8

Rome, 1, 7, 83
Roloff, M.E., 159
Roosevelt, Franklin D., 91; Roosevelt-Truman era, 92
Roosevelt, Theodore, 75, 80, 83, 90, 91, 103
Rosengren, K.E., 163
Rubenstein, E.A., 162
Rubin, Alan M., 164
Ruby, Jack, 94
Rule of exclusion, 66
Rusk, Dean, 108
Russia, 8, 9, 20, 35, 43, 46, 89, 98, 104, 107, 127, 128, 137, 142, 147, 149; Russian Revolution, 3; fifth five year plan, 4; Russian missiles in Cuba, 134

Sadat, Anwar, 98; See Camp David accord
Sanders, Keith R., 159
Satcom K-2, 84
Satellite Conference Network, 124
Satellite technology, 33
"Saturday Night Specials," 119
Saudi Arabia, 34
Saxby v. Washington Post Co., 64
Scarce, R., 159
Scardino, Albert, 156
Schmidt, Benno C. Jr., 157
Schenck v. United States, 38
Schiller, Herbert I., 135, 164
Schneider, Keith, 154
Schram, Martin, 99, 160, 161
Schumer, F., 155
Shuster, Rep. Bud, 105
Sears & Roebuck, 27
Sedition, 40; Sedition Act of 1798, 55
Selective adaptation, 3, 4
Selective exposure, 82, 83
Self-creativity, 7
Self-halluciantion, 138
Self-inferential, media as, 139
Self-referential, media as, 139
Self-referring systems, 7
Senate Select Committee on Presidential Campaign, 97
Service-sector economy, 13
"Sesame Street," 121

Shah of Iran, 127
Shales, Tom, 82, 161
Shapiro, 85, 154, 160
Shaw, D. L., 76, 159
Sheehan, Margaret A., 160
Sheep-and-shepherd concept, 25
"She-Ra," 121
Sheppard, Sam, 67; Sheppard v. Maxwell, 67-69
Sherman Anti-trust Act, 45
Shorenstein Barone Center on the Press, Politics, and public Policy, 101
Simon, H.A., 109, 161
Singer, R.D., 119, 163
Sitcoms, 46, 47, 114
Sixth Amendment, 66
Sky Channel, 135
Smith, Hedrick, 99, 161
Smolla, Rodney A., 54, 157
Social Security Administration, 27
Social systems, as power systems, 4
Sociopoiesis, 95
"Soldiers of the Future," 121
Solidarity, 132
Sontag, Susan, 37
Soul-searching, 141
South Africa, 8, 9
South America, 34
Southern Living, 41
Soviet Russia, 9, 14; Soviet Union, 19; Soviet communist party, 43; Soviet Red Army, 132; Soviet psychiatric ward, prison system, 63; Soviet space shuttle, 34. See Russia
Sovietization, 42
Sovietization of American society, 43
Space Media Network, 34
Space-time, 10
Special interest groups, 75
Spectrum, electromagnetic, 56, 57
Spitz, David, 156
Sports Illustrated, 32
Stahl, Lesley, 99
Stanley, Manfred, 35, 155
"Star Trek," 111
Star Wars, 34
Statistical Abstracts, 27
Stengel, Richard, 160
Stevens, Justice Paul, 64

Stevenson, Adlai, 92
Stewart, Justice Paul, 64
Stewart, Surgeon General William, 121
Stinger missiles, 133
Story-tellers, 112, 114, 116, 135, 151
Story-telling, industrialization of, 116
Stroh, 47
Structure-preserving systems, 10
Stuart Oskamp, 164
Style of Radical Will, 37
Subcommittee on Communications, Senate's, 117
Subcommittee on Television, House's, 140
Subliminal Seduction, 47
Sullivan, L. B., 54
Super Tuesday, 84, 87
Superconductivity, 19
Superman, 111
Superpowers, 34
Supra-party, 43
Supra-state, 6
Surgeon General's Scientific Advisory Committee, 117
Surrogacy, 15
Surrogate motherhood, 15
Sven Jansen crystal, 47
Switzerland, 8
Symbiosis, 9
Symbolic convergence theory of communication, 112
System of Freedom of Expression, 39

Target clustering, 27
Target-seeking messages, 25
Taste collectivities, 27
Taylor, Elizabeth, 48
Technology, Janus-faced, 12
Telecommunications Subcommittee, House, 40
Teleconferencing, 124, 126
Teleology, 4
"Tele-public relations," 98
Texas, 27
Thayer, Lee, 159
"Thirtysomething," 47
Thomas v. Collins, 53
Thoreau, Henry David, 63, 143
Three Mile Island, 14

Tibet, 112; decimating Tibet, 135; genocide, 134; Tibetans' collective nervous system, 135
Tiedge, James. T, 162
Time, 18, 41, 85
Time-shifting, use of the VCR for, 128
Timothy, Crouse, 161
Toll-free calls, 16; Toll-free Live-Aid for Africa, 16
Tolstoy, 143
Tornillo, Pat, 58
Totalitarianism, 7, 8
Tower Commission Report, 14
Toy-based programs, 120
"Transformers," 121
Tribune Entertainment Co., 121
Truman, Harry, 91
TRW Inc., 26
TV Guide, 43.
20th Century-Fox Film Corp., 41

U-2 spy crisis., 91
U.S. LANDSAT, 33
U.S. News and World Report, 45, 101
Ulbright, Walter, East German Communist boss, 123, 135
United States Constitution, 66
United States Department of State v. Washington Post Co., 62
Universal Product Code, 26
University of California at Berkeley, 40
Uribe, Richard, 7, 153
USA Today, 3
"USA Today," 3
Uses and gratifications, technology's, 127
USIA 133
USIA's Worldnet, 132

Varela, Francisco J., 7, 153, 164
VCR, 126-130
Video-conferencing, 73
Video & Library Privacy Protection Act, 26
Video-tex, 73
Vietnam War, 54, 91, 94
Virgil, Mike, 32; Virgil v. Time Inc., 32
Voir Dire, 66, 5. *See* Impartial jury

Waddington, Conrad H., 153
Wall Street, 9, 17, 40
Wall Street Journal, 104
Walley, Wayne, 30, 155
Warren, Samuel D., 24, 154
Washington Post, 41, 82, 96, 104
Washington Post Study, 41
Watergate, 95-98; Watergate crisis, 36; Watergate hearings, 105; the hell of, 91; Watergates, cyclical events, 28
Waters, Harry F., 120, 163
Webster, J. G., 162
Wenner, L. A., 163
Westin, A., 155
Westmoreland, William, 48
Whitehead, Alfred North, 1
Whitney v. California, 39
Wiener, Norbert, 4, 5, 153
Williams, Frederick, 126, 159, 163
Windahl, S., 163
Woodward, Bob, 97
Wright, Jay. B., 157

Yale University, 83
Yarrow, Andrew L., 16, 154

Zukin, C., 78, 159

About the Author

N.D. Batra (Ph.D., communications and dramatic arts, Gujarat University, India) has been a columnist, magazine editor, freelancer, director of an institute, and a communication consultant. He has published *The Hour of Television: Critical Approaches* (Scarecrow Press, 1987). The new book is second of a projected series of three books on American society. He is now working on *Preface to America: The Twenty-First Century*, which will complete the trilogy. Now a faculty member and chairman of the department of communications at Norwich University (VT), he teaches television programming and criticism, communications law and ethics, and communications technology and the informations society. Calling himself a professional stranger, he plays tennis, golf, likes long walks and meditates amidst the green mountains of Vermont.

OHIO UNIVERSITY LIBRARY

Please return this book as soon as you have finished with it. In order to avoid a fine it must be returned by the latest date stamped below.

QUARTER LOAN

JUN 9 1991

JUN 10 1991

JUN 3 1995

QUARTER LOAN
DEC 29 1994

RETURN BY 1999

NOV 1 4 2000

NOV 1 4 2000